SOCIAL WORK PRACTICE IN NONTRADITIONAL URBAN SETTINGS

SOCIAL WORK PRACTICE IN NONTRADITIONAL URBAN SETTINGS

Melvin Delgado
Boston University

New York   Oxford
OXFORD UNIVERSITY PRESS
1999

Oxford University Press

Oxford   New York
Athens Auckland Bangkok Bogotá Buenos Aires Calcutta
Cape Town Chennai Dar es Salaam Delhi Florence Hong Kong Istanbul
Karachi Kuala Lumpur Madrid Melbourne Mexico City Mumbai
Nairobi Paris São Paulo Singapore Taipei Tokyo Toronto Warsaw

and associated companies in
Berlin Ibadan

Published by Oxford University Press, Inc.,
198 Madison Avenue, New York, New York 10016
http://www.oup-usa.org

Oxford is a registered trademark of Oxford University Press

Library of Congress Cataloging-in-Publication Data
Delgado, Melvin.
  Social work practice in nontraditional urban settings/Melvin
Delgado.
    p. cm.
  Includes bibliographical references and index.
  ISBN 978-0-19-511248-1
  1. Social case work. 2. Sociology, Urban. I. Title.
HV43.D47 1998
361.3′2—dc21   97-43521
                                                              CIP

Printed in the United States of America
on acid-free paper

This book is dedicated to the three most important people in my life: my wife, Denise Humm-Delgado, who is my partner, source of constant support, and a colleague, and my children, Laura and Barbara, who have not only supported me through their sense of humor, but also inspired me because of the importance of having a future that embraces values of diversity and social justice. This book, as a result, is just as much their creation as mine, and I thank them!

Contents

Acknowledgments

A book of this nature is not possible without the support and assistance of numerous individuals from within and outside of the academy. A number of graduate student assistants played important roles in conducting literature reviews and field visits, interviewing key informants, and development of case illustrations. Michael Novack, Irene Fassler, Ashley Mead, Kiva Barton, and Myrna Fong were much more than just "student assistants." They helped bring the concept of nontraditional setting to life. DiAna DiAna, Dr. Bambi Gaddist, Dr. Guillermo Vicuna, Dr. Martin Manalansan IV, Paul Cotten, Maureen Piwowarski, and Carlos Santiago played instrumental roles in the development of case studies by giving of their time and sharing materials during the field visits. Financial support for this book was made possible by the Center on Substance Abuse Prevention Faculty Development Grant and Richard Goldblatt of the Carlisle Foundation. Administrative support was provided by Dr. Wilma Peebles-Wilkins (Dean) and Suzanne Hogan (Administrative Assistant) at the Boston University School of Social Work. The author also wishes to acknowledge the anonymous reviewers of the prospectus and draft whose comments and insight made this book stronger.

SOCIAL WORK PRACTICE IN NONTRADITIONAL URBAN SETTINGS

I

SETTING THE CONTEXT
FOR SOCIAL
WORK PRACTICE WITHIN
NONTRADITIONAL URBAN
SETTINGS

The chapters in this section provide the reader with a historical and conceptual understanding of why nontraditional urban settings are an important dimension of social work practice within communities of color. Each chapter will stand on its own. However, there is a degree of overlap inherent in a book of this type.

The first chapter (Introduction) examines the concept of the nontraditional urban setting by placing it within a developmental history of this topic's importance. Chapter 1 also examines how caring and help seeking have been viewed over time, provides a definition of community, and gives a brief overview of the demographics of communities of color in the United States.

Chapter 2 (Urban Communities) provides more in-depth demographics. It analyzes the reasons why the social work profession has not been successful in reaching needy residents in urban communities, and describes the need for the profession to embrace a strength- rather than deficit-based paradigm. Chapter 3 (Caring and Helping) examines the concept of nontraditional settings and why these institutions have played such a critical role in communities of color. In addition, this chapter identifies the factors that facilitate or hinder social workers and agencies as they work in these settings. Chapter 4 (Principles and Strategies) provides the reader with a framework for developing partnerships within nontraditional settings. This chapter takes a developmental approach to collaborative activities, with each stage representing unique challenges and rewards for the practitioner.

1

Introduction

History of Interest

My professional interest in social work practice within nontraditional settings can be traced back to my first year in graduate social work school. I was attending a prestigious university, with an initial (micro-focused) field placement in a public welfare agency on the Upper West Side of New York City. Most, and at times all, of my clients were Puerto Rican, and I had ample opportunity to work with the community. Much of my field experience entailed visiting clients in their homes or meeting them in community settings, such as parks and local eating establishments.

My New York-Puerto Rican background facilitated my entry into and engagement with this community. I quickly discovered that my clients had no difficulty consulting me about such systemic issues as unresponsive teachers, sub-standard housing, lack of recreational outlets for children, missing public assistance checks, and so on. In short, they were very willing to have me act as their "broker" or "advocate." However, they were not willing to discuss their emotional problems or interpersonal conflicts. They took these problems to a Puerto Rican medium who operated out of her apartment approximately two blocks away from my office. She had an outstanding reputation in the neighborhood as someone who was "caring," "effective," and "accessible." Further, she did not charge exorbitant fees; she utilized a sliding-scale fee based on ability to pay. In short, she was a formidable competitor for me.

At the time, I had great difficulty accepting this "competition." I would come to find out that she had only a third grade formal education. True, she was considerably older than me. However, I did not consider her to be any more "Puerto Rican" than me. In addition, I was attending a prestigious school, spending three days per week in a field placement, and taking five graduate-level courses. In short, I believed myself to be a better social worker than the medium, and was completely at a loss about how to deal with this situation.

It wasn't until I came across an article written by Lloyd H. Rogler and August B. Hollingshead (1961) titled "The Puerto Rican spiritualist as a psychiatrist," that I finally understood why the medium was so much more trusted with personal issues and problems. She was not only a mental health provider with solid skills; she lived in the community, was caring, and received her legitimacy as a helper from God—clearly a more prestigious and powerful source than myself. Since that eventful day in 1971, I have devoted most of my professional career to learning more about indigenous resources and nontraditional settings in Latino and other communities of color across the United States.

My interest has focused on developing a better understanding of how people like this medium transcend conventional boundaries and accept a helper role, with all its attendant responsibilities. It has meant learning more about how to bring social work and other helping professions together with these "colleagues" to better serve undervalued communities. Bridging these two worlds becomes increasingly important when the communities served by both are in great need and marginalized.

My professional interest has evolved over the years from research with folk healers and use of natural support systems to work within nontraditional settings, which is the focus of this book. Nontraditional settings are places in a community where individuals gather to purchase a product or service or congregate for social purposes. These settings facilitate conversation and exchanges of concerns, advice, and assistance, minimizing stigma for those seeking help. All communities, regardless of their degree of "disintegration," "upheaval," and "ills," have nontraditional settings that play an important role in caring and helping. As social workers, we just need to be open and see these settings.

Goals

This book seeks to accomplish five goals: (1) inform social workers about the settings in which social work knowledge and skills may be useful; (2) identify social networks of groups that historically have been ignored and can be mobilized to collaborate with social work; (3) provide social workers with the "tools" to better identify and enlist indigenous resources in the helping process; (4) identify challenges and potential barriers to working with indigenous resources, in this case, nontraditional settings; and (5) provide social workers with a vision of practice and corresponding models to assist them in developing more responsive and, possibly more innovative, services that go beyond collaborative practice within nontraditional settings.

Although this book is intended specifically for a social work audience, it should have relevance for other professionals struggling to find more competent, empowering, and efficient ways of reaching out to people in urban areas across the United States. Thus, I write also about sharing a vision for a new form of social work practice that involves partnerships formed within nontraditional urban settings as a central goal of service provision. This partnership involves a process of validation, acceptance, affirmation, and mutual learning. It is predicated on mutual respect and trust, though unfortunately, these two elements are often missing from urban social work practice in the United States (Delgado, 1974; Martin & Martin, 1995).

My intent is not to romanticize these settings as fulfilling nothing but "good" in a community. There are nontraditional settings that, under the guise of helping, cause more harm than good. So we must approach these settings, as we would any agency, with an open mind, and utilize appropriate tools to help us determine whether collaboration within a setting is the right strategy for the worker, agency, profession, and community.

Although it is impossible to write about communities of color without addressing issues of oppression, marginalization, and exclusion, this book's emphasis is on the challenges and opportunities associated with inclusion. There are numerous excellent books in the field examining issues of oppression. However, there is a paucity of scholarly material on how these same undervalued communities have reached out to provide help to each other in a harsh, turbulent, and demanding world.

Work with communities of color must transcend the boundaries of "traditional" social work practice, so that interventions are welcomed and meaningful for these communities. This book is about redefining these boundaries and creating collaborative activities that are central to any form of urban-based practice. Practice in nontraditional urban settings will present innumerable challenges for the profession. However, it will also prove very rewarding!

The relationship between formal (agencies) and informal (nontraditional settings and other forms of indigenous resources) systems can be conceptualized as the two rails of a railroad track. Each system represents a rail, and the two rails stretch from Boston to San Francisco without ever meeting. The only segment that intersects with both rails is the tie in the middle that connects them. This section of the track, in turn, can be thought of as the client or community. Undervalued communities do not have the luxury of allowing these two rails to parallel each other without meeting. The needs of these communities require both systems to work together cooperatively to maximize existing resources and create opportunities for services that would otherwise not exist.

The use of urban-based nontraditional settings by social workers will influence the way people of color and other undervalued groups view the profession, and serve to energize and influence other helping professions. A proactive and participatory approach (empowerment and capacity enhancement) will set the standard for other helping professions engaged in communities of color. Social work not only borrows from other professions, it also contributes to them. This exchange of knowledge serves to bring helping professions together through the sharing of common foundations and approaches. Community, in combination with nontraditional settings, provides a context, or arena, for the exchange to take place.

There are countless numbers of individuals in communities providing a wide range of informal services for residents (Martinez-Brawley, 1990). Unfortunately, these acts of caring and service have largely gone unnoticed outside of their immediate communities (Snowden & Lieberman, 1994). These informal helpers have played instrumental roles in assisting fellow residents to meet the challenges of urban life, and have often done so under the most difficult circumstances and at great sacrifice to themselves.

In this book I address caring in communities of color and the role social work can play in learning from the experiences of informal helpers and organizations. I believe social workers can develop approaches to support and enhance local efforts at helping (capacity enhancement). These efforts will provide the profession with an opportunity to rediscover its past in the community and to embrace a new vision of urban practice with undervalued groups.

Still, there are challenges, barriers, and potential pitfalls to introducing innovative strategies. This book will attempt to minimize these pitfalls by highlighting potential sources for practice in nontraditional settings, identifying and assessing challenges, and providing strategies and examples of how this form of practice can take shape in urban areas of the United States. No book can totally prepare a practitioner for all possible barriers and sources of resistance. There are no guarantees. However, the best a social worker can do is to minimize the consequences of resistance and barriers, and be better prepared to address them when they do arise.

Although this book will address various undervalued populations (groups who, because of their beliefs, physical characteristics, or abilities, are not considered important and worthy of maximizing their potential contribution to society), its emphasis will be on communities of color, particularly people whose first language is not English. These groups face the additional barrier of not being able to communicate in their language of choice. However, other undervalued or "at-risk" groups will also be discussed. Issues related to socioeconomic status, gender, sexual orientation, and disability will be integrated throughout, and within the context of color.

This book utilizes a strengths perspective as a unifying paradigm. This perspective requires utilization of a multi-method approach to assessment and intervention. As a result, every effort will be made to provide examples of micro- and macro-methods of practice. The primary research method is qualitative, with an emphasis on ethnographic tools, although quantitative methods will also be used. These combined approaches facilitate painting a picture that captures the richness and complexity of nontraditional settings and the communities they serve.

An effort is made to balance prescriptive and descriptive approaches by providing a context and case illustrations of social work interventions whenever possible. Extensive reviews of the literature will set the context for each of the nontraditional settings selected for discussion and analysis. Small survey generated data will be utilized as applicable, and case studies will be presented and analyzed to help social workers better appreciate indigenous efforts at contributing to community helping. The case studies are particularly critical in facilitating identification of indigenous resources.

Social Work Partnerships Within Nontraditional Settings

The profession's embrace of partnerships within nontraditional urban settings has the potential to redirect practice from deficits to strengths, from an education to an enhancement model, and may align social work with its historical roots: practice with urban-based groups. The thrust toward vendorship and licensing, and the impact of managed care, have resulted in a profession that, with some exceptions, has abandoned capacity enhancement work within communities, and focused instead on addressing problems at their most serious level. Thus, engagement within nontraditional settings provides an avenue for the professional to engage in strengths-based practice, enabling a preventive and early intervention perspective to take hold as an integral part of social work.

Partnerships of any kind are difficult and often require considerable expenditure of time. Professional social workers must seek new avenues for engaging undervalued groups, and develop strategies and techniques that are much more relevant to urban realities. The more "professional" the profession becomes, through greater educational and credentialing requirements (which translate as more "sophisticated" designated procedures and interventions), the more it has withdrawn from community-based work and work with marginal groups. Nontraditional settings are not staffed by professionally credentialed people. They are staffed by individuals who possess excellent caring skills, which are most likely to be legitimized by the community or, in the case of those with metaphysical abilities, God.

Unfortunately, the concepts of outreach, home visiting, and other community-based interventions are often relegated to the "nonprofessional." Professional social workers, like many of their counterparts in other helping professions, often prefer to work out of offices, which, incidentally, are not based in the community or in areas that are easily accessible. Any further effort to "pull back" from communities will ultimately result in a profession that has lost touch with its historical roots and which is no longer part of a community. Practice involving nontraditional settings will facilitate the reestablishment of the profession's connectedness with undervalued communities.

Partnerships between social workers and those in nontraditional settings offer much promise for minimizing this rift. These partnerships have profound implications for both community and profession. Undervalued communities will be provided with an opportunity to identify their assets and engage in collaborative ventures from a strengths perspective. The profession benefits from these partnerships through the energy and purpose these relationships engender.

Both social work practice and education will increase in relevance for undervalued groups in urban areas. Schools of social work located in urban areas will find it easier to undertake research that addresses the needs and priorities of urban communities. In addition, this model of practice serves as a basis for unifying all methods of practice. It would further inform courses in social policy, human behavior, and the social environment. Schools of social work teaching collaborative practice within nontraditional settings can play a leadership role in helping agencies, through field placements, developing partnerships, and affording opportunities for student interns to practice in this arena.

Application of Concepts to Cases

The development of an in-depth understanding of nontraditional settings is enhanced by the use of case studies that illustrate key practice principles and considerations. Case material can also help practitioners develop a better understanding of the steps and approaches to working within nontraditional settings.

There is never a good substitute for a case study to illustrate difficult conceptual material (Stoke, 1995; Yin, 1994). The case study method has long been criticized as the weak sibling among social science methods, as lacking specificity, objectivity, and rigor. Those who undertake case studies are often regarded as having deviated from their academic disciplines. Nevertheless, case studies continue to be used extensively in social science research, and are particularly relevant to the study of nontraditional settings (Yin, 1994).

There are four essential properties of a qualitative case study that informed the development of nontraditional setting cases addressed in this book: (1) Particularistic—emphasizes cases highlighting practice within nontraditional settings; (2) Descriptive—provides details of the collaboration with nontraditional settings to permit examination of various practice-related issues; (3) Heuristic—develops readers' understanding of the nature of practice within nontraditional settings; and (4) Inductive—emphasizes discovering new forms of relationship rather than verifying predetermined hypotheses (Black & Walter, 1995).

Case studies do not have to be universally representative to have value. Case study research, in essence, is not sampling research. At times, a "typical" case works extremely well, but an "unusual" case may be far superior in demonstrating key points often overlooked in typical cases (Stake, 1995). Consequently, using unusual cases to demonstrate key concepts and processes provides the researcher with sufficient flexibility in selecting the most "appropriate" case for the concept being elucidated.

There are many reasons why case studies are popular for teaching various types of material. Case studies allow a writer to take both a descriptive and prescriptive approach to content, facilitating analysis for readers. Good case studies have a way of bringing to life dry and, at times, boring theoretical concepts and statistics. They allow readers to journey through place and time and put themselves in a "real" situation. They also allow readers to consider if they would do things in the same or in a different way. However, regardless of the writer's ability to convey both the excitement and challenges of "being there," it is still not the same as actually "being there." Good case studies, as a result, serve as a motivator for readers to attempt involvement as described in the text. Even more important, case studies serve to stimulate readers' creativity.

Highly illustrative case studies depend on their availability and accessibility. The examples used in this book were selected to represent different regional, urban, ethnic, and racial groups. It must be noted that most of my research on some of these nontraditional settings was undertaken over a period of three years with Latinos (Dominicans and Puerto Ricans) in New England, and more specifically Massachusetts. Nevertheless, this book attempts to have a "national" and "multicultural" perspective by presenting cases involving other groups and geographical regions of the country.

Case studies were selected through a variety of means. Some of the cases were specifically developed for this book, others were found in the professional literature or in newspapers. The cases obtained from newspapers do not provide the depth of detail associated with case studies in professional literature. However, it is fair to say that nontraditional settings have not found their way into the professional publications. Consequently, newspapers are at least a few years ahead of the scholarly literature. The popularity of newspaper stories involving nontraditional settings reflects the public interest in these places and the increasingly important role they play in communities across this country.

Several of the cases included in this book have been published in various forms by the author. These cases were selected for inclusion because of their teaching value. The cases provide readers with access to the process, considerations, and techniques used in facilitating accessibility and engagement within nontraditional settings. In addition, these cases very often complement each other and serve to broaden the definition of the nontraditional setting as it has been conceptualized by the author in a variety of geographical areas, types of settings, and among various population groups.

Regardless of their source, cases were selected because they illustrate practice within nontraditional settings. Most of these cases reflect how people in nontraditional settings address the impact of AIDS within their respective communities. The emphasis on HIV/AIDS emerged early on in the selection of the cases. The epidemic of HIV/AIDS in marginalized communities has necessitated the development of new approaches to community outreach and education on the part of agencies. Nontraditional settings, too, have had to marshal their resources in the fight against AIDS.

The case studies from Massachusetts derive from community-based research initiated by the author. These studies were the result of research and demonstration grants that were awarded to the author. Case studies from other parts of New England and the United States, which were specifically developed for inclusion in this book, were selected based on a four-step process: (1) identification based on a review of the literature, in all likelihood newspaper accounts, or recommendations from key informants (colleagues and community residents); (2) telephone contact and initial screening; (3) request for, and review of, written materials, if any; and (4) site visits for observations and interviews with key individuals. These site visits required the use of a questionnaire that consisted of semi-structured and open-ended questions. In addition, written materials were obtained to give the cases greater depth. Sometimes these materials consisted of "official" reports, local newspaper articles, forms developed specifically for the services, leaflets and other materials related to publicity, and correspondence, as appropriate.

Undertaking a book of this nature brings with it a whole host of limitations that must be acknowledged. To provide a glimpse into the world of nontraditional settings, a number of compromises had to be made: (1) Case illustrations represent a snapshot of nontraditional settings—namely, the cases do not have a historical perspective and, in rare circumstances, do not provide readers with a developmental perspective; (2) No effort was made to evaluate the nature and quality of the services provided—if someone in a setting stated that counseling was offered, for example, the success or failure of the activity would not be ascertained; (3) When those in a nontraditional setting indicated a willingness to collaborate on future projects, with a few exceptions, this willingness was not tested; (4) The case studies did not have the depth and breadth they warranted, had sufficient time and resources been available—consequently, the nuances and complexity of a setting could not be captured and studied, thus not doing justice to a setting; (5) The author would have liked the cases to reflect greater diversity pertaining to their geographical area of the country, particularly concerning the southwest and south; and (6) As already noted, some of the case illustrations were borrowed from the literature (professional and newspaper), limiting the extent that these examples could be used to illustrate different phases of the framework presented in Chapter 7.

Nevertheless, in spite of all of these limitations, the author cannot help but marvel at the work and commitment of people in nontraditional settings in addressing the needs of the communities they serve. These individuals have taken on tremendous responsibilities with minimal resources to aid their communities; much can be learned about how and why they accomplished this.

Caring and helping take place within a context that can best be understood if examined from a variety of perspectives and methods. The case studies involved a variety of quantitative (small-scale survey), and qualitative (ethnographic) research methods, reinforcing the importance of researcher training in both methods, with area of interest dictating method, rather than method dictating area of interest (Allen-Meares & Lane, 1990; Sells, Smith, & Newfield, 1997). Maintaining an open mind concerning the best approaches to research will enhance the quality of the research and minimize disruption to nontraditional settings and the communities they serve.

The intensive work that must be done before enlisting (engaging) the support of those in nontraditional settings, combined with the paucity of literature on them, makes large-scale survey work difficult, if not impossible, due to expenditure of time and funds and the importance of extensive local involvement in the research. However, this does not minimize the importance of small-scale research, which lends itself very well to the use of qualitative methods to provide depth and meaning to data generated through surveys. This form of research is not expensive and is well within the reach of most social service organizations, regardless of size. Though it severely limits the generalizability of data, and most agencies are only interested in serving a well-defined catchment area, small-scale research is not labor intensive and can be shaped to meet local needs and circumstances.

The importance of seeing the world, the community, and nontraditional settings through the perspectives of the residents and within their cultural context is referred to as ethnography (Burawoy, 1991a, 1991b; Sells, Smith, & Newfield, 1997). According to Spradley (1979, p. 25): "An ethnographer seeks out ordinary people with extraordinary knowledge and builds on their common experience. . . . Ethnographers view these research participants as 'informants' rather than 'subjects' . . . Informants, as a result, become teachers for ethnographers."

Ethnographic research methods lend themselves well to the study of nontraditional settings. Practitioners and researchers most be cognizant of both the tangible and intangible factors that shape the character of their communities. A skilled ethnographer is able to see the world and assess its problems as would members of their constituencies. This does not necessarily mean everyone is in agreement. Constituents will be better able to see more clearly the practitioner's point of view within the appropriate context (Martinez-Brawley, 1990).

Ethnographic research methods used in carrying out studies for this book primarily involved review of printed materials, observations, interviewing, and listening, to develop an in-depth appreciation of the community. A well-rounded understanding of communities brings with it fresher insights about interventions. Equally important, engaging in ethnographic studies makes us want to keep learning, because what we discover is so intriguing, important, and rewarding (Hardcastle, Wenocur, & Powers, 1997). This new knowledge will help us better design, deliver, and evaluate services to undervalued communities.

The combination of quantitative and qualitative methods of research can complement each other very well in the study of nontraditional settings.

Each of these methods' limitations are minimized when they are combined. In addition, neither method requires hugh expenditure of time, energy, or resources—they can be as extensive or as focused as needed. The combination of methods lends itself to the use of a team effort, with each member bringing skills and strengths that complement those of other team members.

Conclusion

This book will likely elicit a wide range of emotions and responses, from delight to indignation. At times, it will strike a provocative and profound chord; at times much of what is said is just plain "simple." However, the book is intended to provoke thought and debate, and to inspire others to undertake similar scholarly ventures.

The quest for a model involving nontraditional settings in urban areas represents an effort to better understand the everyday phenomena of caring and the provision of help. To obtain a better appreciation of help giving and receiving, it is necessary to view the topic from a multifaceted perspective, defining numerous concepts. This chapter sought to provide the reader with an appreciation of how the author arrived at this point in a long journey, as well as to provide a context for the book.

2

Urban Communities

Urban areas have a unique place in U.S. history, playing a prominent role during all critical phases of the country's development. However, the term "urban" is elusive, having many different definitions and ways of being applied in practice. Unfortunately, most of these are negative and highly biased. Demographic profiles of population composition reveal distinct patterns in cities, as compared with suburban and rural sections of the country. Urban areas are not only more densely populated, they also have a disproportionate number of groups of color and other undervalued groups in this society (George, 1992).

Social work practice is influenced by geographical area and population composition. Service design and organizational structure are based on geography and population composition. This chapter will highlight how historically the profession of social work has missed opportunities to fill a vacuum in urban-based practice, and will discuss the need for a new paradigm to inform new approaches to service delivery.

Definition of Urban Community

As the focus of this book is on urban-based, nontraditional settings, it requires that a definition of urban community be given. The concept of "urban," unfortunately, engenders negative images in the minds of many individuals in this country (Campbell, 1996). It is not unusual to hear of urban poverty, crime, mayhem, drug abuse, dropouts, blight, flight, fear, etc. These conditions and situations are not restricted to urban areas; they can also be found in suburbia and rural areas of the country. Yet the bias persists, severely limiting the potential of urban areas to provide models and solutions to their problems.

The concept of the urban community encompasses many different dimensions. It is impossible to find a unifying definition that scholars, practitioners, and residents all embrace (Abrahamson, 1996; Badshah, 1996; Chavis & Wandersman, 1990; Haymes, 1995; Keating, 1996; Unger & Wandersman, 1985; Zukin, 1995). There is an elusive and emotional nature to community that is fraught with meaning. For many of us it elicits memories of school, worship, play, major life cycle stages, and interactions, both pleasant and unpleasant. Community is where we learned that we were part of a group, much larger than our family, composed of neighbors, friends, shop owners, and strangers we saw but never spoke to. We were part of life in a much broader context than family (Hardcastle, Wenocur, & Powers, 1997).

Thus, any definition of urban community must encompass a multitude of dimensions, including physical locality, resident composition, and transactions of various kinds (business, personal, educational, recreational, spiritual). In addition, urban areas are not static, they are ever changing internally and in the ways they relate to society (Lyon, 1989). McKnight (1995), Fellin (1995), Hoffman (1994), and Flanagan (1993) provide different, yet complementary, definitions of community.

McKnight's (1995) definition of community complements that of Lyon (1989) and centers of collective associations, formal and informal, that can transcend geographical space. One form of informal association is an enterprise or business. Associational activity transpires in grocery stores, restaurants, laundromats, beauty parlors, barbershops, bars, hardware stores, and other local places of business. These interactions serve an important function in defining community and determining which residents "feel" they belong. In fact, the formation of the United States Constitution was discussed and debated in taverns and inns before it was discussed "formally." These settings provided an atmosphere that facilitated the exchange of ideas.

Fellin's (1995) definition of the term "personal community" includes dimensions that are important for social work practice: namely, the individual in multiple communities. An individual's "personal community," by necessity, must consist of all of the communities—locational, identificational, interest—in which an individual engages in meaningful social interaction, in the use of services and resources, in employment activities, and in recreational pursuits. This "multiple" dimension broadens the scope and depth of potential social interactions and social resources, including formal and informal helping networks. Abrahamson's (1996) concept of "enclave" is similar to Fellin's "personal community," and refers to concentrations of individuals who do not have the same ethnic status, but share many commonalities such as income, lifestyle, or other attributes.

Hoffman (1994) addresses why a definition of neighborhood is problematic because of the variety of ways it has been used in the literature. Most scholars agree that, at the very least, the definition requires an urban spatial unit with geographical boundaries, a name, and some sense of psychological unity among its residents. "Neighborhood" refers to an area larger than a street, or other small unit, but smaller than the city as a whole. Consequently, the term "neighborhood" is equivalent to the term "local community."

It must be noted that neighborhoods are much smaller in scale than a community, usually refer to personal space and networks, and take on the qualities of a primary group (Fellin, 1995). Nevertheless, neighborhoods have long been an important venue for addressing urban problems. Neighborhood initiatives can be considered both a strategy and a metaphor for how America deals with its most significant urban problems (Keating, Krumholz, & Star, 1996).

Flanagan (1993) brings into the definition of urban community the influence of ethnicity and its relationship to indigenous organizations. Ethnic cohesiveness increases community visibility. Large numbers of co-ethnics can support (socially, financially, and politically) an array of services such as retail shops, religious institutions, voluntary organizations, communications media, and so forth. These establishments, in turn, reinforce the identity of a community internally and externally. It should be noted that the formation of a community identity does not require a majority of co-ethnics for the community to become identified with a particular ethnic group. A small, but highly visible population may be sufficient to establish and maintain an identity specific to an ethnic group.

Any perspective of urban community in America must place emphasis on three key elements, which may vary at times in degree of importance: (1) geographical area (which may or may not be a critical dimension, depending on the situation); (2) social rather than physical space; and (3) presence of interactive links binding individuals to each other, as well as to the larger society. Thus, the concept of community can involve multiple perspectives, in addition to what is generally regarded as geographical locality and commonality of residents, i.e., ethnicity, race, socioeconomic status, etc. The community concept can also involve the degree to which there is a "psychological" sense of belonging among residents, their participation in events, and the concentration of facilities they use (Zukin, 1995).

The latter refers to settings that provide an opportunity for meeting significant needs within the community:

> Several types of communities have been identified by the social sciences . . . For all these types of community, there exists a process for improving the quality of community life as portrayed in such terms as "community development," "community building," and "community organization." A central mechanism in this process is individuals' participation in voluntary organizations which produce collective and individual goods. These groups include neighborhood organizations, professional associations, self-help groups, churches, political parties, advocacy organizations, or unions. (Chavis & Wandersman, 1990, p. 56)

Consequently, a "sense of community" can transcend geography, commonality of background, and use of common institutions, but will always involve quality of interactions. It also enables members to create a shared history and common destiny (Allen & Allen, 1987; Herszenhorn & Hirsh, 1996).

Demographics and Communities of Color

This section focuses on providing a demographic profile of four major groups of color in the United States (African Americans, Asians, Latinos, and Native Americans). These four groups have been selected because of their numbers and propensity to reside in urban areas, and their projected increase in representation in the twenty-first century. Whenever possible, every effort will be made to differentiate within these groups to provide the reader with an appreciation of how differences in country of origin impacts socioeconomic status. The term "communities of color" serves as a unifying concept for groups whose members may differ by country of birth, language, culture, and the circumstances of their arrival in this country, but who share similar stressors as a result of oppression based on the color of their skin.

The professional literature contains a number of publications outlining in great detail the problems, needs, and issues confronting these communities. Thus, the social needs of these groups will not be addressed here. Communities of color in the United States face constant struggles in meeting a wide range of challenges. These communities are very often viewed as consisting of nothing but problems and unmet needs, and are disproportionately represented in statistics related to crime, drugs, teen pregnancy, poverty, etc. (Butterfield, 1992; Goldberg, 1997; Lee, 1994a, b, c; Terry, 1992a). Nevertheless, these communities have made significant, and often valiant efforts at addressing their needs, and have done so without significant outside resources. Nontraditional settings gain in importance when the communities they serve are marginalized and, as a result, undervalued in this society (Delgado, 1997b).

Communities of color in the United States are undergoing rapid and dramatic demographic changes as the twenty-first century approaches. The racial composition of the American population has changed more dramatically in the past decade than at any time in this century; nearly one in every four Americans has African American, Asian, Pacific Islander, Latino, or Native American ancestry. In 1980, one in five Americans had such backgrounds (Barringer, 1991). These changes are reflected in numerical representation, diversity within and among groups, dispersal patterns, urban concentrations, and population projections for the next century.

Numerical Representation

Communities of color can be found throughout all regions of the United States, and in all fifty states (Abrahamson, 1996; Barringer, 1993). Urban areas across the United States are experiencing dramatic changes in composition, and nowhere is this more apparent than in New York City (Bouvier & Grant, 1994; Dugger, 1996; Gonzalez, 1992). The racial and ethnic composition of cities has changed in the past 40 years, with 80 percent of all people of color living in metropolitan areas. A majority of all African Americans, Asians, and Latinos live in just thirty cities (Rusk, 1995). In 1970, New York City's white, non-Latino population represented 60 percent of the residents. However, it is estimated that by the year 2000 their number will decrease to 35 percent (Firestone, 1995). These demographic changes can be traced to three key factors: (1) birth rates; (2) immigration; and (3) out migration.

The death rate for white non-Latinos is higher than the birth rate, and more whites are moving out of the city than are moving in. Latinos, on the other hand, have a birth rate that far exceeds their death rate, and more Latinos are immigrating to cities than are moving out. African Americans have a moderately high birth rate that exceeds their death rate, but more leave the city than move in. Last, Asians (more than half of whom are Chinese) have a very low birth rate but a very high immigration rate (higher than Latinos). Among Latinos and Asians, there is tremendous diversity in country of origin.

The population increase among Latinos in New York City can be found in other urban areas across the United States (Roberts, 1994). The increase among Latinos parallels a national trend in which they now outnumber African Americans in Los Angeles, Houston, Phoenix, and San Diego. The Latinos in those cities are primarily of Mexican or other Latin American origins. In New York City, most are either from Puerto Rico or the Dominican Republic (Firestone, 1995).

Recent estimates suggest that these trends can be expected to continue well into the next century. By the year 2020, more Latinos will be added to the population each year than African Americans, Asian Americans, and Native Americans combined; starting in 2019, the Latino population, being relatively youthful, will have the nation's lowest death rate (Seelye, 1997).

The topic of undocumented status, or "illegal aliens," has been the source of considerable tension across the United States, with no major region or urban area escaping its impact. However, the Southwest is widely considered to have more than its share of undocumented residents (Verhovek, 1996). If we include undocumented residents, the population of Latinos in the United States is that much greater.

African Americans

The common perception of the black community in the United States is that it is homogeneous (Staples, 1995). Differences among African Americans can be quite extensive as a result of culture, experience over generations, migration pattern, and access to quality education, services, and meaningful employment (Black, 1996).

The African American population is estimated to be 30 million, representing an increase of 13.2 percent during the 1980s, with a median age of 28, six years younger than the national median age. African Americans represent sizable populations in the District of Columbia (399,600), Mississippi (915,050), Louisiana (1,299,300), South Carolina (1,039,900), and Georgia (1,746,600) (Barringer, 1991). Their largest percentage increase occurred in New Hampshire (80.4%), Minnesota (78%), Vermont (71.9%), Alaska (64.6%), and Maine (64.3%). These increases, although significant percentage-wise, reflect an influx into states where African Americans were generally not present in sizable numbers prior to 1980, as is the case in the three New England states.

Like many other groups of color, African Americans are generally concentrated in urban areas of the United States (Rusk, 1995): New York, Chicago, Los Angeles, Philadelphia, Detroit, Atlanta, Houston, Baltimore, Miami, Dallas-Fort Worth, San Francisco, Oakland, Cleveland, New Orleans, St. Louis, Memphis, Norfolk-Virginia Beach-Newport News, Richmond-Petersburg, Birmingham, Charlotte, Milwaukee, Cincinnati, Kansas City, Tampa-St. Petersburg-Clearwater, and Washington, D.C. If San Antonio, San Diego, El Paso, and San Jose are added to the above cities, they account for the majority of Latinos in the United States; if Honolulu is added, these cities will account for a majority of Asians and Pacific Islanders.

Asian Americans and Pacific Islanders

The category of Asians and Pacific Islanders is very broad and often does a disservice to the twenty-two groups that comprise this category (Browne & Broderick, 1996). This population may be the most diverse of this country's major groups of color. Segments of the Asian American population have been in the United States for many generations, while others are newcomers who arrived only recently. This community comes from more than two dozen different countries. As a result, they do not share a common language, religion, or cultural background. While a large segment of this population is financially well-off, many are poor (O'Hare & Felt, 1991).

Although Asian Americans and Pacific Islanders can be found throughout all sectors of the country, the western region has the highest concentration (Barringer, 1991; O'Hare & Felt, 1991; Portes & Rumbaut, 1996). The states of California (2,845,700), New York (693,800), Hawaii (685,200), Washington (210,960), and Alaska (19,700) have the highest concentrations (Barringer, 1991). However, these states do not account for the highest percentage increase in the 1980s. The states of Rhode Island (245.6%), New Hampshire (219%), Georgia (208.6%), Wisconsin (195%), and Minnesota (193.5%) recorded the highest increases (Barringer, 1991).

Cities tend to attract Asian groups, with particular cities attracting specific groups. The cities with very high concentrations of Asian Americans are Honolulu, Los Angeles, San Francisco, New York, Chicago, and San Jose.

Various subgroups favor particular cities, with Chinese favoring San Francisco, Boston, New York, and Washington, D.C. Japanese prefer Honolulu, Los Angeles, and Seattle. Filipinos favor San Diego, San Francisco, and San Jose. Vietnamese are concentrated in Orange County (California), San Jose, Houston, and Minneapolis (Lee, 1996).

However, it is very important to remember that Asian American groups differ in terms of their migration history, population, language, religion, educational level, income, degree of acculturation, preferred residential location, political involvement, and so forth (Onishi, 1996). These differences require that increased attention be paid to intra-ethnic differences among Asian American groups.

Latinos

The Latino population, like its Asian and Pacific Islander cohorts, is also very diverse in background (Frisbie & Bean, 1995; Hurtado, 1995; Ortiz, 1995; Valdivieso & Davis, 1988; U.S. Bureau of Census, 1992). The term "Latino" can refer to any individual who was born in or can trace ancestry to South America, Central America, or the Caribbean islands of Cuba, the Dominican Republic, or Puerto Rico. Latinos, unlike Asians and Pacific Islanders, do share the same language, the influence of Spain, Indian roots, and, depending on their history, African heritage. However, the differences sometimes appear much more significant than the similarities (Oboler, 1995; Ojito, 1997). Latinos are very young (26) when compared with the national median age (34). Mexican Americans are the youngest (24) of the three major sub-groups, followed by Puerto Ricans (27) and Cubans (39) (U.S. Bureau of the Census, 1991).

The Latino population in the United States is estimated to number 26,646,000, excluding those who reside in Puerto Rico (IPR Datanote, 1995). They are the most urbanized (92%) of any ethnic group in the United States. The three largest groups of Latinos are Mexican Americans (17,090,000), Puerto Ricans (2,776,000), and Cubans (1,111,000). However in the United States, there are approximately 3,725,000 Central and South Americans, and close to 2 million other Latinos. Dominicans are the largest subgroup, and are heavily concentrated in New York City, which has an estimated Dominican population of 500,000 (Gonzalez, 1992; Kaplan, 1997). Estimates predict that the Dominican population in New York city will double by the year 2005, surpassing the Puerto Rican population as the largest Latino group (Kaplan, 1997).

Three out of the top five states that experienced the largest percentage increase in Latino population are in New England (Rhode Island, 132%; Nevada, 130.9%; Massachusetts, 103.9% [Rivera, 1992; With, 1996]; New Hampshire, 102.8%; Virginia, 100.7%). Nevertheless, the states of California, Texas, Florida, New York, and Illinois accounted for 78 percent of the Latinos in this country. Latinos account for 25 percent of the population of

California, and are projected to increase to 45 percent by the year 2030 (Hayes-Bautista, Schink, & Chapa, 1988).

Mexican Americans can be found throughout the United States, with 91 percent residing in urban areas (U.S. Bureau of the Census, 1991). However, the states of California (approximately 7.7 million) and Texas (4.3 million) have the highest concentration. As a result of political forces, Mexican Americans have moved to other sections of the United States (With, 1996). Puerto Ricans are concentrated in the northeast, primarily in New York (1,047,000), New Jersey (304,000), Massachusetts (146,000), Pennsylvania (144,000), and Connecticut (140,000). However, Florida (241,000), Illinois (147,000), and California (132,000) have sizable concentrations of Puerto Ricans (Barringer, 1993). The vast majority (95%) of Puerto Ricans in the United States reside in cities (U.S. Bureau of the Census, 1991).

Approximately 90 percent of Cuban Americans live in four states: Florida (60%) has the highest concentration, with Miami being the city most favored for residence, followed by New Jersey, New York, and California (Bernal & Shapiro, 1996; Perez-Stable & Uriate, 1997). Dominicans tend to reside in New York, New Jersey, Massachusetts, and Rhode Island; Nicaraguenos tend to settle in Florida (Miami); and El Salvadorians in Los Angeles, California (Novas, 1994). Approximately 95 percent of El Salvadorians live in urban areas (U.S. Bureau of the Census, 1991).

Native Americans

Native Americans communities can be found throughout the country (U.S. Bureau of Census, 1991). However, their greatest concentration is in the western states, which account for 66 percent of all Native Americans in ten states. The largest concentration can be found in Oklahoma (252,400), New Mexico (134,400), South Dakota (50,600), and Montana (47,700). Their largest increases, nevertheless, can be found in other states, with Alabama (117.7%), Tennessee (96.7%), Florida (88.7%), Hawaii (84.2%), and New Jersey (78.3%) experiencing the biggest jump during the 1980s (Barringer, 1991).

The terms "Native American" and "American Indian" are often used interchangeably. However, there is tremendous difficulty in obtaining an accurate numerical account of this group. These labels encompass a wide range of languages, lifestyles, religious kinship systems, and organizations. In addition, there are a variety of ways of defining "Indian": (1) a genetic definition is based on percentage of Indian blood as established by the Federal register of the United States; (2) community acceptance, being recognized as Indian by other Indians; (3) enrollment in a recognized tribe; (4) and self-declaration, the method used by the Census bureau (Sutton & Broken Nose, 1996).

Only about 35 percent of Native Americans live on reservations (U.S. Bureau of the Census, 1991). Over 50 percent live in urban areas, with New

York City being home to approximately 30,000 Indians from over 60 tribes (Sutton & Broken Nose, 1996). The mean age of Native Americans (24.2) is considerably younger than the general population (34) (Indian Health Services, 1993).

Projections for the Twenty-first Century

Much has been written about the future composition of the United States (Barringer, 1991; Hayes-Bautista, Schink, & Chapa, 1988; Pears, 1992; Spencer, 1986). Although reports, newspaper accounts, and scholarly publications may differ concerning numbers, there is generally agreement that this country is not just "graying" (getting older), but also "coloring" in the process. Immigration and rapid population growth are expected to make Latinos the nation's largest group of color by 2020, totaling 51.2 million (15.7% of the population), up from 9.7 percent in 1993. African Americans will be the second largest minority at 45.4 million people, or 13.9 percent (up from 12.5%). Asians and Pacific Islanders, too, will experience significant population growth, rising to 22.6 million, or 6.9 percent, up from 3.4 percent. Native Americans will increase their share of the population from eight-tenths of 1 percent to nine-tenths of 1 percent, rising to 3.1 million in 2020 (The New York Times, 1994).

An examination of the projections for the year 2050 reflects a continuation of the trends reported for the year 2020, with whites accounting for a declining share of the population. The non-Latino population will stop growing by 2029, when it is expected to reach a peak of 208 million. By contrast, the African American population will nearly double in 60 years, from 32 million to 62 million in 2050. The Asian American population will grow even faster, from 8 million today to 12 million in the year 2000, and 41 million in 2050. The Asian American population will double by 2009, triple by 2024, and quadruple by 2038. Latinos will account for more than 40 percent of all population growth in the next 60 years. Their numbers will rise to 49 million by 2020 and 81 million by 2050 (Hayes-Bautista, Schink, & Chapa, 1988; Pears, 1992; U.S. Bureau of Census, 1983, 1986).

Social Work and Urban Practice

The social worker's professional search for meaning and direction regarding practice with urban-based, undervalued communities can be described as a critical issue. According to Meinert (1994), an issue can be classified as critical when it meets three criteria: (1) it appears in the public consciousness of the profession's members and is the subject of open and frank discussion; (2) it is not trivialized or marginalized, and is considered important by the profession; and (3) neglecting it will have deleterious consequences for the viability and continued growth of the profession, requiring that it be addressed in a carefully planned and strategic manner. There is no question in this author's mind that social work practice with urban-based undervalued groups would meet Meinert's definition of a critical issue.

It can be argued that the social work profession, although having great potential for reaching and engaging undervalued groups, has not succeeded in so doing. There are a number of reasons for this, some of which are broad and not restricted to the profession, others of which are profession specific. The nation's move away from addressing the needs of undervalued groups provides social work with an opportunity to consider other paradigms and strategies for working within communities that will improve the lives of undervalued people by building community and addressing issues of social justice. In short, we must reconnect with our historical mission (Weil, 1996).

A Profession in Search of Meaning in Urban Areas

The social work profession is at a critical juncture as it approaches the twenty-first century, considering the major social, political, technological, and demographic changes occurring in the United States (Kreuger, 1997). Nowhere are these changes more striking and challenging for practice than with undervalued groups and communities in urban areas. Cities have historically been a refuge for undervalued groups in search of better schools, better jobs, better health care—in short, a better life. Cities represent the land of opportunity in America (Rusk, 1995).

The profession, like other helping professions, is struggling to address major social problems such as HIV/AIDS, alcohol and other drug abuse, homelessness, violence, under- and unemployment, to list just a few, in an era of diminishing resources, political will, and lack of creative solutions (Van Soest & Bryant, 1995). These social problems increase in severity when found in undervalued groups residing in urban areas of the country. Thus communities of color, one such group, have had to struggle to make the profession meet their needs within a context of respect (Iglehart & Becerra, 1995; Paulino, 1994).

Professional socialization affects the process of care giving by stressing such terms as "objectivity," "professional distance," and "overidentification." In fact, any strong sense of social justice often can be interpreted as "unprofessional." It is a remarkable achievement to retain a capacity to care as a professional in light of all the mechanisms that have been developed, through graduate school and employment, to temper these feelings (Schwartz, 1997).

Several scholars have been critical of the profession. In the 1970s, Galper (1975) critiqued social work from a "radical" perspective, addressing his concerns from a professional stance rather than practice method. In their critique of social work, Specht and Courtney (1994, p. 23) comment on how the profession has abandoned its historical focus:

> The objective of social work is to help people make use of social resources—
> family members, friends, neighbors, community organizations, social ser-

vice agencies, and so forth—to solve their problems. However . . . social workers generally look at use of groups, community associations, and voluntary associations as of secondary importance to change. At best, they provide "social support" and "helping networks"; somewhat less importantly, they are good information resources and recreational experiences, and they provide respite for caregivers and backups and reinforcement for individual treatment.

A central mission of social work must be to build a meaning, a purpose, and a sense of obligation to the community. The community will then become both the setting and the vehicle through which the development of commitment, obligation, and social support can be developed (Delgado, in press e; Specht & Courtney, 1994). The community will be enhanced, as will a new vision for the profession.

Iglehart and Becerra (1995), too, are highly critical of the social work profession. However, their perspective focuses on the professions historical relationship with communities of color. The reluctance of society to understand and address major social problems in a systematic and comprehensive manner spills over to the helping professions. The importance of culturally competent service delivery has increased over the years in direct response to the "benign neglect" practiced during this time (Iglehart & Becerra, 1995). Van Soest and Bryant (1995) raise questions about social work's reluctance to address urban-based violence, a problem that is very salient in communities of color.

Trolander (1988), in analyzing how the settlement house movement has changed since its nineteenth-century origins, attributes professionalism, changes in the composition of cities, and a decreased emphasis on social change as key factors in the movement of social work away from social change. The profession has received increasing criticism during the past decade from a variety of sources in and out of the profession. Margolin (1997) argues that social work has shifted away from social reform and has, instead, embraced strategies focused on social control of undervalued individuals, who most likely are either poor or of color, or both. The embrace of a deficit perspective, with roots in a medical model, hindered the profession from entering into partnerships within the communities and groups it seeks to help.

The failure of social work to include systematically people of color and their perspectives has resulted in a profession adrift from urban realities, struggling to reconcile decisions made over the past hundred years. The future of the profession is predicated on our willingness and ability to identify historical developments; this awareness and acknowledgment, in turn, can be the basis from which the errors of yesterday will not be repeated in the service delivery of tomorrow. Tomorrow will present far greater challenges to society and the profession, necessitating a shift in how communities are viewed and social work is conceived (Iglehart & Becerra, 1995).

Delgado (1974), in sharing his observations as a social work student more than 20 years ago, painted a picture of a profession struggling with contradictions:

> I entered the profession in hopes of acquiring the necessary skills to return to the South Bronx and alleviate some of the misery and despair of those who are forced to live in abandoned buildings, suffer starvation, and contend with repressive institutions. Instead, I found myself in a profession that concentrated on manipulating the individual rather than social institutions, a profession that is run by the middle class for the middle class, while it considers itself the protector of the poor and powerless. (p. 123)

Although social work's origins are deeply rooted in community-based practice, there has been a slow but steady shift over the years away from community to organization and private practice (Fellin, 1995; Iglehart & Becerra, 1995; Specht & Courtney, 1994). A shift away from the community has been further accelerated by the profession's adoption of clinical interventions that fail to place the individual within a community context (Trolander, 1988). The thrust toward professionalism further reinforced the importance of social service organizations, and thereby professionals, as the principal source of assistance to urban-based communities (Margolin, 1997).

McKnight (1995, pp. 103–104), in critiquing helping professions and the labeling process they rely on, notes:

> Human service professions focus on deficiencies, call them "needs," and have expert skills in giving each perceived deficiency a label . . . As a result, we are generally aware that to be diagnosed and labeled . . . carries a heavy negative social consequence . . . For those whose "emptiness" cannot be filled by human services, the most obvious "need" is the opportunity to express and share their gifts, skills, capacities, and abilities with friends, neighbors, and fellow citizens in the community. . . [Professionals] inevitably harm their clients and the community by preempting the relationship between them.

Effective service organizations do not view individuals as the source of problems and practice interventions focused on fixing, remedying, controlling, or preventing risky behavior. Individuals are too complex to be viewed within a narrow perspective that has a single focus and is problem-based (McLaughlin, 1993). Consequently, "effectiveness" must encompass a context broader than that which traditionally has been regarded as the "client." This context must take into account family, community, and society.

An emphasis on professional credentials often works against meaningful involvement within communities of color by limiting who is "qualified" to provide assistance. Bureaucratic requirements of "professional qualifications" make it difficult to hire community residents who have innate abilities to help. Rather, professionals are hired who may not represent the same ethnic and economic backgrounds of the community they serve. They are individuals who, with some exceptions, view employment as part of a career, with advancement often meaning leaving an organization and community (McLaughlin, 1993).

The deemphasis on community (indigenous) resources has resulted in an overemphasis on formal institutional help. As a consequence, this shift has further removed the profession from community-based settings that are meaningful for residents. In addition, the shift has resulted in social workers displaying a reluctance to venture out into the community for fear of personal injury and in the name of "efficiency," that is, more clients can be served if time is not spent on travel.

Need for a New Paradigm

Social work is in need of a paradigm that builds community capacity as a central goal. Such a paradigm requires a philosophical foundation that embraces the belief that communities are capable of helping themselves if provided with the opportunity to do so. A number of social work scholars have put forth their vision for the profession of social work, and in the process critiqued various aspects of the profession. Specht and Courtney's (1994) vision for social work in the twenty-first century encompasses community-based services, with capacity enhancement as a central tenet of practice. They argue that community-based practice must be based on the assumption that, first and foremost, the community has the capacity to address most problems through a variety of indigenous efforts. Further, those indigenous efforts are preferred whenever possible as a means of capacity enhancement.

Weil (1996) also puts forth a vision for community practice in an age of diminishing government responsibility when issuing a challenge for social work to be proactive, advocating for vulnerable groups and emphasizing community-focused practice that connects empowerment strategies with social and economic development. Smith (1996) challenges social work to develop a paradigm that is much more in tune with the reality of being African American in this society, and advocates the use of participatory action research that involves inputs from African American families and indigenous institutions.

Van Soest and Bryant (1995) address how important it is for the social work profession to shift paradigms to better understand and address urban-based violence. This shift would require the profession to develop an understanding of the deeply embedded and submerged structural foundation of violence, and to use tools of astute skepticism and critical thinking. Social workers will then have increased awareness of how institutions socialize their members with cultural norms that foster structural inequality based on gender and race.

A shift from provision of care in an office to capacity enhancement entails adoption of this new paradigm, and involves development of services and approaches that are community-based and in settings that historically have not been utilized by social workers (Badshah, 1996; Billups, 1994; Logan 1996b; Sullivan & Rapp, 1996). This new form of practice will result in modification of existing intervention techniques, and the creation of new techniques that are better suited to the new arena of practice.

Social work, like other professions, has historically relied on a paradigm of scarcity, limiting its ability to enter into meaningful dialogue, engagement, and partnership with undervalued communities (Saleebey, 1992). A paradigm of scarcity is predicated on a view that communities, in this case those that are undervalued, need outside resources and assistance to meet their needs. These resources are best delivered within established social service settings and by professionally credentialed staff, and are based on conventional views of community.

Conclusion

Any definition of "urban" must include a multitude of perspectives if it is to capture the term's essential meaning. The importance of cities for groups of color and other undervalued groups is undisputed; this importance will, in all likelihood, increase in the next century.

The profession of social work must come to terms with its historical roots before it can embrace new paradigms concerning urban practice. This form of practice will require bold and highly creative approaches that are based on a clear and in-depth appreciation of the communities it seeks to engage and help. Further, this form of practice must take into context urban factors, boundaries, and dynamics for it to have relevance.

3

Caring and Helping

The process of caring can be placed within a number of contexts, one of which is community (Chavis, 1997; Williamson, 1997). The literature on community settings, spaces that are unique, therapeutic, and socially welcoming, has highlighted a variety of interesting perspectives on this topic. Oldenburg (1991) calls these places "third places," or "Great Good Places." The "Great Good Place" is a generic designation for a great variety of public places that host the regular, voluntary, informal, and happily anticipated gatherings of individuals beyond the realms of home and work.

A setting qualifies as a "Great Good Place" by meeting five criteria: (1) it serves to "root" individuals, because it is a context, space, or setting where one is known when present and missed when absent; (2) it lends itself to possession and control; it is a setting that belongs to those who patronize it: it is "their" beauty parlor, grocery store, house of worship, etc.; (3) the setting serves socially to rejuvenate the patron, who can unwind and relax; (4) patrons experience no fear of being themselves, but are fully and unconditionally accepted; and (5) the setting exudes warmth, friendliness, support, and mutual concern. These criteria highlight the special qualities of these places. However, these settings take on added significance when the patron has only home as the "other place"; those individuals who are oppressed may not have the second place, work, to call their own.

Indigenous and Professional Caring and Helping

Community caring can best be categorized as either indigenous or professional. The former represents localized, unorganized or organized, efforts to reach out to and help residents. The latter represents efforts on the part of professionals, legitimized by society, to offer assistance that can be expected to meet minimal standards, with accountability to designated bodies.

Indigenous Caring

Indigenous efforts at providing assistance within undervalued urban-based communities are important to the field of social work. The importance of urban areas in the lives of people of color is undeniable, and so is the care giving process. This context for caring is very much community- and urban-based and has a long and distinguished history. Smith (1996, p. 35) posits a provocative yet insightful question that has direct applicability to the central purpose of this book:

> The basic issue or question is: How does social work (and other helping professions) build on the strength of African American families and communities [and other undervalued groups] in such a manner that the perception of "outsider" is minimized or nonexistent? Perhaps a more fundamental question is: Is this possible? The answer to the latter question is yes.

Any effort to learn from or enlist the services and support of nontraditional settings in undervalued communities is significant for social workers; it helps the professional shift from "outsider" to "insider" in an urban context. Demographic patterns suggest a continued emphasis on people of color living in large urban areas. Undervalued groups are searching for a way to have their voices heard in a crowded urban landscape. When heard, these voices shed light on the pain and the trials and tribulations of being part of an undervalued group. However, these voices also speak to strengths and pride. Nontraditional settings are but one community strength, and complement many others.

The shift from "outsider" to "insider" will prove challenging and will require much soul searching and acceptance of "blame" for past injustices on the part of social workers. Nevertheless, as the saying goes: "The truth shall set you free, but in the meantime it will make you feel miserable."

The concept of caring is not relegated to any one particular time, sector, or profession. Caring is widespread and can be found in any community in the United States. An ability to care is usually a key indicator of a community's health and well-being. Care giving is a direct manifestation of the stability of a community. After all, the community is the central meeting ground for relationships, and thus is the place to examine care giving. If a community is overwhelmed by the trials and tribulations of daily life, and dominated by external forces, it will not have the ability to care for itself. This failure will manifest itself in a whole range of social problems, which can only be solved through the development of partnerships between residents and external forces (McKnight, 1995).

Albrecht (1994) also views community from a care giving perspective, and highlights how spontaneous help is mobilized by close and distant ties, as well as by the supportive messages communicated among friends and family. In large part, this support is a function of a shared moral code, reinforced by networks of interaction and mutual influence.

The topic of community residents helping fellow residents is not new in the United States (Chase, 1990; Forte, 1997; Williamson, 1997; Wuthnow, 1996). In fact, the last three presidents have made volunteerism an important element of their national campaigns and administrations. There are a number of national organizations, such as Points of Light Foundation, City Care of America, and the Corporation for National and Community Service, that have stressed volunteerism and developed numerous projects stressing self-help.

The self-help movement in the United States started with Alcoholics Anonymous and has expanded over the past 60 years to include other groups (Powell, 1987, 1990). These established self-help movements, it should be noted, have generally not been embraced by people of color, so these communities had to develop their own systems of helping (Bacon, 1993, Boyce, 1990; Graham & Boyce, 1989; Gutierrez, 1990, 1992; Lazzari, Ford, & Haughey, 1996; Logan, 1996a; Saulnier, 1994; Simoni & Perez, 1995).

There is a need for established self-help organizations to make a concerted effort to reach out into communities of color and to devise formats that appeal to these groups. This can be accomplished by modifying belief systems and practices to incorporate the cultural outlook of these groups (Simoni & Perez, 1995; Snowden & Lieberman, 1994).

Having people in a community come together to help one another has become an increasing challenge in the 1990s. A sense of community is elusive or short-lived due to the high rates of moving, changing employment, and divorce. Stability is rare in many peoples' lives, particularly those who are marginal socially and economically (Brown, 1995).

Why take time from one's own busy schedule, personal demands, family needs, and so on, to help others? There are multiple benefits to be derived from helping others, and service to community can change a person's life. Service helps us understand people with different backgrounds and different perspectives. This knowledge allows us to learn more about ourselves. We learn about our strengths, shortcomings in our backgrounds, and we grow and adapt to an ever-changing environment. Further, we get the opportunity to develop relationships outside our immediate, and highly "safe," surroundings. Bonds are reinforced when we work together in search of common goals (Segal, 1994).

Turning to external sources for assistance is not the solution to getting communities to be better care giving places. Solutions depend on how ordinary citizens respond to their neighbors in daily interactions, rather than on "total strangers" associated with "professional" care givers, funders, and other stakeholders (Brown, 1995; George, 1992; Jones, Newman, & Isay, 1997). Care giving can be accomplished only through the development of partnerships between the community and external sources: a partnership that respects the community's willingness and abilities to get involved in the help giving process. The types of people who have made a difference are ordinary men and women who believe that all people must share their intellectual and creative resources to make our communities better places to live (Chavis, 1997; Fiffer & Fiffer, 1994).

Caring takes many shapes and forms in this society. There is the formal side of caring, which is often represented by government, professionals, organizations, and funding sources. There is also the informal side of caring. This type of caring is often referred to as volunteerism. However, this perspective may be too narrow, as formal volunteering is only one of the ways in which individuals and communities can show care and compassion. Millions of Americans extend an informal helping hand to their neighbors, relatives, and friends, although the level of caring shown to strangers is not equal to that given to relatives and close friends. Nevertheless, the efforts of the many people who have done a kind deed for some stranger in need are not to be minimized. Many of these kindnesses do not require a huge expenditure of energy, and may require only a few minutes of one's time. Other acts of caring require much time and energy (Wuthnow, 1991).

Indigenous efforts at providing care can also be placed within a self-help paradigm. Efforts at self-help are often motivated by shared concern and the belief that assistance is beneficial to both the individual in need and the one providing help. This form of assistance often emerges from spontaneous interaction or planning by those who share similar concerns. Cultural traditions involved with help seeking and help provision may play a strong role in shaping how a group or community comes together in search of common pursuits (Weber, 1982).

Much has been written about our society's inability or unwillingness to care for others who have suffered misfortune (McKnight, 1995). Rarely does a week go by during which the popular press does not report some tragedy, need, interethnic conflict, or act of selfishness in our society (Boyce, 1991; Wysocki, 1991). Nevertheless, "random acts of kindness and caring" can be found in any community across this country. Many of these acts of caring, unfortunately, are rarely identified and validated by the press and society.

This oversight is most glaring in undervalued communities, especially communities of color (Belluck, 1997; Chideya, 1995; Jones, Newman, & Isay, 1997; Kostarelos, 1995; Logan, 1996; Snowden & Lieberman, 1994). The African American community, for example, has historically relied on practices such as home care and mainstreaming for people with disabilities, predating human service applications of these approaches to care. African Americans value caring for others within the family and community, providing a source from which successful coping strategies have arisen (Daly, Jennings, Beckett, & Leashore, 1995).

Harper (1990, p. 240) sums up the African American experience of providing health care to its community very well when stating:

Blacks have always cared for the sick at home, yet it was never labeled "home care." Blacks have been dying at home and receiving care in the process, yet it was never called "hospice care." Blacks have relieved each other from the caring and curing processes, yet it was never seen as "respite care." Blacks have cared for each other in their homes, in their neighborhoods, and throughout their communities, yet it was never referred to as "volunteerism."

Self-reliance may have a cultural basis, but it also may be reinforced by external factors such as racism in the United States (George, 1992; Yamashiro & Matsuoka, 1997). Racism can take on various forms, from an "inability" to service the needs of a group to an unwillingness to understand and utilize cultural factors in treatment. So what may start out as a cultural pattern, in this case self-reliance, gets reinforced, even when detrimental to the group, because of barriers in service delivery.

Lazzari, Ford, and Haughey (1996), in their research on Latinas who had been identified as active in the community, found four key factors that motivated care provision: (1) seeing the need, (2) feeling personal satisfaction, (3) receiving support from others, and (4) believing in it personally. Acts of caring and kindness do occur within communities of color, and are often performed by individuals who may not be substantially better off than the individuals they help (Delgado & Humm-Delgado, 1982; Hill, 1972; Kostarelos, 1995; Lazzari et al., 1996; Martin & Martin, 1985). Nevertheless, there is a common misperception that people in communities of color have no success stories or are incapable of acts of kindness toward each other. When and if such acts occur, the help provided is often classified as "misguided" and as causing more trouble than it addresses. Fortunately, this bias, has not been accepted by communities of color, where the tradition of helping stretches across centuries and continents (Cox, 1995; Kostarelos, 1995; Neighbors, Elliot, & Gant, 1990).

Sometimes helping occurs out of a good "business" sense, and at other times because it is the "proper thing to do." Regardless of motivation, it is necessary to identify situations in which assistance is provided to learn under what conditions it occurs and to develop approaches for working with helpers. Schwartz (1997, p. 70), eloquently sums up the role of caring within a context of community when stating:

I am convinced that there is nothing special about my neighborhood. I have begun to realize something similar to what you discover about pond water in sixth-grade science. The water in the pond looks just like the processed water that comes out of the tap. But when you dip a test tube in any pond and look at it under the microscope, you discover a very great difference. The water in the pond is teeming with life. I have come to believe it is the same with neighborhoods and communities. Despite the tremendous assault on vernacular life . . . if you look with the right lens you usually find that significant ignored remnants of hospitality [caring and assistance] still exist.

Professional Caring

Professions in general, including social work, have lost part of their glamour in this society (Schwartz, 1997). Schon (1983, pp. 11–13) places this loss within a broader context:

> Professionals claim to contribute to social well-being, put their clients' needs ahead of their own, and hold themselves accountable to standards of competence and morality. But both popular and scholarly critics accuse the professions of serving themselves at the expense of the clients, ignoring their obligations to public service, and failing to police themselves effectively. . . . The crisis of confidence in the professions . . . is bound up with the questions of professional self-interest, bureaucratization, and subordination to the interests of business or government. But it also hinges centrally on the questions of professional knowledge. Is professional knowledge adequate to fulfill the espoused purposes of the profession? Is it sufficient to meet the societal demands which the professions have helped to create?

Caring demonstrated by professionals has been largely unsuccessful at reaching communities of color in urban areas. Why are indigenous efforts more acceptable to these groups? Several key themes address this and must be incorporated into urban social work practice: (1) importance of mutuality; (2) accessibility; (3) affirmation versus stigmatization; (4) multifaceted mission; and (5) primary role of helper is not doing "social work."

Importance of mutuality. A community's breakdown in care giving may be the result of major social, economic, and demographic changes. Communities may have become more fragmented, resulting in breaks in the naturally occurring linkages among indigenous support systems; these linkages provide support and nurturance to individuals and families and create opportunities for them to participate meaningfully in their communities (Benard, 1990; Delgado, 1995b).

In houses of worship, for example, strength derived from mutuality between minister and congregation, among congregation members, and between congregation and community, is a very powerful factor in attracting and maintaining members (Roberts & Thorsheim, 1992). Participation refers to more than involvement and entails both receiving and providing help.

The role of mutuality in the helping process involving nontraditional settings cannot be overlooked in an analysis of why these places are so attractive. Mutuality has two dimensions—obligation and responsiveness. Delgado (1995b), in a study of Puerto Rican elders, found the influence of mutuality to be very strong in the exchange of assistance: (1) communities of color must be willing to seek and receive help from internal resources; (2) a sense of community is found when residents feel they belong to a community, are able to help others, and have others care about them; and (3) when mutuality is an integral part of cultural values, it takes on increased significance in the help seeking and giving process.

Accessibility. The concept of accessibility is multidimensional and covers more than just physical barriers. The concept also consists of geographical, psychological, cultural, and operational factors. These factors are very often interrelated and can be present at any time, some with greater or lesser intensity.

Geographical. Geographical accessibility is probably the simplest to understand regarding nontraditional settings. Simply stated, most nontraditional settings are located within the community and offer relatively easy accessibility. Access to these settings may entail walking only a short distance down a street. However, it is not unusual to have social agencies located in a downtown area of a city or strategically located between several communities. Accessibility in these instances is usually possible only through private or public transportation. Nontraditional settings also offer the additional geographical advantage of possibly being clustered closely together, making multiple accessibility that much easier. If one setting cannot provide assistance, then another setting can.

However, the reader is cautioned that just because a nontraditional setting is physically located in a community does not make it accessible to residents. The following example illustrates this point. It would be perfectly reasonable to assume that an African American church located in the heart of an African American community in a West Coast city would be an asset to the community. However, on closer study, it was seen that this church had a congregation of African Americans who were residents of the community, but were also upwardly mobile. When members of the congregation left the community for a more economically advantaged community located a short distance away, they continued to worship at the church. The church was an asset for the congregation, but was not an asset for the community in which it was geographically located.

Psychological. What makes an agency or nontraditional setting welcoming to the community? Nontraditional settings in general (with some exceptions, most notably botanical shops and folk healing centers in Latino communities) have achieved psychological accessibility. Psychological accessibility refers to the degree of comfort and trust engendered by the setting. This aspect of accessibility is particularly important because it translates into a positive state of mind for the customer.

There is a cultural dimension to a comfort level, with comfort being facilitated by key cultural values such as *personalismo* (the need to relate to individuals versus institutions) and *familismo* (the importance of family as providers). These values reinforce help seeking and help provision within a context that maintains the dignity of the individual in need.

DiAna (1995, p. 32), the owner of an African American beauty parlor, explains why these establishments are natural nontraditional settings for conducting outreach and education in communities: "Most women visit a salon some time in their life or may go with a friend to sit and wait or take their children for services. Women have always found the beauty shop to be a place where they can go to get some reinforcement and advice, either from the hairdresser or from other ladies in the salon."

Psychological accessibility may be the result of the interplay among several factors: (1) strong historical associational experiences; (2) consumers may personally know the individuals who own and operate the setting; (3) people have successfully sought and obtained assistance on previous occasions; (4) the setting fulfills a multitude of needs, thereby not stigmatizing the patron when help is sought; (5) individuals seeking help do not have to fear being discriminated against based on their racial or ethnic background; (6) individuals patronizing these settings are much more than customers or clients; they are known for who they are rather than the problem they are seeking help for; and (7) nontraditional settings provide customers with the opportunity to provide help in return—in short, there is mutuality.

Social service agencies have struggled with how to make their settings more welcoming. There even may be agencies located in the heart of the community that still have great difficulty attracting clients of color. The negative psychological state created in clients can be quite formidable. Clients will always remain "clients." Clients will never be expected to reciprocate when the situation presents itself or to enter into social relationships once their case is closed. Social workers rarely, if ever, live in the community. Consequently, the community is deprived of knowing the worker as a fellow human being. The lack of personal relationships seriously limits the attractiveness of social agencies when compared with nontraditional settings.

Cultural. Cultural accessibility requires an understanding, appreciation, and affirmation of the values and beliefs that are held by the community. It also refers to the use of nonverbal communication, metaphors, symbols, etc. To communicate at this level, there needs to be a very strong grasp of cultural values and history, as well as empathy with the individual seeking help.

Needless to say, a social worker with the same cultural and socioeconomic background as the community will find it much easier to achieve cultural accessibility. However, it is important to note that having the same background does not automatically result in unconditional acceptance. Professional education has a way of creating distance between worker and community. In fact, professional socialization may put the worker in the difficult position of not feeling comfortable in the agency or in the community.

Nontraditional settings have a clear understanding, appreciation, and willingness to exercise cultural factors to increase accessibility. These settings "do what comes naturally" to them, and what comes naturally to them is what the community is seeking. In all likelihood, the individuals working in nontraditional settings are also living in the community and engaging in all aspects of community life. Consequently, they just have to be themselves. Social workers, on the other hand, will have to do a great deal of unlearning and relearning of what it means to be "natural."

Operational. Operational accessibility represents a serious challenge to the social work field and all other helping professions. Operational accessibility focuses on the service structure consumers encounter and the time limits during which they can seek services. Translated into everyday operational terms, it means the experiences encountered when someone seeks services. Nontraditional settings are informal in the way they provide services. There are no forms to fill out or eligibility criteria to meet before a consumer qualifies for services.

Social service agencies require that a person fill out numerous forms and answer very personal questions before qualifying as a "client." This process makes it very difficult, if not at times impossible, to have the worker develop an understanding of who the person seeking help really is.

Days and times of operation are also very limiting when compared with nontraditional settings. Most social service agencies operate during regular working hours and days. It is true that more and more agencies have developed procedures to cover nonstandard operating times. Nontraditional settings, however, can operate 10 to 12 hours per day, or even longer, 6 to 7 days per week. Thus, there are ample opportunities for someone to access these settings.

Accessibility differences between nontraditional settings and social agencies are quite significant. This does not mean that agencies will never be able to compare favorably with nontraditional settings. There are changes that agencies can make to minimize the differences. These changes are possible, as will be explained, but they require a dramatic shift in perspective and a willingness to engage in a new form of practice.

Affirmation versus stigmatization. There is little debate in the social service field that people of color have a propensity to be negatively labeled when seeking and receiving social services (Iglehart & Becerra, 1995). The tendency to label people places the profession of social work at a distinct disadvantage when compared with nontraditional settings. The former invariably requires a client to answer very personal questions before a relationship based on mutual trust and respect is formed. Stigma is inherent on the receiving end of most services provided by social workers.

The process of affirmation is the cornerstone of service provision within nontraditional settings. People in these settings know the individual in a more holistic fashion than do social workers. These individuals may have patronized an establishment for many years before actually seeking services when confronted with an emergency. Thus, the client does not have to fear developing a reputation as someone in constant trouble. Also, the help seeker will share as much information as comfort level allows—an important safeguard against unnecessary intrusion.

Multifaceted mission. Nontraditional settings fulfill multifaceted roles within the community. These roles can consist of most, if not all, of the following: (a) maintenance of cultural heritage; (b) providing a social outlet; (c) selling a product or service; (d) an employment outlet; and (e) community leadership.

Maintenance of cultural heritage. Nontraditional settings fulfill an important role in transmitting cultural values between generations. These institutions very often serve as a bridge between the "old ways" and the "new ways," and help younger generations to keep their cultural values. These establishments are among the few institutions that cater to consumers who speak a "foreign" language.

Nontraditional settings, as well as other forms of social and natural support systems, serve to transmit cultural values, while providing assistance to communities of color. There is a serious gap between generations pertaining to identity, language preference, and help seeking patterns, with youth preferring formal services and their parents and grandparents preferring natural support systems. Natural support systems provide an avenue for socialization into the culture, as well as a resource for help provision (Delgado, 1995b).

Providing a social outlet. Nontraditional settings provide excellent opportunities for community residents, particularly those who are non-English speaking, to create, maintain, and renew friendships. These settings are safe places where patrons can be themselves and not fear discrimination. Nontraditional settings that target racial, ethnic, or other undervalued groups must be prepared to provide an environment in which cultural heritage is valued, and news from the homeland is offered. They must serve as a vehicle for residents to connect easily with each other.

The social outlet that nontraditional settings provide takes on added significance when the community they serve has few "free spaces" where members can interact and be themselves. Too often, people do not have the necessary funds to pay for recreational/social outlets. In essence, communities of color, particularly those whose first language is not English, can rarely venture outside of the community and feel safe and free to be themselves without fear of negative social consequences.

Selling a product or service. The term "merchant" connotes someone who operates a facility where primary function is the selling of goods or services to the community in which it is located. This purpose increases in importance when the service or goods have an ethnic or cultural base. These nontraditional settings may well represent one of the few places where certain products, foods, or other items can be purchased in this country.

Even in circumstances in which such a nontraditional setting makes available a product or service that can be widely purchased, the cultural nature of the setting facilitates economic transactions. For example, beauty parlors can provide a service that appeals to a wide number of ethnic or racial groups. However, this nontraditional setting caters to a particular group, and because the owner and staff are of the same group, the service takes on greater importance because of its cultural context.

Employment outlet. Although most nontraditional settings are relatively small, they do serve as employment outlets for community residents, particularly those with language limitations. People whose knowledge of English and/or lack of formal education limits their employment opportunities to settings that do not require English proficiency may use these outlets extensively.

Businesses play an important role in providing employment opportunities for co-ethnic groups. Some small businesses that are labor intensive (clothing, restaurants, construction, or retail), often attract immigrant entrepreneurs. These small firms, however, need to increase their hiring of workers who are capable of learning required skills and who are willing to remain with the business once they are properly trained (Waldinger, Aldrich, & Ward, 1990).

If the business is located within the geographical area from which it solicits employees, the establishment is not only in a strategic position to hire residents, but also to serve other functions within the community simply by virtue of its location. Thus, examination of community social networks will in all likelihood uncover places of employment playing a prominent role in the lives of workers, their families, and other relevant contacts.

Community leadership. Nontraditional settings can play leadership roles within their communities. The individuals who own, operate, or staff these establishments are in a good position to have in-depth knowledge and understanding of community issues. Their daily contact with residents increases their importance in shaping community opinions, sharing information, and soliciting and encouraging participation in community events.

Depending on their leadership skills, their reputation within the community, and their willingness to assume roles that transcend that associated with nontraditional settings, they can play important roles as leaders. In communities where there are no elected officials or few agency heads of similar ethnicity and background, nontraditional settings may prove to be fertile grounds for leadership development, if leadership doesn't already exist.

Primary role is not doing social work. This dimension of nontraditional settings is probably the simplest to understand, yet will present the most problematic challenges to the profession. By assuming a role other than that of a helper, with few exceptions nontraditional settings are in a position to offer assistance or to be solicited for help, with an understanding that either party can turn down the request. Thus, no one is obligated to enter into a role as provider or receiver of help.

This flexibility in roles, in combination with factors outlined earlier in this chapter, makes the help seeking and help providing completely contingent on the degree of trust and respect that is present. Trust and respect do not have to be present in a social work–client relationship, although it is unquestionably highly desirable. This is particularly true in situations in which the individual receiving help is coerced into the relationship (Rooney, 1988, 1992). Involuntary clients, which is generally the case with people of color, present significant challenges for social workers.

The development of a partnership within this new, nontraditional sector offers much promise for the social work profession, for those in greatest need of services, and for communities. The needs of social service organizations very often seem to be the priority, rather than the needs of the consumer and community. The needs of urban-based communities of color do not come tied in neat bundles, nor do they have tidy problem definitions. Social service organizations based in these communities must connect residents with the larger society, promote a positive sense of purpose and personhood, and provide much needed resources to address a multitude of issues. These organizations must serve multiple roles, one of which is that of being a "family" that meets needs, and promotes growth, much in the same, inclusive way a family would (McLaughlin, 1993).

Personal Qualities and Qualifications of Individuals in Nontraditional Settings

What are the qualities that make people who work in nontraditional settings so attractive? Collins and Pancoast (1976, p. 53) provide one perspective on this question when they state:

> The natural neighbors . . . differ in the degree of interaction they stimulate within their networks. Their helping styles differ according to their sex, their settings, and their individual personalities. But they are alike in their spontaneous response to the needs of others and in their willingness to listen and act on their behalf. They do not view themselves as "doing anything," yet . . . they reach individuals who are not reached by professional social workers. They take on the responsibility of the helping role willingly and carry it out consistently and conscientiously over time, making use of everything they can learn to improve their performance.

These individuals can be referred to as "guides" who have key qualities in common. Guides do more than just introduce one person to another; they broker a person into the web of associational life. Guides tend to be people with a "special eye" and the capacity to recognize those who are in need. Effective guides are also well connected in the interrelationships of community life. These helpers are successful because they are trusted by their community peers, not because they have institutional legitimacy. They share the belief that the community is a reservoir of hospitality waiting to be offered. All they need to do is connect the individual in need with the right community resource. They learn they must say goodbye to the person they guide into community life, and they do not foster dependence. In essence, they are guides and not servants (McKnight, 1995).

McLaughlin (1993) raises points similar to those of McKnight when he examines the importance of what he calls "local leaders" in understanding community needs and issues of youth. These leaders use local knowledge and credibility to craft programs and resources that provide the connective tissue between estranged, cynical, inner-city youth and broader social institutions essential to their productive futures and positive conceptions of self. These leaders have in-depth knowledge of social, political, and economic resources in the larger community. Their roles can easily encompass those of brokers, catalysts, and coaches. These roles facilitate making contacts and linkages to enlarge the opportunities available to youth, and they provide the prerequisite introductions and confidence necessary for access (McLaughlin, 1993). Schwartz (1997, p. 78) acknowledges the presence of individuals who are "natural" helpers: "In informal worlds there are certain people to whom others turn when they have problems in living. These were the kinds of people I stumbled over in the nonprofessional sectors of the mental hospital and who seemed to me to be natural therapists."

The qualities identified by Collins, Pancoast, McKnight, and McLaughlin go beyond the learning that transpires in classrooms, and reflect both personal qualities and the importance of knowing and residing in the community. Community connections make a variety of contacts possible. Most successful guides come from the community rather than service systems. A person interested in human services can spend money and receive training to be able to help others. However, there is no formal curriculum that can connect a person to associational community life. This capacity is enhanced through years of experience and contributions to community life (McKnight, 1995).

Regardless of whether these special individuals are called guides, lay health advisors, natural support providers, helpers, or leaders, they represent a vast untapped resource for the field of social work. There is much that can be learned about how and why they help, how they view the community, and why the community allows them to practice. In addition, the fact that these individuals are rarely academically trained to provide assistance opens up further avenues of inquiry.

There invariably is an initial distrust social workers may have about people in nontraditional settings and other "natural helpers." However, professionals who come into contact with natural helpers will soon become admirers and advocates of their efforts, assuming social workers are willing to be open-minded and take the time to get to know them. These helpers are often central figures in neighborhood networks, perform unique and important human services, and are potential colleagues in a partnership with social workers (Collins & Pancoast, 1976).

Practitioners' reluctance to embrace nontraditional settings and other forms of social and natural supports also may be the result of the late stage at which they get involved in providing assistance. This may be due to social workers and other human service workers typically being at the end of the help seeking process. Before seeking formal help, clients often have engaged in considerable, but ineffective, coping activity. Often, indigenous resources such as social support systems may be absent, nonresponsive, or deficient, inhibiting an individual's ability to function effectively (Pearson, 1990). Seeking assistance from formal services is often undertaken after a series of efforts to get help from natural sources.

Nontraditional settings can provide help to all age groups within a community. Nontraditional settings provide nontraditional services, during nontraditional times, with nontraditional personnel. They are not bound by such traditional considerations such as eligibility, catchment areas, staff qualifications, and other bureaucratic factors. In essence, nontraditional settings are effective and attractive because they are attuned to local needs and considerations.

Barriers to Collaboration

Although the rewards of collaboration within nontraditional settings are immense, so are the formidable barriers that must be surmounted. One of the primary reasons such partnerships are so rewarding is because collaboration is so rare in the human service field in general, let alone within nontraditional settings. The professional literature on interagency collaboration identifies numerous obstacles to successful collaboration (Delgado & Humm-Delgado, 1980; Gans & Horton, 1975; Gray, 1989; Kraus, 1984).

Effective collaboration between social service agencies and those in nontraditional settings requires negotiating at least four significant barriers: (1) lack of trust on the part of both parties; (2) different conceptual underpinnings for assessment and intervention; (3) lack of knowledge and appreciation of each other's mission (purpose) and nature of work; and (4) different structural and operational nature of services. These four barriers will likely be present in any initial effort at developing a partnership. The degree to which each is significant, ranging from slight to formidable, depends on the situation; specifically, on the reputation of the people in the setting seeking to develop collaboration, and the nontraditional setting's history of interaction with social service organizations. If past interactions have been positive, then problems are less significant; if negative, problems may be insurmountable.

Lack of trust. Undertaking any cooperative venture, whether formal or informal, requires that all parties involved trust each other (Lenrow & Burch, 1981). This trust takes on added significance when plans go astray, and some party bears a disproportionate amount of distress or loss as a result. If there is a high level of trust, it makes such situations much easier to weather. However if the trust level is low or nonexistent, then a mishap will be reason enough to dissolve a partnership and create lifelong enemies.

Lack of trust is manifested in many ways, and results in misinterpretation of actions on the part of those in formal and nontraditional settings. Culturally appropriate behaviors and attitudes may be misinterpreted as resistance, hostility, pathology, ignorance, lack of sensitivity and appreciation of what the provider can offer, and of distrust. Nontraditional settings are not immune from stereotyping and bias against formal systems, and this may seriously undermine the development of trust essential to any cooperative venture (Delgado, 1994).

Lack of trust becomes an insurmountable barrier when one or both parties have entered into a collaborative partnership without serious thought about the work and time needed for success. It arises when they have not taken the implications of a partnership seriously and are prepared to dissolve the relationship at a moments notice. This is usually the time when misunderstandings arise, and lack of trust is to be expected.

Trust is developed by successfully negotiating misunderstandings or "incidents." That is why it is so important to plan an initial collaborative activity that is time limited, has a high probability of success, and allows all parties to terminate the agreement without major expenditure of time and effort. Examples of these activities will be presented in Section III.

Different conceptual underpinnings for assessment and intervention. One cannot minimize the importance of how problems are conceptualized (Cohen, Mowbray, Gillette, & Thompson, 1992; Eng & Hatch, 1992). Social workers who are part of a multidisciplinary team will quickly realize that other professions have a "different world view," which can often be traced back to professional education and socialization. Differences between social workers and informal helpers like those found in nontraditional settings can be quite striking. Professionals and informal helpers often have two quite different perspectives on how assistance should be provided. The professional generally views assessment as based on standards acquired through training and experience. Knowledge and expertise are valued in establishing the credibility of the help provided. These standards may have little meaning for informal helpers, as their form of helping is predicated on informal personal relationships, shared experiences, and altruism. Further, their credibility and acceptance are determined by the norms of exchange within the network (Froland, Pancoast, Chapman, & Kimboko, 1981).

Different conceptualizations do not necessarily represent an insurmountable barrier. Both parties, social workers as well as informal helpers, need to develop a system that conveys to the other the goals and approaches used to provide assistance. How one helper views the presenting situation needs to be translated for the other. Once this "code" has been cracked, it is possible to share information and perspectives.

It would be a mistake for social workers to expect helpers in nontraditional settings to change their world view and adopt the conceptualization of the professional. Such a view change may invalidate the work that is accomplished in nontraditional settings. In addition, if a social worker attempts and fails to bring about this conversion, it may seriously undermine any current or future effort at developing a partnership. Social workers must learn how informal helpers conceptualize presenting requests for assistance.

Delgado (1977) in studying Puerto Rican mediums (a kind of folk healer), concludes that these helpers have a great deal in common with social workers. Both have a propensity toward task-oriented therapy, place heavy emphasis on recognizing the impact of environmental factors on psychic functioning, and utilize similar treatment modalities (individual, family, group). Help sessions can range from immediate crisis intervention to long-term help. Treatment is essentially a social process that may be delineated, for the purposes of analysis, as consisting primarily of three basic, interdependent factors: a system of beliefs and concepts, a set of techniques, and a system of social relations. Although parallels can be drawn between these two systems, the conceptualization of the etiology of a problem is different.

As already indicated, informal helpers do have a conceptualization that guides their interventions. Social workers may subscribe to theories of relationship; mediums subscribe to interventions by the metaphysical (Singer, 1984). Different credentialing processes are in operation. For the social worker, credentialing involves universities and accrediting bodies; in the case of the medium, it involves God.

Lack of knowledge and appreciation of each other's mission and nature of work. The lack of exposure and contact with each other often results in misinformation and ignorance concerning each party's purpose and ways of working (Lavoie, Farquharson, & Kennedy, 1994; Stewart, Banks, Crossman, & Poel, 1994). In all likelihood, people in formal and nontraditional settings either know nothing of each other's purpose or, if they do, it would tend to be some horror story that discourages contact, let alone collaboration. Neither party has access to documents, reading material, and other forms of information that can serve to eliminate stereotypes.

Consequently, increasing awareness can only be accomplished through lengthy conversations and extended visits at each other's settings. Social workers can extend invitations to staff and owners of nontraditional settings to visit the agency. These visits will provide ample opportunities to share and learn. Social workers, in turn, can spend time in nontraditional settings, learning more about the setting's operation and its customers. This aspect of learning is labor intensive. However, there are no shortcuts to learning and developing a relationship.

Different structural and operational nature of services. Not only do nontraditional settings look very different from social agencies, their method of operation is also dramatically different. Nontraditional settings have very extensive hours and, depending on the setting, may even be open 7 days per week. Further, these settings do not have extensive intake procedures, rules and regulations, and do not subscribe to the concept of "catchment area." These operational factors minimize distance between consumer (client) and helper (provider).

Social service agencies generally have very formal hours and days of operation. These settings must abide by formal rules and regulations, one of which is a catchment area requirement. These settings must first determine eligibility and do so by asking numerous and, at times, very embarrassing questions. Such a process does not engender the development of a positive and trusting relationship.

The barriers outlined above may seem quite formidable. However, there are various strategies that social agencies and social workers can employ to move beyond these obstacles to achieve meaningful and productive partnerships within nontraditional settings. Nevertheless, it is important for those in agencies to take note of these barriers and realize that they will not go away on their own.

Critique of Nontraditional Settings

Although much can be said about the value and importance of nontraditional settings in the lives of people of color, these establishments are not without their limitations. Interestingly, the concept of nontraditional setting has much appeal to both "progressives" and "conservatives" alike. Gottlieb (1988, p. 13) sums up this appeal quite well when analyzing the concept of social support:

> For conservatives, the concept of social support resonates because it connotes reliance on voluntary and private arrangements for the delivery of human services because it smacks of a self-help ethos. For liberals, social support represents one avenue to empowering citizens, enlarging their control over their lives, and eventually leading to reforms in the community's health and welfare institutions that are predicated on greater public participation.

Saleebey (1996), a leading proponent of a strengths perspective, outlines several areas of critique in using such an approach: (1) positive thinking in disguise (the goal is to build a perspective that is long-lasting rather than short-term to overcome a crisis); (2) reframing misery (reality is faced, but within a context of understanding survival and other coping mechanisms); (3) pollyannaism (there is an understanding that clients are not without faults or strengths); (4) ignoring reality (a strengths perspective does not discount problems, but examines them within a context); and (5) yes, but . . . (strengths may be addressed to a limited extent but are not core or systematically identified and used in interventions).

Whittaker and Garbarino (1983) raise similar concerns about social support networks. They note that social support networks offer no panacea or quick solution to the problems faced by human service practitioners. Networks can be destructive as well as supportive, and an improper infusion of professional expertise can seriously undermine or quickly eliminate informality, mutuality, and reciprocity—vital elements in the care giving process.

Olsen (1983) raises concerns similar to those of Whittaker and Garbarino, stressing that the thrust towards volunteerism does not result in government and professional abdication of their responsibility to provide resources, services, and coherent welfare policies. Community-based networks cannot be expected to fill in the gaps caused by lack of funds or lack of professional competence. Efforts must be made to distinguish between the respective and complementary roles of the professional and community network sectors, maintaining accountability and sufficient distance to enable each party to remain the severest critic of the other.

Logan (1996b) issues a warning to the profession about relying solely on finding African American solutions to African American needs and problems. It is by no means a responsibility that belongs solely to African Americans; solutions must be multifaceted and targeted toward the achievement of structural changes in society.

Delgado (1996a, p. 58), in advocating collaboration between agencies and Puerto Rican food establishments (grocery stores and restaurants), raises a point of caution:

> It is necessary, however, to pause and examine the implications of utilizing "self-help" and "natural support systems" concepts with undervalued communities. . . . Concepts such as the aforementioned are receiving a great deal of attention at the national and local levels. Both the political "right" and "left" have stressed the importance of empowering communities as an approach for meeting social and economic needs. Nevertheless, the manner in which empowerment practices are operationalized and the meaning they have for government intervention, will vary depending upon one's political perspective.

Rothman (1994) echoes Delgado's sentiments when emphasizing that the use of indigenous resources alleviates reliance on formal systems and professional experts. As a result, providers must recognize the value of informal support, without reducing public commitment to formal supports for groups requiring it. Schwartz (1997) cautions us not to get into a "bad" versus "good" stance when examining formal and informal systems of care by drawing a contrast between formal and informal worlds and concluding that the former is all bad and the latter is all good. It is the severely skewed imbalance between the two that has negative consequences. Cultural factors exercise great influence over people's lives. Thus, as professions have risen in dominance, they have assumed authority over aspects of life that the ordinary rules of one's culture once governed, creating tension between these two systems.

Popple's (1996, p. 152) summary of the critiques of the British model of community care is similar to those of informal care on this side of the Atlantic:

> . . . community care has been actively promoted by the Right for a number of reasons. These usually revolve around the need to avoid the expense of institutional care, but also because this form of care is perceived as the most "appropriate" and "natural" form of care for the dependent. This view is derived from the residualist or anti-collectivist approach to welfare whereby the family is seen as the locus of care, and the role of the statutory sector only comes into play when the unit has broken down in some way.

Development of Innovative Community Approaches to Practice

The relearning of new approaches for practice within nontraditional settings is necessary if social work is to be successful in engaging these institutions:

> We must begin by reorienting our perspective because our training and culture impose conceptual baggage that stands in our way. One of my favorite metaphors is the saying, "If the only tool you have is a hammer, then you tend to treat every problem as if it were a nail." . . . Our principal tool is one-to-one intervention, professional to client . . . few professionals have reoriented their basic thinking about helping . . . They continue to see most, if not all, of their clients and their problems as nails for which the hammer of direct dyadic intervention is the appropriate tool . . . The hammer–nail metaphor is powerful because it highlights how our investment in professional roles and practices blind us to other tools and resources for improving the quality of human life." (Garbarino, 1983, pp. 16–17).

The metaphor of hammer and nail illustrates the narrowness of view of the helping professions regarding needs and solutions. They thereby eschew a multitude of approaches that are often considered "radical" and "unorthodox." It is necessary to dare to think in a new way, to shift from an old to a new paradigm, even though it causes a great deal of discomfort and tension for social workers and their agencies.

Conclusion

Urban-based nontraditional settings have increased in importance during the last decade, as government and other funders of social services have taken a much more punitive approach toward consumers of social services. People in nontraditional settings have experienced this change in climate, and many have responded to make up for diminished formal services.

Nontraditional settings can be found in any community, urban or rural, and can take a variety of forms. These settings do not have bold neon signs describing the social services they provide. Instead, they are camouflaged as everyday types of establishments. This not only increases their attractiveness to the community, it also increases the challenges for social workers in identifying and engaging people in these settings in collaborative activities.

Those in nontraditional settings have many organizational and personal qualities that make them attractive to communities. The factors outlined in this chapter must be taken into account in the planning of collaborative partnerships within nontraditional settings. However, as will be addressed in Chapter 10, identification and engagement of people in these institutions may not result in collaborative activities.

4

Principles and Strategies

Strategies of Intervention in Urban Communities of Color

Professional intervention, when needed, must take into consideration four key factors: (1) it must not replace or undermine local (indigenous) efforts; (2) it must be undertaken with extreme care and consideration of its impact on the greater community; (3) it must ultimately achieve the goal of helping; and (4) it must stimulate indigenous healing capacities (Schwartz, 1997). Social work intervention strategies in urban communities of color especially must take these considerations into account.

Levels of Community Service Delivery

Interventions can occur within four levels of community service delivery (Fig. 1). Social service delivery at the community level must be conceptualized within these four dimensions. Each level of service delivery, or arena, represents a primary area of dominance and influence. Their boundaries, however, are permeable, and do not preclude any form of interaction or relationship among the different levels. Consequently, nontraditional settings can be conceptualized as coexisting with a variety of other formal or informal sources of care.

Movement along the service delivery continuum from Level 1 to Level 4 represents a shift in the formality of services, structure of the setting, degree to which cultural factors have or will be taken into consideration, and the personal nature of the relationship between the consumer and the provider. Service delivery transpires within a context influenced by the culture, values, and ideologies of the groups and individuals initiating intervention. Consequently, these actors determine what legitimate problems are to be solved and the means through which to address them (Iglehart & Becerra, 1995).

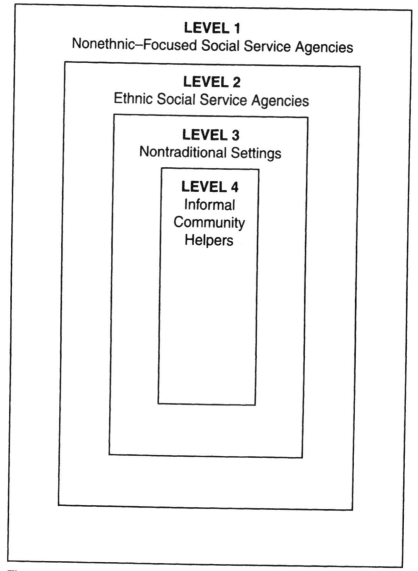

Figure 1. Service Delivery at the Community Level.

Level 1 consists of nonprofit, public or private, nonethnic agencies. These institutions are generally government related or receive most, if not all, of their funding from conventional funding sources. These organizations are the most common form of service delivery in communities, regardless of their ethnic composition. They rarely will have many staff members or board members who are residents of the community they serve. As a result, services generally will reflect a standardized quality, with minimal effort to accommodate cultural values and traditions. The organizational climate tends to be formal and highly structured, severely limiting the nature of the client-worker relationship. Most of these organizations rarely subscribe to empowerment and participation principles. When they do, these principles tend to be operationalized along very narrow, nonthreatening lines. This level also includes organizations that may have a social action mission, and may, in the course of organizing communities, provide services that may be considered conventional. Their primary mission, however, is oriented to social action.

In Level 2 are ethnic social agencies, which represent formalized institutions with roots in the community: agencies developed as a result of a community's need to help its own residents (Iglehart & Becerra, 1995; Jenkins, 1981). These organizations have a clear statement of goals and an open commitment to a defined ethnic group. The ethnic agency serves as an ethnic organization and a "special" form of social agency. To succeed, an ethnic agency must find a way to balance and incorporate both service and ethnic goals in a single delivery system (Jenkins, 1981).

The involvement of ethnic-based community organizations in service collaboration is an effective way of involving communities (Harrington, 1994). These institutions are well situated and enjoy the trust and goodwill of their communities. In addition, they are cognizant of the prevalent cultural values and mores of their communities (Bastian, 1995). Community-based organizations play a critical role in developing and implementing community-based research, with the results being useful in developing follow-up and new programs and services (Van Vught, 1994).

However these organizations, which are often in the best position to reach out and engage residents, might be reluctant to provide help, as they may be regarding HIV/AIDS. This reluctance, or inability, may be the result of fears associated with this disease, of being severely hampered by funding constraints, or being overwhelmed with a multitude of other community needs that they cannot meet successfully (Singer, Castillo, Davison, & Flores, 1990). In short, these agencies may not play an important role in addressing this epidemic. Depending on local circumstances, there may be other population groups not being effectively served, or served at all.

Ethnic agencies are generally smaller organizations and have lower budgets than Level 1 organizations, and there are fewer of them in the community. The ethnic composition of staff and board members is often similar to that of the community, with most staff and board members residing in the community. The staff generally consists of nonprofessionals. Organizationally, they may be closer to primary-type agencies (storefronts and collectives) than bureaucracies. This often translates into a friendly, informal atmosphere, facilitating worker-client interactions and the use of empowerment principles. Agencies at this level can also refer clients to less formal ethnic organizations that provide various types of services that can be considered social in nature, but are primarily or totally staffed by non-professional community residents.

Level 3 consists of nontraditional settings. Nontraditional settings can be defined as places in a community where individuals gather to purchase a product or service or congregate for social purposes. By their very nature, these settings facilitate conversation and exchanges of concerns and advice, minimizing stigma for those seeking assistance. Exchange of advice and assistance is mutual. These settings are generally staffed by individuals who share the same ethnic and socioeconomic background, and other key characteristics such as gender, religion, etc. They are the consumers (maximizing psychological, geographical, and cultural access), and one of their primary roles includes being a "helper."

Nontraditional settings tend to be small, although numerically are probably the most represented institutions in the community. They do not have to be the most centrally located place in a community, and can be found throughout all sectors. Nevertheless, most communities of color have a section of the community where residents congregate, or businesses and other types of institutions are located. As a result, it would not be out of the ordinary to find multiple nontraditional settings located within one city block; in fact, it is quite possible to find similar types of settings close to each other and competing for the same customers.

Level 4 represents those individuals who have assumed important helper roles within the community but do not have any institutional base or affiliation. These individuals can be folk healers, neighbors who act as advocates, those willing to help in case of emergency, etc. By not having an institutional base, these helpers are very often "invisible" to the outside world and, as a result, are very difficult to locate and engage. Nevertheless, they may well represent the fabric, or glue, that is necessary for a community of color to survive through difficult times.

The four levels of service delivery differ according to their visibility, ubiquitousness, and willingness to collaborate with social workers in the development of activities or projects targeting the community. Rothman (1994) acknowledges that the availability and function of a wide range of informal-based (nontraditional) community resources can transcend all four levels of help. Groups can include ethnic organizations; neighborhood associations; block associations; and social, political, religious, and fraternal organizations. Activities can include all or some of the following: discussions, sharing recreational or cultural interests, field trips, and community involvement.

Level 1 and 2 institutions are very similar. In fact, Level 2 ethnic agencies may parallel those of Level 1, with the exception of staffing composition and some modification of service delivery, which reflects cultural values. Nevertheless, these institutions are still formal social service organizations, with all the associated advantages and disadvantages. Their private, nonprofit status requires them to follow most, if not all, of the rules and regulations associated with the Level 1 type of organization, although they will in all likelihood reflect a cultural affinity for the community.

Their attractiveness to the community may, in part, stem from a reliance and preference for hiring nonprofessional staff. Professional staffing, as a result, is seen as a barrier that distances the worker from the client. This distance becomes a significant impediment to understanding and engaging clients (Iglehart & Becerra, 1995). Hiring staff who are not too dissimilar from people in the community is often viewed as an advantage for service delivery. In addition, these agencies may not be able to afford professional staff with the same community background.

Level 3 institutions, on the other hand, will not be staffed by social workers or other helping professionals, nor will they have a rich history of collaborating with human service organizations, although they may not be averse to doing so if approached. However, many of these settings have never been approached, or visited by social workers. These institutions will never look like a typical social service agency, nor will they operate like one. A high degree of informality and personalized service will typify the interactions in these settings.

Level 4 helpers, however, are difficult to generalize because their individuality is both a strength and a weakness. These community helpers may not currently be working in the social service field but may have done so at some point in their lives. As a result, they have a good working knowledge of the social service system. Community helpers may also be individuals who are bilingual and possess the necessary qualities to act as advocates for others. They may also be individuals who are healers or who possess the qualities of good listening, empathy, and advice giving and, as a result, are well respected and valued by the community.

The professional literature has numerous examples of these and other types of helpers. Lazzari, Ford, and Haughey (1996, p. 202) provide an excellent description of the multifaceted roles Level 4 helpers play within a Latino community they studied:

> The women in this study serve as role models not only for young Hispanic women and men, but also for social work professions. Their knowledge and skills are vast, yet their contributions go largely unrecognized. Although many of the women had the equivalent of a high school diploma, they were actively engaged in the roles of generalists in social work practice, including educator, advocate, mediator, counselor, grassroots organizer, consultant, social conscience, liaison, case manager, facilitator, and director.

Mendoza (1980) also provides an excellent example of a Level 4 helper in the identification of a "servidor," or individual who serves his or her community. These individuals were next door neighbors, family friends, or just community residents. Her research among Latino elders found a type of informal helper who provided various forms of expressive and instrumental assistance. These "servidores" substituted for family members who, because of geographical distance from elders or because of their own needs, could not help their elder family member. The servidores' assistance played a pivotal role in keeping elders living in the community when they were at risk for placement in nursing homes or other institutional settings. These helpers required no monetary payment or had no expectations of reciprocal help. Care was provided because it was the "right thing to do."

Intervention Strategies and Communities of Color

There are a number of significant strategies that, if incorporated into urban social work practice, will help the profession reaffirm its mission of addressing oppression of undervalued groups: (1) empowerment; (2) utilization of a strengths perspective; (3) use of a community focus for service delivery; (4) use of multicultural principles and concepts; and (5) development of new arenas for collaborative practice.

Empowerment. The concept of empowerment has been widely accepted within the profession (Lee, 1994d; Solomon, 1976). This concept strikes at the heart of what social workers consider to be a key aspect separating the profession from other helping professions. Solomon (1976, p. 19), who is widely considered to be one of the first social workers to use the principle of empowerment as a mechanism for changing the power relationship between worker and client/community, defines empowerment as: "a process whereby the social worker engages in a set of activities with the client . . . that aim to reduce the powerlessness that has been created by negative valuations based on membership in a stigmatized group."

The literature on empowerment has addressed it from a multifaceted perspective (Gutierrez, GlenMaye, & DeLois, 1995; Gutierrez & Ortega, 1991). Empowerment can be viewed as a process (including the development of self-esteem), method (participation), approach (strengths- and asset-based), and a goal for practice. These four perspectives can exist individually or in combination, making for a dynamic and highly localized way to operationalize empowerment. Thus, the concept of empowerment does not have a fixed, universal meaning. Nevertheless, as a principle for practice it has far-reaching implications for work with undervalued, urban-based communities.

Critical consciousness, a crucial component of empowerment and multiculturalism, can be defined as a process for developing and exercising power that results from greater self-awareness (Gutierrez et al., 1995). Thus, greater awareness of self is a fundamental component of any effort to operationalize empowerment. Self-awareness brings with it a better understanding of one's potential for achieving change and all of the ramifications that spring from these actions. Critical consciousness is also an important dimension of multiculturalism and is manifested through greater self-awareness of one's ethnic/racial heritage.

Gutierrez et al. (1995) attribute the rise of empowerment practice within the past two decades to a concerted effort on the part of human services to address undervalued groups. Moore (1992) views the African American church as playing an empowering role within that community by being a source of mutual assistance and a center for considerable social change. Brashears and Roberts (1996), too, view the African American church as a source and vehicle for change at the micro- and macro-levels.

Empowerment can be accomplished only through the recognition of the power imbalance between worker and client. It necessitates having consumers take greater responsibility for bringing about positive change in their lives and community (Gutierrez, 1992; Gutierrez, Alvarez, Nemon, & Lewis, 1996; Gutierrez & Ortega, 1990). There is no question that there is a need for policies designed to empower clients and to preserve their ability, freedom, and dignity. A strengths perspective toward social policy can assist social workers in accomplishing these essential tasks (Chapin, 1995). In essence, empowerment not only allows for participation, it relies and solicits it; in the process it seeks to maintain the dignity of the person and community (Holmes, 1992).

It is critical to stress the importance of community as a context in which members are empowered. This is where individuals strive to meet their needs, pursue self-interests, and exert the greatest self-determination and control over their lives. The community becomes a resource for discovering and joining with others who share the same needs and interests (Gidron & Chesler, 1994).

Social workers who subscribe to empowerment principles will quickly realize the tension inherent in working with consumers and communities to bring about purposeful change. For example, in the construction of research models, we must take care that those groups or populations that are the subjects of study do not become objects of study (Editorial, 1994).

In the arena of social planning and program development, empowerment represents the difference between planning for and planning with clients (Forester, 1989). The difference is much more than semantic. Planning with clients entails entering into a co-equal relationship with a community. It is a form of partnership that is time consuming, requiring tremendous flexibility on the part of the worker. Planning involves sharing and an understanding that the community is the best judge of what it needs. Nevertheless, the rewards can be most impressive.

Lee (1994d) and other scholars (Gutierrez et al., 1996; Staples, 1984) have outlined a three-pronged rationale for using empowerment principles in social work practice: (a) development of self-esteem; (b) increased knowledge and skills; and (c) cultivation of indigenous resources. However, the addition of a fourth prong, community participation, provides a more comprehensive approach toward empowerment.

Development of self-esteem. It is widely recognized that the first step in achieving independence and control over one's life and community begins with the desire to do so (Mecca, Smelser, & Vasconcellos, 1989). This critical initial step is only possible when one believes one is worthy of a better existence and is capable of achieving it (Smelser, 1989). Thus, achievement of self-esteem, in the context of empowerment in communities of color, requires cultural and ethnic pride (Delgado, 1997c; Gordon, 1996).

To achieve this goal services must be well grounded in cultural history as a component of general self-esteem and social competence. Unfortunately, within the broader community context there is often little with which to ascribe value or pride to African American or Latino youth (McLaughlin, 1993). Thus, achievement of self-esteem cannot be accomplished without enhanced cultural and ethnic pride.

Increased knowledge and skills (capacity enhancement). The strategic development of community knowledge and skills is often referred to as capacity enhancement. The term "capacity enhancement" is used increasingly in the field of human services. Community capacity enhancement can be defined as development of initiatives to identify, support, and enhance local capabilities in addressing locally identified needs (McKnight & Kretzman, 1990). Capacity enhancement's appeal to social work and other helping professions stems from: (1) its embrace of a strengths/assets perspective; (2) its stress on community participation; (3) the importance it places on partnership development; and (4) its reliance on indigenous resources as the foundation for development.

Capacity enhancement is predicated on a belief that there is a retrenchment on the part of government toward undervalued communities, particularly those that are urban based, requiring these communities to seek alternatives to "outside" community resources. By turning to internal (indigenous) resources, these communities can be empowered to develop and control avenues for developing their capacities.

Capacity enhancement is a multifaced concept that consists of five distinct, yet complementary, levels: (1) goals for practice; (2) philosophical stance (set of guiding principles); (3) methods (participation and skill enhancement); (4) process (further development of self-esteem); and (5) approach (strengths-based/assets). These five levels for viewing capacity enhancement provide practitioners with a variety of perspectives on how best to conceptualize and operationalize this concept in service to community. The concept has particular relevance for undervalued communities that, as a result of historical and current developments, have been systematically taught that they have no marketable skills or history worth saving and learning about. Communities of color are a prime example of these destructive processes. Collaborative practice within nontraditional settings is one form of enhancing community capacity.

Boyte and Kari (1996, p. 25) highlight the importance of capacity enhancement in describing a session between deaf youngsters and two social workers:

In one session, a group of deaf youngsters listed dozens of problems . . . Afterwards, the social workers . . . told our workshop leader that in more than twenty years of combined work with the deaf, they had never heard anyone ask hearing-impaired teenagers what they themselves could do about the problems that they experience . . . Most disability programs view those whom they serve as people at risk, in need of help. The idea that people with a disability might be capable of creative problem solving . . . is not normally part of the training that professionals receive.

Cultivation of indigenous resources. When Benson (1996, p. 9), a leading researcher on asset (indigenous resources) building for youths, was asked what can people do to create assets, he noted: "We need purposeful asset building across the community, and we also need 'random acts' of asset building by individuals . . . There is a common core of commitment to things that matter. As communities, we must take time to name it, to share it, to talk about it and to keep it visible—for the future of our young people."

When applied to communities of color, this statement refers to a wide range of potential indigenous resources. These resources have generally been conceptualized as natural support systems of various kinds (Baker, 1976; Delgado, 1995a, 1996a). Some of these support systems can be classified as nontraditional settings and others as helpers. Although the operationalization of natural support systems, which are cultural variations of social supports, will vary according to ethnic and racial groups, they still fulfill key roles within communities.

Social work intervention within communities of color must emphasize increased usage of indigenous support structures and decreased reliance on external structures. Logan (1996c) advocates the development of an integrated, four-part set of strategies, one of which emphasizes capacity enhancement, for addressing African American needs, but that is also applicable to other groups of color: (1) support of executive (primary functions of families) systems; (2) strengthening generational boundaries (role-specific responsibilities and expectations); (3) strengthening or changing contextual (social and political) concerns; and (4) provision of individual (self-worth and self-esteem) support.

Community participation. Empowerment and purposeful change cannot be achieved without meaningful consumer and community participation (Aldrich & Waldinger, 1990; Florin & Wandersman, 1990; Sarri & Sarri, 1992). The concept of community participation in decision making took life and form during the 1960s, when government sought and provided avenues for participation and made efforts to renew and reinterpret neighborhood-based services (Halpern, 1995).

Individuals, organizations, and communities resist or reject change when participation is either seriously limited or discouraged: (1) there is a lack of active, ongoing involvement in innovation and change; (2) there is a sense of powerlessness, actual or perceived; (3) there is a lack of information and knowledge about the goals of the effort to change; and (4) there is lack of active participation and empowerment of the target population (Sarri & Sarri, 1992). Participation in decisions impacting on the community, particularly those that influence how a "problem" is defined, represents an important dimension of empowerment.

Empowerment, in addition, necessitates possessing a vision that is predicated on a new way of thinking about old problems. Empowerment forces us to view the world differently, as it abandons the limits and distortions of the pathology model and focuses on human strengths and abilities as the proper starting point for social work practice (Holmes, 1992). This new thinking fosters development of innovative forms of practice that are community based, actively solicits involvement of community sectors not normally involved, and creates opportunities for partnerships. Social work, in essence, needs to view the environment as an invaluable helping resource and not as a source of problems (Sullivan, 1992).

Community participation can be undertaken in a variety of ways, one of which is employment of local residents and former consumers. Koester (1994) and Vazquez (1994), for example, report that staff, in this case former drug users who were indigenous to the community being studied or served, were the single most important component in their AIDS prevention program. These staff members knew the history, values, and concerns of drug abusers and residents who were at greatest risk for sharing needles. Current drug abusers, in turn, knew and respected staff who were in active recovery, minimizing distrust. Staff were also well aware of the culture of the street, shared language, and had a desire to help their community. This desire went beyond that usually associated with employment. Participation in this example empowered both the workers and the community.

Utilization of a strengths perspective. The decade of the 1990s has witnessed exciting developments regarding the use of natural support systems/assets/resiliency approaches for reaching undervalued communities across the United States (Eckenrode, 1991; Freeman, 1997; Glugoski, Reisch, & Rivera, 1994; Kretzmann & McKnight, 1993; Williams & Wright, 1992). These developments have highlighted the importance of human service organizations collaborating with indigenous community resources (Barrera & Reese, 1993; Daley & Wong, 1994; Gutierrez & Ortega, 1991; Martin & Martin, 1985; Mason, 1994; Thompson & Peebles-Wilkins, 1992; Weick, Rapp, Sullivan, & Kisthardt, 1989). These indigenous resources, in turn, are deeply rooted in cultural traditions of care giving and care seeking (Ghali, 1982; Longres, 1988; Morales, 1992; Rivera, 1990), and take on greater significance when a group has been uprooted to an alien land and culture (Gutierrez, Ortega, & Suarez, 1990).

Kozol (1995), in his book *Amazing Grace,* examines the lives of children in the South Bronx, New York City. The author paints a portrait of hope and survival and, in several cases, thriving children living in a sea of untold dangers and despair. The ability to see through the most obvious signs of need and problems to identify strengths and resilience is a philosophy or world view that has tremendous implications for consumers and providers of social services (Sandler, Miller, Short, & Wolchik, 1989).

A strengths perspective has far-reaching implications for clients and workers by making workers understand that, however "disadvantaged" or in need, individuals have survived, and in some cases thrived. A person's ability to survive must be examined and be well understood and appreciated. Only through a better understanding of how people survive can we identify their internal strengths. As social workers we must tap into these assets and build on their possibilities (Saleebey, 1992).

The concept of strengths is represented in the professional literature in a variety of forms, with assets (Benson, 1996; McKnight & Kretzmann, 1990), resiliency (Denby, 1996; Newcomb, 1992; Reed-Victor & Stronge, 1997; Rutter, 1987; Werner, 1991), coping (Daly, Jennings, Beckett, & Leashore, 1995; Eckenrode, 1991; Hathaway & Pargament, 1992; Lazarus & Folkman, 1991; Monat & Lazarus, 1991), protective factors (Mathias, 1996), and natural support systems (Delgado & Humm-Delgado, 1982; Gottlieb, 1988) being the most popular manifestations of this concept.

Strengths-based practice offers a tremendous potential for reaching undervalued and underserved communities (Chapin, 1995; Freeman, 1997; Hill, 1972; Logan, 1996a; Pollio, McDonald, & North, 1996). Gutierrez et al. (1996) have used community strengths from an organizing perspective by identifying areas of positive functioning, and using them as a central focus for organizing initiatives.

There is a need for a strengths-based paradigm for communities of color that have non-Eurocentric cultures. This paradigm must identify successful coping strategies that can be incorporated into more effective intervention strategies, which can be offered (Daly et al., 1995).

A strengths perspective can also be used to analyze how families adjust to life in the United States by focusing on client's self-reliance and their motivation to address concerns within their own communities, as in the case of Central American refugees in Los Angeles, California (Dorrington, 1995). It is also important to use a strengths perspective in policy formation, to develop in policy practitioners the mind set and skills to create options for inclusion and empowerment (Chapin, 1995).

A strengths perspective, unlike the more commonly used deficit approach, serves to identify, mobilize, reinforce, and enhance existing resources (expressive, informational, and instrumental) in the development of community solutions to community concerns. This perspective offers an alternative conception of the environment, and promotes matching the inherent strengths of the individual with naturally occurring resources in the environment. Tapping these strengths serves to maximize the potential of clients and communities. When viewed from a strengths perspective, the environment serves as a source of opportunities for clients, and increases the number of helping resources (Sullivan, 1992).

Saleebey (1996), one of the leading social work proponents of a strengths perspective, attributes the emergence of this concept to the nation's preoccupation with pathology. The evolution of a more strengths-based perspective comes from an increased awareness that United States culture, and helping professions, is rife with diagnostic approaches predicated on individual, family, and community pathology, deficits, problems, abnormalities, victimization, and disorders. A deficit approach views individuals, families, and communities as the primary source of problems, with solutions possible only if derived and directed by external sources (Chapin, 1995). In essence, meaningful participation on the part of the community is neither valued or sought. The assumptions a strength paradigm are predicated on have relevance for both micro- and macro-practice.

There are a number of key assumptions influencing a strength perspective. These assumptions can be translated easily into all forms of social work practice: (1) all people and environments possess strengths that can be utilized to improve the quality of clients' lives; (2) it is much easier to motivate clients if their strengths are emphasized; (3) strengths-based work necessitates cooperative exploration between clients and workers, with clients being the "experts" on their lives, not the professionals; (4) a strengths perspective discourages "blaming the victim" and focuses on coping strategies; and (5) all environments, regardless of circumstances, contain resources (De Jong & Miller, 1995).

These five assumptions require practitioners, regardless of method, to shift roles, becoming partners not "experts," explorers not predictors, catalysts for building rather than labelers, and community directed rather than individual focused. Consequently, a strengths perspective requires social workers and agencies to develop the required structure and process to facilitate this shift in paradigms.

The challenges that beset communities of color are largely the result of powerful national forces that are beyond their immediate control, and have resulted in major socioeconomic restructuring. Community building should begin with an asset-based approach, which systematically uses indigenous resources. This approach, however, does not mean a community must struggle in isolation or proceed without assistance from outside resources (Cisneros, 1996).

Use of a community focus for service delivery. Social problems do not occur in a social vacuum but in an existing context with particular frames of reference and expectations. The concept of community is such a frame of reference and is particularly important in understanding social problems (Hardcastle et al., 1997). The use of community knowledge informs strategies for intervention, with equal applicability for all age groups (McLaughlin, 1993).

Community problems, concerns, and needs, must be addressed within the context in which they are found. Interventions must address all sectors of a community and seek to enhance capacity:

> Professionals who claim to do social work should not be secular priests in the church of individual repair. They should be working to build communities . . . We must not concentrate our resources on helping individuals increase their self-esteem and realize their potential. We must use our resources to help groups in the community to build a community-based system of social care that leads to the creation of healthy communities. That is how we can help to make people healthy. (Specht & Courtney, 1994, p. 175)

There is a need for the profession to develop an in-depth knowledge base of communities. The knowledge base pertaining to communities is not sufficiently well developed within social work, particularly when compared with our knowledge of individuals and families. More research needs to be undertaken concerning how communities function and how their capacities can be built to complement, or replace, some of the functions of the federal social welfare system (Coulton, 1995a).

Any effective system of community-based social care must mobilize all sectors of the community from formal to informal. The system must not focus exclusively on solving problems, but must also seek to enhance community capacities for self-renewal and help. Communities have become more fragmented, resulting in breaks in the naturally occurring linkages among social systems. These linkages provide support and nurturance to individuals and create opportunities for them to participate meaningfully in their community. Further, these linkages help communities define themselves and serve both to reduce unnecessary stress and enhance social competence.

Community-based interventions are complex, requiring considerations of the following factors to achieve success: (1) an in-depth understanding of people comprising the community and how they conceptualize their needs, resources, and the desired intervention strategies; (2) involvement of all sectors (formal and informal); (3) use of a process that facilitates and encourages participation in all aspects of the intervention; and (4) the building of social infrastructure (capacity enhancement) as a key element in all forms of intervention.

Use of multicultural principles and concepts. There is no paucity of scholarly material on the topic of multiculturalism and the social work profession (Devore & Schlesinger, 1996; Ewalt, Freeman, Kirk, & Poole, 1996; Greene, Jensen, & Jones, 1996; Iglehart & Becerra, 1995; Keys, 1994; Lum, 1996). The literature on this topic is expanding in scope and complexity, reflecting the challenges and tensions this country, and the profession, are facing as they approach the next millennium (Atherton & Bolland, 1997; Grant, 1996; Grant & Gutierrez, 1996). Multiculturalism can be defined simply as a perspective, with a philosophical, knowledge, and practice base, that stresses the importance of examining behavior and attitudes within a context that uplifts culture. The concept of multiculturalism can be operationalized in various ways, engendering considerable debate in the profession and drawing attention to the complexity of the concept (Gould, 1995).

Critical consciousness, an element discussed earlier regarding empowerment, is also instrumental in better understanding multiculturalism. The development of greater awareness of our heritage results in a better appreciation of ourselves and, indirectly, others. Appreciation of other cultures cannot occur successfully without a corresponding awareness of our own cultural values, beliefs, and practices. This consciousness-raising process can be uplifting and confusing, can create anger and elicit other reactions, both positive and negative. Nevertheless, the personal growth that results from exploration of one's cultural background cannot be achieved without undertaking a journey of self-exploration and reflection. This journey can be painful because it often necessitates examining basic beliefs and behaviors that may be considerably different from those of other cultures.

Multicultural-based practice refers to goals and methods that actively and systematically seek to address issues of social and economic justice as an integral part of any form of service delivery (Gutierrez et al., 1996). This form of practice represents the antithesis of ethnocentric-based practice, which is founded on the values, beliefs, and approaches of Euro-American culture.

As already noted, multiculturalism is not without controversy, with considerable debate about the degree of cultural behavior patterns, beliefs, and attitudes that should be accepted and reinforced through service delivery (De La Cancela & Zavalas, 1983). Cultural beliefs concerning gender roles and folk healing, for example, have engendered much discussion and disagreement.

The ethnic and racial composition of the country is changing and is projected to continue to do so well into the next century. These demographic trends have resulted in urban areas across the United states becoming increasingly more of color, putting increasing pressures on social care giving systems to meet the needs of a very diverse population. Professional social work education, too, has had to struggle with the development of curriculum reflecting these changes and the need for the profession to recruit greater numbers of workers of color to serve these communities (Browne & Broderick, 1996; Manoleas, 1994; Ronnau, 1994; Singleton, 1994).

Gutierrez et al. (1996, p. 507) stress the importance of a multicultural perspective for social work practice:

> The promise of multicultural practice will remain unfulfilled if social workers continue to only react to societal changes and maintain the current structure of profession and education. Multicultural community practice will require redesigning social work education and practice. Significant changes

must occur in how social workers educate students . . . It also requires the participation of social workers in *nontraditional settings.* (italics added)

It is widely accepted that for social work education to maintain its relevance, it must seek new models for educating practitioners for urban-based practice with undervalued groups (Browne & Broderick, 1996; Glugoski et al., 1994; Longres & Seltzer, 1994; Marshack, Ortiz-Hendricks, & Gladstein, 1994). Jarman-Rohde, McFall, Kolar, and Strom (1997) challenge social work educators, and indirectly the profession, to build new partnerships within and outside the profession and to create new paradigms and fresh approaches to providing advocacy, service, and student education.

The literature on community-based intervention is equally explicit about the importance of organizations and practitioners knowing more about groups in greatest need (Hardcastle et al., 1997; Rapp, 1992). An emerging knowledge base shows a diversity of perspectives that can be developed into a multicultural approach. These perspectives fall into four categories: (1) definition of culture; (2) resiliency; (3) natural supports; and (4) cultural competence. Multicultural practice serves to highlight and identify a variety of innovative methods for engaging undervalued communities and stresses that there is no one way of providing assistance or collaborating.

Definition of culture. A consensual definition of culture is as elusive as any concept in society: "since culture is a dynamic phenomenon and subject to change, aiming at the positive end of the continuum [culturally competent] is an ideal state requiring a lifelong commitment. The caveat, however, is that an organization's staff may be proficient with one given cultural group but may need to work on enhancing their abilities to work with emerging or other existing groups within their catchment area" (Mason, 1994, p. 6). This is the concept of culture within both a historical and present-day context (Marin, 1996).

There is really no disputing the importance of culture in all aspects of macro- and micro-assessment and intervention. The concept of culture in community organizing can be identified by three key factors that must be considered if organizing is to have meaning and be effective within communities of color: (1) an understanding of the uniqueness of ethnicity, race, and culture, and the need to individualize whenever possible; (2) the unique qualities within and between groups has implications for practice; and (3) organizing must utilize empowerment methods and be based on the development of critical consciousness (Rivera & Erlich, 1992).

Ortiz-Torres (1994, p. 111) comments on the importance of using culture as a key component of initiatives targeting HIV/AIDS in the Latino community, stressing how it can influence all stages of a research process: "A real understanding of the ways in which cultural processes interact with HIV-related risk behaviors should be reflected in the particular ways research questions are chosen, in how these questions are posed, and studies are designed, to reflect culture and ethnicity not only as background variables but as active and crucial elements of participants' socioeconomic realities and contexts."

Resiliency. The concept of resilience has recently received considerable attention in the professional literature (Kaplan, Turner, Norman, & Stillson, 1996; Luther & Ziegler, 1991; Newcomb, 1992; Werner & Smith, 1992; Zunz, Turner, & Norman, 1993). The field of education has made significant strides in embracing and studying this construct (Garbarino, Dubrow, Kostelny, & Pardo, 1992; Rutter, 1987; Werner, 1991). The use of a resilience construct has generally been applied to micro-level intervention with individuals and families (Mathias, 1996). The concept of assets represents the transformation of resilience into a macro-level intervention.

Resilience can be defined as those factors that either effectively shield an individual from the impact of tragedy or trouble or allow them to recover with minimal consequences. Resiliency is an ability to ward off toxic circumstances or consequences, and it resides in the ways in which people deal with life changes and in what they do about their stressful or disadvantageous circumstances. Attention must be paid to the mechanisms operating at key junctures in a person's life when a risk trajectory may be averted and a more constructive path taken (Rutter, 1987). Scholars have identified three areas, or domains, of resilience: (1) internal resources (temperament and self-esteem); (2) family climate (warmth, affection, emotional support, clear and reasonable structure and limits); and (3) social environmental (extended family, friends, participation in community groups and activities) (Brooks, 1994).

Brooks (1994, p. 547) summarizes the interrelated, and dynamic nature of these arenas for children. However, the themes have applicability for all other age groups:

> It is obvious that many factors residing within the child, in the family, and in the larger social environment interact in an ongoing and dynamic way to determine whether early vulnerabilities give way to a life of productivity, success, and happiness—a life truly characterized as resilient—or whether these vulnerabilities intensify, resulting in a life punctured with disappointment, despair, envy, underachievement, and ongoing failure. As these factors are articulated more precisely, increasingly effective programs can be developed and implemented for harnessing the unique strengths of individual children.

Ideology is part of resilience, but it is rarely used by professionals when they discuss resilience. Ideology contributes to resilience because it provides a context and meaning to risky behaviors and toxic environments, and highlights an ability to function under extreme conditions. This ideological dimension can be witnessed in accounts of families under stress. Strong religious beliefs in families, for example, can bring stability and meaning, particularly during times of hardship (Garbarino et al., 1992).

Natural support systems. Baker (1976, p. 139) defines natural support systems as follows:

> In most communities there exists a network of individuals and groups who band together to help each other in dealing with a variety of problems in living. Such groupings which provide attachments among individuals or between individuals and groups such that adaptive competence is improved in dealing with short- term crises and life transitions are referred . . . to as *natural support systems.* The word *"natural"* is used to differentiate such systems from the professional care-giving systems in the community . . . Natural support systems include family and friendship groups, local informal caregivers, voluntary service groups not directed by care-giving professionals and mutual help groups. (italics added)

The concept of natural support is very similar to that of social support. However, natural support systems represent culturally-based care giving resources. Unlike their social support counterparts, which are available and accessible to most if not all groups in a community, natural supports are constructed based on cultural values, history, and belief systems.

There are primarily three practice-oriented interventions involving these systems: (1) examination of the nature and extent of interpersonal ties and how they make up the support system; (2) determination of how these support systems function and impact on the helping process; and (3) identification of methods that can be developed to increase access to support systems (Pearson, 1990). The latter can take one of two approaches—increase the willingness of individuals and indigenous institutions to offer assistance or increase the willingness of individuals and communities to turn to these resources for assistance.

The concept of cultural competence has currency in the field. Cultural competence refers to a set of congruent behaviors, attitudes, and policies that come together in a system, agency, or intervention, and which work effectively in multicultural situations (Cross, 1988). Competency is viewed as the goal all service providers must achieve, and can be viewed as the final stage from a developmental perspective. This stage is one step ahead of cultural sensitivity, which indicates a proclivity and knowledge base. However, competence reflects skills and abilities. In short, sensitivity sets the stage for competence.

Organizations need to achieve cultural competence by subscribing to the following basic principles (Cross, 1988): (1) valuing diversity; (2) conducting a self-assessment; (3) understanding the dynamics of differences; and (4) adapting to diversity (attitudes, practices, policies, and structure).

Cultural competence. The concept of competence is not new to social work or the field of human services. The desirability of a competency model for social services can be traced back to the early 1980s model that stressed ecological (community-oriented) competencies that have applicability for practice (internal and external based) and consists of three arenas for competencies (Maluccio, 1981): (1) skills and capabilities (this component consists of personal qualities as well as cognitive, perceptual, language, and physical abilities); (2) motivational aspects (ability to cope with challenges and be self-determining); and (3) environmental qualities (ability to identify and enlist environmental resources and supports).

The term "cultural competence," however, reflects the evolution of service delivery to communities of color (Campinha-Bacote, 1991; Delgado, 1998a, 1998b; Hernandez & Isaacs-Shockley, 1997; Yee & Weaver, 1994). It refers to a set of congruent behaviors, attitudes, and policies that come together in a system, agency, or intervention to work effectively in multicultural situations (Cross, 1988). Cultural competence represents the latest manifestation of cultural sensitivity, and is applicable to work with consumers, students, organizations, and research (Grant, 1996; Grant & Gutierrez, 1996; Manoleas, 1994). Cultural competence can be viewed as a process, and "not an end-point" (Campinha-Bacote, 1991).

There are at least five critical elements that require the development and operationalization of cultural competence: (a) increasing diversity of consumer populations; (b) the influence culture has on help seeking behaviors; (c) differential service utilization rates of various cultural and racial groups; (d) the impact of diverse perspectives on the conceptualization of the etiology of behaviors, emotions, or thoughts that dominate how culture describes problems; and (e) the necessity for culturally relevant services to differ from conventional services that ignore cultural differences (Mason, 1994).

The lack of culture-specific methods for prevention, early identification, and intervention that reflect community values and beliefs severely limits the effectiveness of any effort at helping. Culture-specific methods must reflect "local reality" in their design and goals. To ensure this, it is necessary to minimize cultural distance between organizations and residents.

For social services to be culturally relevant, they must by necessity eschew a deficit model and undergo dramatic changes in conventional attitudes about culture and how it influences client and community perceptions. Deficit models regarding groups of color have resulted in negative biases about their respective realities. Discarding these biases is very hard, even for the most well-intentioned individuals (Mason, 1994). Cultural competence, as a result, covers worker and organizational knowledge, skills, and attitudes.

Development of new arenas for collaborative practice. The rediscovery of community as a context for practice has consequences for social work in that it requires the profession to learn more about settings in which residents feel comfortable, and which are possible arenas for practice (Hardcastle et al., 1997). These settings are very often owned, staffed, and patronized by residents. Coulton (1995b) suggests that community-based research be used as a method to develop a knowledge base for community-based practice focused on strengthening families, creating economic opportunity, and protecting vulnerable individuals.

This form of community-based practice necessitates the development of new strategies for intervention that are based on a new set of guiding principles (Badshah, 1996). These principles require social workers to accept the new role of partner rather than sole provider of services. Coulton (1995b, p. 439) raises a series of questions that can be answered only through community-based partnerships:

> Does social work as practiced today have ways of connecting workers in poor communities to training and labor markets, creating networks to meet family needs, building communities' internal controls, generating community-supported emergency and other types of assistance, and restoring communities as climates for economic opportunity? That is what a community social worker will need to do, not alone, of course, but collaboratively with leaders and residents. Practice research must support the development and enhancement of social work methods that can be embedded in and use the strengths of the community context.

Four factors emerge as prime motivating forces for the initiation of collaborative efforts for addressing community needs: (1) failure of existing efforts to address needs; (2) resource scarcity: given the lack of public resources allocated to alleviating current social problems, the pooling of resources in terms of time and money has been the only viable option for individuals and organizations concerned with social change; (3) mandates: there have been a growing number of state legislatures that have mandated interagency collaboration; and (4) leaders with a vision: perhaps most influential at initiating collaborative efforts are leaders who have a vision and who are willing to take the first step in implementing their vision. Leaders often provide the critical and/or institutional support necessary for building an effective collaboration.

Besides these motivators, the benefits accrued from collaborative efforts also serve as motivators for further collaboration. Benefits commonly identified in the literature are: (1) program effectiveness; (2) economic savings: and (3) empowerment of participants. The process of collaborating—communicating, planning, problem-solving, decision making, and socializing—breaks down the isolation people often experience and builds nurturing, supportive relationships among participants (Gray, 1989; Kraus, 1984).

There is another motivator for developing collaborative partnerships within nontraditional settings:

> Professionals are organized; those of us in "communities" with weak social ties are not. Nonetheless, the argument that only professionals should intervene is quite lame. Whatever the strengths and weaknesses of professionals, there are simply not enough of them, nor can we afford to pay the bill to hire enough of them no matter how much we prefer to remain uninvolved and delegate . . . problems . . . to public agencies. (Brown, 1995, p. 148)

Delgado's (1994; 1995a) work in the field of alcohol, tobacco, and other drugs, stressed the importance of agencies collaborating with indigenous resources, in this case natural support systems, as a means of opening up new arenas for practice and research. Interventions based on collaboration with natural support systems offer much promise and are predicated on respect and faith in a community to help itself. They stress infrastructure (social and physical) development whenever possible.

Collaborative practice takes on greater significance when applied to groups that have historically not accessed conventional social services. Consequently, this form of practice has more potential when applied to undervalued groups and involves institutions that have generally not been considered "worthy" of involvement in collaboration.

However, collaboration of any kind is very difficult to achieve and often fraught with pitfalls if not carefully planned and implemented. Collaborations between social agencies are also difficult because we live in a society that values individualism and competition, inculcated at an early age (Triandis, 1995). Rarely are school assignments or rewards tied to group or team efforts. In fact, the longer one stays in school, the more individual-oriented and competitive the educational process becomes. Academic training in social work and other fields is not an exception. Ultimately, doctoral-level social work education requires the completion of a dissertation that is the student's responsibility. Upon graduation, the student obtains employment in a social service agency and is asked to become part of a team.

Unfortunately by that time, a social worker does not possess the experiences, skills, knowledge, and trust to be part of a team. The transition to being a team member is a greater challenge when a social worker becomes part of an interdisciplinary team. Thus, collaboration between a social agency and a grocery store, beauty parlor, or house of worship becomes even more challenging.

Conclusion

The profession has struggled, generally unsuccessfully, in reaching out to undervalued groups. There is a tremendous need for new paradigms and models for reaching and engaging these marginalized groups. However, as is the case with any approach, it is necessary to take a highly critical stance on current practice and to have the political will to acknowledge there is something wrong before exploring alternatives.

Nontraditional settings have a potential to serve as an important bridge between the profession and undervalued communities. Involving nontraditional settings does not have to be an exclusive form of practice. Rather, it can complement other forms of reaching and serving communities.

The use of nontraditional settings is not a cure for all of the issues confronting communities of color and other undervalued groups in urban areas. However, the hope is that embracing this form of practice will result in other innovative modes of practice. Involving nontraditional settings can best be conceptualized as one step in a long journey, rather than a destination itself.

II

NONTRADITIONAL SETTINGS: CONCEPTUAL FOUNDATION AND APPLICATION

Section II provides readers with a conceptual foundation from which to better understand the boundaries, roles, and implications for practice. Chapter 5 (Nontraditional Settings: Conceptual, Dimensional, and Services) provides a theoretical foundation from which to better understand the importance of these settings on community life.

Chapter 6 (Nontraditional Settings: Literature and Case Illustrations) reviews the literature on nontraditional settings and provides vivid examples, where available, of how these settings provide assistance in the daily life of a community. Chapter 7 (Framework for Practice) delineates an approach for how practice can unfold when involving nontraditional settings.

5

Nontraditional Settings: Conceptual, Dimensional, and Services

The topic of social work practice within nontraditional settings owes a great debt to the work undertaken over the past two decades by various social work and other professional scholars. Practice within these settings must be placed in an evolutionary context to be appreciated fully. Collins and Pancoast's (1976) book, *Natural Helping Networks: A Strategy for Prevention*, introduced this concept to the profession. Their classic book served multiple purposes for the profession: (1) it developed bridges between community and social agencies; (2) it outlined a series of issues and considerations in this form of practice; and (3) it raised implications for the education of social work students.

This last purpose provided a vision for this form of practice that will stretch into the next century: "At the start of the 1970s, when social work students appeared dissatisfied with traditional approaches and were seeking ways to help bring about social change, it seemed logical to introduce concepts about natural networks to them. Those students to whom the ideas were presented, first in field placement . . . and then in an elective course, were remarkably quick to understand and make use of them."

Their work served as a foundation for practice in the 1980s, which witnessed the further development of natural helpers and the broadening of this concept to include social support and natural support systems. The research and publications by Gottlieb and colleagues (Froland, Pancoast, Chapman, & Kimboko, 1981; Gottlieb, 1981, 1983, 1988; Whittaker & Garbarino, 1983) provided the field of social work with rich illustrations of practice and a well-developed conceptual understanding.

The concept of "behavior setting" is used to describe places or institutions within a neighborhood that facilitate active informal helping (Froland et al., 1981). These settings encourage residents to congregate in the course of their daily lives, facilitating the help seeking and giving process. The concept, however, was not fully operationalized, and relied on a summary of several neighborhood-based projects. Consequently, the concept of behavior setting, when translated into a nontraditional setting, needed a more in-depth analysis and critique.

Work within nontraditional settings represents a continuation of the work by these social work pioneers and broadens the concept of help to include new arenas. A focus on nontraditional urban settings brings to the foreground people of color, a group that has generally not been addressed in the literature. This shift in focus results in a practice that emphasizes culture, issues related to exclusion and devaluation, empowerment, and participation.

"Community care" is a formalized type of practice in England. This practice involves planned social work collaborative activities with informal community-based resources. These resources can encompass nontraditional settings as part of efforts to cultivate social networks and voluntary services for vulnerable population groups, particularly older people, persons with disabilities, and children under the age of five. This model focuses on developing self-help concepts to address social and welfare needs and utilizes staff as organizers, or brokers, to encourage people to care and to volunteer (Popple, 1996).

The role of professional staff in community care work varies according to intensity and duration of involvement and can take shape in three possible roles: (1) professionals are not expected to fulfill permanent supportive or monitoring roles by relying on volunteers and low-paid helpers; (2) professionals plan to be supportive for only a short period, so that community care can be continued without them; and (3) professionals provide minimal assistance to laypeople, who, in turn, take major responsibility for providing assistance (Popple, 1996).

Nontraditional settings lend themselves to analysis from a variety of theoretical approaches due to their all-encompassing nature. These approaches generally overlap and provide a rich context in which to analyze nontraditional settings. The following conceptual approaches increase their relevance for analysis by placing nontraditional settings within a community and cultural context: (1) social embeddedness; (2) urban sanctuaries; (3) free spaces; and (4) social/natural support systems.

Although these perspectives make minimal reference to each other, in combination they take into account key social, economic, cultural, and psychological factors that help explain the influence these settings have within communities of color. Each theoretical approach can stand on its own in developing a better understanding of nontraditional settings. However, in combination they add a prodigious amount of depth to the appreciation and understanding of why nontraditional settings have grown in importance in this society, particularly when they address the needs of undervalued communities.

Social Embeddedness

The concept of social embeddedness first appeared in the professional literature during the 1980s (Wolchik, Beals, & Sandler, 1989). This concept was further developed by Portes and Sensebrenner (1993), and provides a solid theoretical foundation for examining nontraditional settings. Portes and Sensebrenner's (1993) use of the construct of "social capital" to study factors that lead to the creation and success of ethnic economic establishments has great potential for use within nontraditional settings in communities of color. Social capital can be applied to the creation and consolidation of small businesses. A solitary ethnic community represents a market for culturally specific goods, a source of reliable labor, and a source of start-up capital (Portes & Sensebrenner, 1993).

The greater the distance (cultural and linguistic) between the "old" country and the receiving society, the greater the tension and clash. This ultimately may result in a group developing its own network (bounded solidarity), with minimal contact with the host society. This tension is further exacerbated if the group is largely undocumented. Bounded solidarity serves both to reinforce cultural traditions and to minimize the influence of the "outside" world through fostering internal reliance on goods and services.

Nontraditional settings represent an important source of "social capital" in communities of color. In addition, they provide business owners with an opportunity to assume the role of "social buffer" (Pfeffer, 1994). This construct fits well within Portes and Sensebrenner's (1993) "bounded solidarity." Social buffers are individuals within a community whose social role is to reinforce norms and values, provide access to the external community, and thus stabilize a community.

Bounded solidarity and social buffers provide a context for examining how nontraditional settings have developed and thrived. They represent a culturally accepted way for achieving entrepreneurship, and are a vehicle for meeting a wide range of health and social service needs for residents, who may either mistrust the "host" society or have very limited access to quality health and social service resources as a result of discrimination, poverty, lack of English language skills, or their undocumented status (Drachman, 1995).

Urban Sanctuaries

The concept of "urban sanctuaries" has significant meaning for urban social work practice and complements the work of Evans and Boyte (1986). Urban areas in the United States are facing tremendous challenges as the twenty-first century approaches. A rather disturbing, and widely accepted, picture of the world is the unmet needs of urban-based youths, a group often referred to as at-risk. The absence of a community, and of the sense of loss of community that is so evident throughout the United States, is an even more spectacular fact of life in the inner city (Gardner, 1994).

McLaughlin, Irby, and Langman (1994) introduce the concept of community builders. These individuals create environments in which people care and in which the young person has an identity, a role, and pride in membership. Family-like environments in which youth find protection and security are consciously developed and nurtured. Youth, as a result, share a sense of responsibility and purpose (Gardner, 1994).

According to the Compact Edition of the Oxford English Dictionary (1971, p. 2634), the word "sanctuary" has many meanings, particularly as it relates to religious themes. However, the simplest definition of sanctuary is "a place [where one can take] refuge . . . or privileged place of protection." McLaughlin et al. (1994) have taken the concept of sanctuary and applied it to an urban context. Urban sanctuaries are settings other than a home (either formal or informal) to which individuals can retreat; where they can feel safe, accepted, and understood; where they can grow emotionally and intellectually, socialize freely, and reflect on their circumstances when and if they choose. Every community has such places; some communities more than others. These places can take many different forms, which can vary during their life cycle. Places such as houses of worship, social and recreational clubs, libraries, public pools, schools, playgrounds, or any other settings that are accessible within a community can qualify as urban sanctuaries. Individuals may have access to multiple sanctuaries within the course of a day, week, year, or life. Unfortunately, some people may have minimal or no access to such places.

Urban sanctuaries not only provide refuge, but can also enrich a person's life. McLaughlin et al. (1994) identify seven key characteristics that make urban sanctuaries successful in reaching inner-city youths: (1) these settings foster family-like values and have clear expectations for membership; (2) participation is actively sought and is directed toward activities that have meaning for youths and the greater society; (3) they are aware of and take into consideration the operative reality of youths in an urban environment; (4) they are able and willing to respond to the types of crises often prevalent in an urban youth's life; (5) settings are community based and accessible geographically, psychologically, culturally, and operationally; (6) they challenge youths educationally and emotionally; and (7) they are in tune with the hopes and aspirations of youths.

Free Spaces

Evans and Boyte (1986, p. 17) define "free spaces" as:

> . . . particular sorts of public places in the community, what we call free spaces, are the environments in which people are able to learn a new self-respect, a deeper and more assertive group identity, public skills, and values of cooperation and civic virtue. Put simply, free spaces are settings between private lives and large-scale institutions where ordinary citizens can act with dignity, independence, and vision.

Research on inner-city gardens and gardeners (community gardens are literally free space) highlights the appeal of this concept by stressing how important it is for people in a community to have a place they feel is their own (Hynes, 1996). Spencer (1995) describes the importance of an urban garden in a low-income community in Stockton, California and, indirectly, stresses the importance of free space this garden provides the community.

Delgado (1996b), ties in the concept of free space with nontraditional settings by noting how marginalized communities have few settings and opportunities to come together to discuss common hopes and fears. Free spaces represent vehicles for expression and action that are not controlled by "elites." In essence, indigenous institutions provide a free space in which community members come together. They provide services that go beyond what is typically expected, and in a manner that stresses self-respect and cultural understanding.

Delgado and Barton (in press) utilized this concept in their research on Latino murals in urban areas of the United States. According to the author, the theoretical work of Evans and Boyte serves as an excellent foundation from which to analyze the importance of these murals in Latino and other communities of color. They developed the concept of "free spaces" to describe places where community residents can come together and articulate common concerns, hopes, and shared values.

Applying the concept of free spaces to Latino communities highlights numerous institutions and places controlled by and for the community. These places can be a beauty parlor or barber shop, grocery store, social club, fundamentalist house of worship, to list a few. Building walls, internal and external, must also be considered free spaces. Murals are often painted on these free spaces in urban communities. Some are painted on and in official buildings such as schools and police stations. However, most are painted on building walls that have been "claimed" by the community as its own, even though they are not owned by community residents. These spaces are transformed from their original purpose as part of a building to a message board for those in and out of the community to see, read, and learn from.

It is important to note that, with rare exceptions, the author did not encounter a nontraditional setting that had taken on a political agenda as part of its service to the community. A political agenda is action for social justice focused on changing any of the following: policy, policy makers, or actions of corporations (Weil, 1996). Thus, the author agrees with Fisher and Kling's (1987) critique of Evans and Boyte's contention that these settings often do not play instrumental roles in initiating change.

Because of their accessibility, nontraditional settings are in a unique position to engage in political action of various types. However, political action is not often taken. There may be a variety of reasons for this reluctance, or perceived inability, to bring about change. Nontraditional settings may be patronized by newcomers who may be more interested in the politics of the country that was left behind rather than the politics of their new country.

Owners of commercial establishments may be reluctant to engage in political action for fear of alienating customers who do not share the same sentiments, or out of fear of retribution from governmental authorities that regulate their businesses. Nontraditional settings such as churches—with the possible exception of the African American church and its long and distinguished history of civil rights actions—may be too focused on achieving justice in the afterlife to be concerned with conditions in the present. Nontraditional settings may have a tradition of eschewing political change in their home countries, and this stance may be transplanted to this country. Finally, urban-based communities may have alternatives to bringing about political change that are not dependent on nontraditional settings; thus, nontraditional settings can focus their attention on personal services.

Social/Natural Support Systems

The concepts of social and natural support systems have been operationalized in a multitude of ways (Wolchik et al., 1989). The research on social support can best be conceptualized in three areas: (1) sociological (social network approach); (2) psychological (perceptual approaches); and (3) communicative (interactional approaches) (Burleson, Albrecht, Goldsmith, & Sarason, 1994). These approaches have generally stressed individually focused roles in providing assistance to others in need (De La Rosa, 1988; Delgado & Santiago, in press; Lazzari, Ford, & Haughey, 1996).

The literature on natural support systems (cultural variations of social support), although not as extensive as that of social support, has taken a cultural perspective on helping, and has addressed both individual and institutional sources of assistance. As a result, this literature has been generally community based and paid more attention to communities of color (De La Rosa, 1988).

The theoretical approaches outlined in this section provide practitioners with a strong conceptual base from which better to understand the role of nontraditional settings within a cultural and community context. These theoretical approaches, although briefly covered in this section, provide practitioners with a set of "lenses" through which to better understand and appreciate indigenous support resources. The nature of nontraditional settings lends itself to a variety of theoretical approaches to developing a better appreciation of their importance in the life of a community, particularly if the community is undervalued by this society.

Help-Seeking Patterns and Nontraditional Settings

Help-seeking patterns very often arise from the interplay of cultural factors and previous experiences in seeking and receiving assistance from formal sources. To no one's surprise, research has shown that most people usually first turn to friends, relatives, neighbors, co-workers, and even acquaintances for help. If and when professional help is sought, clergy, teachers, and physicians rank highest on the list. However, beauticians, bartenders, and the like also rank high on the list (Garbarino, 1983). It is natural for individuals in need to turn to family and friends, if they seek help at all. Professionals must not stand in the way of this form of support for clients but in fact should encourage the natural tendency of individuals to go to the informal sector, nontraditional settings being an example, for appropriate assistance (Maguire, 1991).

The work of these and other researchers suggests that the importance of nontraditional settings lies in their accessibility and the stage at which they are consulted—namely, fairly early on in the help seeking process. Help seeking patterns may also involve social workers, but they are rarely the first and primary source of help. Consequently, social workers can not assume that no one else has tried or is currently assisting a client with a problem. Delgado (1977, 1979-80) notes that in situations in which a client may be seeing a social worker, the client may also be consulting a folk healer. If the client makes significant progress in resolving a presenting problem, the source of the success will invariably be attributed to the folk healer.

Social workers can take one of four approaches to nontraditional settings: (1) ignore them; (2) undermine them; (3) modify their practice to take them into consideration as a resource; and (4) collaborate with them by developing innovative services. The first approach is probably the usual way human service workers address nontraditional settings. They simply do not acknowledge the assistance of nontraditional settings and, as a result, do not ask consumers about them. The second approach is even more harmful than the first. This approach involves the worker in an effort to undermine systematically the importance of nontraditional settings. This can be accomplished by "persuading" the consumer not to use these services and to actively interfere with the client's seeking help from this resource.

The following strategies are excellent examples of culturally competent services because they not only acknowledge the importance of these settings, but also set out to involve them to various degrees (Delgado, 1995a). Modifying practice to take culture into account is not uncommon in the field of practice.

The first approach requires social workers to modify their methods for assessment and intervention based on the cultural background and expectations of the client. Interviewing may necessitate that a worker move from behind a desk and sit next to the client to minimize perceived social distance. During an intake, a worker may have to set aside a form and spend time conversing with a potential client before actually commencing with an "official" intake. This action provides both the worker and applicant with an opportunity to share important information and expectations before engaging in "formal" procedures.

Second, in the research arena modification of practice may mean changing conventional research approaches to take into account a group's experience. Delgado (1997a) shares an experience in conducting focus groups with Latinos. Some Latino groups, depending on their country of origin, will out of fear refuse to participate in focus groups. Their experience with groups in which members share common concerns may be associated with the start of a revolution; participation, as a result, could manifest itself in having members disappear and never be heard from again. In these situations, the author argues, it is recommended that researchers use a key informant as a preferred method.

The third approach, which is the focus of this book, specifically sets out to involve these settings in some form of service collaboration. This phase of collaboration represents the culmination of much time, energy, and resources (Delgado, 1994).

Use of innovative, community-based approaches raises the untapped potential of nontraditional and other indigenous resources. One case study stands out through its description of the work of community volunteers who come together to establish a "cafe" to feed the hungry. Volunteers served as a coordinating body to tap services provided by others in the community, including those from nontraditional settings:

> But Cafe 458 is a bistro with a difference . . . They earn the right to eat at the Cafe by agreeing to participate in programs aimed at getting back into the community . . . It uses the attraction of good food and a pleasant atmosphere to get luncheon guests talking about their problems . . . Toward that end, the Cafe's menu includes more than just good things to eat . . . Participants can take advantage of free services, all provided by volunteers . . . barbers offer free haircuts . . . lawyers offering no-cost legal services. (Garr, 1995, p. 12)

Implementation of innovative services is not without its challenges. Developing a social network program (for example, support groups, strengthening families, connecting with natural helpers, and linking with formal and informal community resources) is no exception: "Thus, the first reaction to social network training . . . was that the workers were already performing the intervention and that they already knew the material. In reality, a tremendous difference exists between spending time in . . . work strengthening clients' ties to significant others and focusing principally on this intervention, which involves considerable new learning and reconceptualization of practice" (Blum, Biegel, Tracy, & Cole, 1995, pp. 184–185). Practice within nontraditional settings may prove an even greater challenge than practice within social networks.

Although, as already noted, the profession has a history of working in communities, this has not meant that social work has strategically reached out to and involved communities of color. A review of social work literature would reveal: (1) the historical development of community social work practice rarely involved communities of color and was only tangentially directed toward them; (2) community organization efforts directed at communities of color and noncommunities of color simultaneously, resulted in the former being less successful; (3) the greatest impetus for social work's increased involvement in organizing communities of color has come from government, more at the federal than local or state level, and, as a result, involvement has been subject to changes in the political environment; and (4) many social problems specific to communities of color have not received significant social work attention (Solomon, 1985).

Types of Services Provided by Nontraditional Settings

Nontraditional settings are very attractive to community residents because of the services they provide. The nature and extent of these services may vary according to setting. Some nontraditional settings may conceptualize services very narrowly and restrict their availability to select patrons. However, other settings may offer extensive services and are quite flexible about who qualifies for them. This determination of service necessitates some form of formal assessment on the part of social workers.

People in nontraditional settings generally provide at least five categories of assistance to those who seek help (Delgado, 1995c; Gottlieb, 1983; Israel, 1985): (1) informational support (suggestions, advice, information); (2) instrumental support (labor, time, money); (3) expressive support (affect, esteem, concern, listening); (4) appraisal support (feedback, affection); and (5) problem solving (assistance in assessing situations and developing appropriate actions). The degree to which these services are provided is very much determined by the settings.

Translating Theory into Practice

The translation of theoretical concepts into practice is very often talked about in social work education (Simon, 1994; Thyer, 1994). The concurrent nature of field practice and classroom instruction seeks to facilitate this process. However, this translation is never easy because often the material that is presented in scholarly books and other publications can rarely be applied to "real life" situations as covered in the class. In fact, theoretical concepts are often considerably modified to take into account factors and situations not addressed in scholarly sources or class discussions.

The difficulties associated with translation of theory to practice can be minimized by: (1) utilizing a set of guiding practice principles; (2) identifying common approaches toward taking the initial step of considering collaboration within nontraditional settings; (3) addressing key organizational factors and considerations; (4) listing the key staff qualities necessary for working within nontraditional settings; and (5) examining how schools of social work can collaborate with community-based organizations and nontraditional settings.

It is important to note that every social worker does not have a predisposition to undertake every conceivable intervention method, nor are all equally facile at addressing every conceivable social problem. Some methods and social problems are easier than others. Thus, not every social service organization or social worker can be expected to work within nontraditional settings; some organizations and workers may feel more comfortable and competent in these settings than others.

Principles for Collaborative Practice

It is impossible to write a book of this nature without culling out a set of guiding practice principles. Principles serve as mechanisms for translating goals and visions into action. A number of authors have developed sets of principles that have relevance for practice within nontraditional settings. Some of the principles were promulgated more than 25 years ago and still have currency today. They can easily be applied to social work practice within nontraditional settings in communities of color (Boston Foundation, 1994; Froland et al., 1981; Garr, 1995; Whittaker, 1983).

1. Consumers of services must be seen as individuals with strengths and assets, not just problems. Consumers are people with multifaceted lives that go beyond the "presenting problems." Many of these individuals have survived multiple traumas and situations that, for others, might have resulted in death at a very early age. In short, survival is an ego strength and should never be minimized by social workers (Boston Foundation, 1994; Froland et al., 1981).

The community must be actively involved in all phases of an initiative (Garr, 1995). Those most directly affected by policies and programs must be at the heart of dialogue and community enhancement (Boston Foundation, 1994). This fosters sustained commitment, coordination, and collaborations based on a shared vision and mutual respect (Boston Foundation, 1994).

2. It is necessary to recognize the importance of an enduring network of social relationships and the role they have played, currently play, and will play in the future. The roles these resources have played are instrumental in communities of color, and must be recognized and involved whenever possible. The fact that a help seeker is a "client" does not necessarily mean that this person does not have an active social network, including those in nontraditional settings, in their lives. Further, it does not mean that they, in turn, are not helping others. Qualities such as reciprocity, mutuality, and informality are central to social supports, though are often missing from formal services (Whittaker, 1983).

3. Informal helpers and, indirectly, nontraditional settings, must be viewed as having equal status with professionals. The former cannot be conceptualized as "paraprofessionals" because they do not have "credentials" or "high levels of formal education." This does not make them any less worthy of possessing "expertise" in helping consumers of color.

These individuals possess intimate knowledge of culture and local circumstances, and can be considered "experts" on context. This level of knowledge is not easily acquired, least of all from books or other scholarly sources.

These sources may devote themselves to providing information on culture. However as any seasoned practitioner knows, culture is dynamic and highly influenced by local circumstances. Thus, informal helpers are often in a position to "update" practitioners on how culture is manifested in the community. Consequently, the profession of social work must expand its vision of who is a "worthy" practitioner and take into account consumer legitimacy.

4. Informal and formal providers must be thought of as a team rather than separate parties to caring and service provision. In the true concept of "team," everyone who is involved in an effort is valued. Effective service delivery can only occur through a creative combination of professional and social support resources (Whittaker, 1983). Partnerships work far more effectively than single organizational efforts (Garr, 1995). Thus, initiatives involving nontraditional settings must coordinate activities whenever possible to minimize the duplication and undermining that often result when parties compete. Team effort does not occur naturally and without considerable practice. It entails clear and frequent communication and understanding of the role and contribution of each team member.

5. Practice within nontraditional settings is founded on the respect and understanding of how people and groups of color define their problems and solutions (Delgado, 1998f). This consumer/community-based approach places problems and solutions within a cultural context; symbols, metaphors, and other forms of expression take their meaning from a group's experience and beliefs.

Practice must be grounded in this context for interventions to have meaning and acceptance and, as a consequence, reflect local circumstances. Practice methods will have to be modified based on local events, history, and available resources. No two urban areas are alike, even when they share similar socioeconomic profiles. Further, for practice to be welcomed and acceptable, it must seek to promote celebration of cultural diversity as a foundation for wholeness (Boston Foundation, 1994). In addition, practice must ensure access to fundamental opportunities and remove obstacles to social justice.

6. Problems must never be compartmentalized. In real life, problems are interrelated. Initiatives must be targeted—one approach cannot work for all (Garr, 1995). Leadership must be exercised to bring about innovative interventions. The most effective grassroots leaders are charismatic, competent, flexible, embrace innovation, and are not afraid to break rules in pursuit of the common good (Garr, 1995).

7. Although the role of the public sector is limited and consumers must have the option to seek assistance from a variety of sources including social supports, government should support, not supplement, indigenous resources (Whittaker, 1983). In addition, government involvement, when it occurs, must also promote active citizenship and political empowerment (Boston Foundation, 1994).

Four General Approaches to Contacting and Involving Nontraditional Settings

There are four general approaches to identifying, assessing, mapping, engaging, and eventually collaborating with nontraditional settings: (1) connections; (2) observations; (3) use of cultural guides; and (4) systematized research. Each of these approaches is highly dependent on local circumstances, including the amount of time and resources devoted to development of collaborative partnerships.

The initial, critical stages of framework building provided in Chapter 7 and applied in Chapters 8–12, provide examples of various ways in which social workers can take the steps necessary to involve nontraditional settings. This approach does not have to be labor intensive. However, it does require practitioners to be much more cognizant of their accessibility to key stakeholders. This orientation toward connections is often associated with getting board members. However, it also has validity in nontraditional settings.

Making connections is one way the process can start. This approach is characterized by a social worker or agency tapping into the community network to identify and access those in nontraditional settings. A program in Cleveland (Men of Color AIDS Project [MOCAP]) provides a vivid example. A bar popular with men of color was used to conduct an educational workshop. This setting was used because a member of MOCAP knew a performer in the bar who got the owner to agree to make space available. In another circumstance, a member of the board of directors knew the owner of a restaurant, and he managed to get space for a support group in that setting. Agency and work connections can facilitate the process of identification and access. However, if an agency or worker does not have meaningful connections within the community, this method is severely limited.

Another method is observational, and entails a social worker entering a community and observing interactions, flow of traffic (people), and noting the presence or absence of nontraditional settings. Social workers have the luxury of undertaking this approach at their leisure and when visiting clients, by taking time to observe the surroundings. This method is unobtrusive and can be integrated into daily activities. In addition, practitioners who are reluctant to take a more obvious approach can do this with relative ease.

Another example involving MOCAP in Cleveland typifies the above approach. The organization selected barbershops for outreach and community education based on whether or not they displayed notices and posters related to human service activities. Those that did were considered more amenable to engaging in other human service-related activities than those that didn't, minimizing efforts at engagement.

The use of cultural guides represents another approach to entering, identifying, and engaging nontraditional settings. This approach necessitates the use of someone who is very knowledgeable about the community, is well respected by residents and owners of nontraditional settings, and is willing to show the worker around the community. In addition, a cultural guide is willing to facilitate the engagement process by "sponsoring" the worker and agency.

Finally, entry into the community and nontraditional settings may be based on a systematized asset assessment derived from a clear definition of the geographical area to be studied, development of a questionnaire, and an in-depth analysis of the results. This approach can be as broad or as focused as the needs of the worker and organization dictate. However, this is the most labor intensive and costly of the approaches identified in this section.

Staffing and Organizational Factors to Consider

Delgado (1996f), based on a case study of a California community-based organization collaborating with African American, Cambodian, and Latino (primarily Mexican American) nontraditional settings, identified a series of key organizational factors that had to be addressed successfully in the planning and implementation of a project. These considerations fell into five areas of applicability for work within nontraditional settings: (1) staff qualities and qualifications; (2) staff embrace of principles and philosophy; (3) supervision and staff development; (4) development of internal institutional support; and (5) development of external support. Each of these areas presented project administrators with a unique set of challenges that went beyond the usual challenges associated with community-based services. Although based in California and targeting youths, the lessons learned have applicability for other agencies wishing to engage nontraditional settings.

Staff Qualities and Qualifications

There is no question that agency staff is at the heart of any successful effort at engaging nontraditional settings. Staff members must possess extraordinary qualities to engage in extraordinary social work. These qualities facilitate work in this arena. An examination of the personal qualities of staff memers is critical for agencies that screen and hire workers. Saleebey (1996, p. 299) identified the personal qualities clients can possess that can prove instrumental in working with a strengths perspective: "A sense of humor, loyalty, independence, insight, and other virtues might very well become the source of energy for success with clients even though their seeds were sown in trouble and pain." A similar set of qualities is also applicable to staff.

A total of thirteen personal qualities have been identified for the "ideal" staff member to succeed in working within nontraditional settings. These personal qualities go beyond the usual employment requirements concerning formal education, language capacities, work experience, etc. As the reader reviews the list of qualities, it is important to note that few, if any, staff members will possess all of them. Conversely, if staff possess none of these qualities, it is recommended that they not be involved with nontraditional settings.

Sense of humor. It is no mistake that the list of personal qualities commences with the importance of workers having a sense of humor. An ability to laugh, particularly at oneself, is critical when undertaking work within nontraditional settings. One often finds oneself trying to unlearn "professional" language, demeanor, and behaviors, the better to interact with ordinary people. As a result, mistakes are made with words or actions that place a worker in a particularly vulnerable position regarding self-esteem.

A sense of humor provides social workers with a cathectic outlet when things do not go the way they originally planned. The author had an experience in social work school that illustrates this point. The author was invited to attend the baptism of a baby born to a Puerto Rican couple he was seeing as part of his case load. The relationship between the author and the couple was excellent, and it was nearing termination. Invitations to baptisms, birthdays, wakes, and weddings, are not out of the ordinary in certain communities, particularly when the worker was trusted and respected. At the celebration after the baptism, the author was introduced to a local resident who was near his age. The worker was not married or engaged at the time. After a while, the author realized that the couple was playing matchmaker. After he spent a reasonable time at the celebration, the author excused himself. After departing, he had to laugh because he got much more out of the visit than he realized.

Ability to tolerate ambiguity. The ability to tolerate ambiguity takes on added significance within nontraditional settings because the individuals working in these places may not act or think the way we believe they should act or think. Consequently, no amount of classroom teaching can possibly prepare social workers for all that can happen in the field. This can simultaneously be a source of excitement and dread. Social workers, as a result, may find themselves in situations that were never discussed in school or books. For some social workers this is exciting because their abilities will be tested. However, for others, an unexpected situation may result in a worker feeling overwhelmed and "freezing" rather than responding naturally.

Practice with undervalued or newcomer populations will very often necessitate the tolerance of ambiguity. An inability to function without clear direction, purpose, and expectation, may typify work within nontraditional settings. A social worker seeking to engage a bartender, grocery store owner, or barber, must be prepared for a wide range of responses, more so than can be expected in engaging fellow human service workers or clients' family members.

Willingness to be flexible. Work within nontraditional settings will be unsuccessful if workers are rigid in carrying out their tasks. Nontraditional settings are flexible by nature, otherwise they would simply be businesses, etc. Thus, having the skill to assess a situation and deciding whether or not a prescribed approach would be successful, would be very handy in engaging and collaborating with nontraditional settings.

The need to be flexible can be operationalized in a variety of ways: (1) ease in which a worker can enter and transact business in a setting that is out of the ordinary; (2) willingness to share of themselves in the process—remember, people in nontraditional settings are not interested in where a degree was obtained, who were mentors, etc. They want to know the worker not as a worker, but as a human being; (3) willingness to work on weekends, evenings, and holidays. Nontraditional settings very often have unusual hours of operation, and this might entail workers being willing to visit these places during very active or inactive periods, depending on circumstances.

Patience. As the saying goes, "patience is a virtue." Nowhere is this more applicable than in nontraditional settings. Remember, these establishments do not abide by the same rules and procedures as social agencies. Consequently, they do not subscribe to any particular ways of doing things. The goals a worker may set out to achieve may have to be modified or may take considerably longer than anticipated.

Social workers must be prepared to be tested in nontraditional settings and to have to answer questions that they normally would not be asked in typical case situations. Thus, those in nontraditional settings may not be interested in a worker's degrees, but in their qualities as a human being. Questions asked may delve into areas that may be considered very personal, such as religious background, marital status, place of residence, and so on.

Perseverance. A willingness to engage in nontraditional forms of collaboration requires perseverance on the part of workers and their organization. Social agencies and workers must realize that just because they are prepared to work within nontraditional settings does not mean that people in nontraditional settings are prepared to work with them. Thus, an element of trial and error will always be present in initiatives involving nontraditional settings.

It would be wonderful to initiate engagement with those in nontraditional settings, to be well received, and to have one's actions result in success. However, as with any planned intervention, things can go wrong. Involving nontraditional settings must be viewed as a long-term investment strategy. Effort must be made not to give up right away when there is failure. Instead of the question being "Do we cut our losses?" the question should be "What did we learn to be successful the next time?" "To plan is human. To implement is divine."

Resilience. The author would love to say that engagement within nontraditional settings will always result in unqualified success. However, this is not case with nontraditional or any form of practice. The ability to bounce back from failure or adversity is a critical quality in working with nontraditional settings, just as it is in working with unresponsive institutions and clients.

Resilience becomes an important factor in a worker's "tool box" if the worker is to meet the challenges of working with undervalued groups in the communities they live in and within the nontraditional settings they patronize. It is important to remain cognizant of the fact that just as there are agencies that do not lend themselves to collaboration, there are nontraditional settings this applies to as well. Failure should never be construed as a message not to continue and move forward with other nontraditional settings.

Creativity. The author realizes that creativity is in very short supply in professional fields. In all likelihood, if a student has an ounce of creativity left before graduating from social work school, the field will make sure that it does not interfere with "business as usual." The process of exercising creativity can be very energizing and an excellent outlet for many social workers and their agencies.

There are people in numerous nontraditional settings across the United States who have not been approached, yet who are willing to work with social workers. Creativity must be closely tied to follow through. This nation, as noted in an earlier chapter, is becoming increasingly more urbanized and diverse in composition. New groups are always reaching our shores, presenting the profession with both an opportunity and a challenge to reach them in an affirming and effective manner (Ryan, 1997). To achieve this goal, we must be creative in developing new settings and approaches!

Willingness to be tested. People in nontraditional settings will rarely be willing to engage in collaborative activities without first testing the worker and the agency. Consequently, a willingness to undertake a "test" should be a quality that agencies and staff must possess. It is an integral part of any practice, and work within nontraditional settings should not be an exception.

The form of the test will undoubtedly vary according to the nontraditional setting, the undervalued group, and the community context. It may manifest itself in the form of being expected to share facts about one's own background and give pertinent details such as family composition, partner's name, etc. The worker may also be asked to perform a "favor" that is clearly not a usual work responsibility. This may entail having to make telephone calls or advocate for a resident or a family member of the nontraditional setting's owner or operator. Tests may be multiple. However, each test can be expected to be progressively easier to address, as the prior test served as a foundation for a relationship based on mutual trust and respect.

Thrill of the quest. Identifying, assessing, and engaging those in nontraditional settings is an exciting enterprise. Social workers wishing to practice within these settings must value this excitement. No two nontraditional settings will be alike or two collaborative projects identical, thus no two days are ever alike in content and character.

The thrill of working within these settings very often is cast within an "adventure" context. The rewards and challenges, however, must be valued to keep up one's energy level, to be willing to have new experiences, and to enjoy the satisfaction of doing a job that is important. True, not every social worker wishes to be part of such a journey. However, every social worker wishing to work within nontraditional settings must be willing both to undertake and enjoy the journey.

Ability to observe. There is far too much emphasis placed on verbal discourse within the profession. That is not to minimize the importance of verbal language. However, signs and nonverbal language are also powerful ways to communicate. Workers, as a result, must possess a keen power of observation to identify potential collaborators within nontraditional settings.

Observing where groups congregate or where clients shop for their food and clothing can provide valuable hints concerning key nontraditional settings within a community. Stores where residents shop and stay to converse may be excellent sites for outreach or distribution of public educational materials. Needless to say, the power of observation must be exercised within a community setting.

The author very often makes it a point to eat in a community restaurant to determine the comfort level of customers with the establishment, their tendency to converse with the owners/managers, and the willingness of the community to patronize the establishment. Much can be discerned in the process of eating in the community.

Focus on strengths. Although there is no need to belabor the point, social workers must feel comfortable with a process that first identifies strengths, and then needs. This approach resonates with the philosophical stance the worker applies to normal life. The ability to start with strengths is very important in facilitating the engagement process and in the development of collaborative activities. This does not mean that undervalued communities do not have needs. However, strengths will represent a critical component of how needs are addressed. As a central part of this process, the worker must be willing and able to seek out these strengths in the development of micro- or macro-focused intervention activities.

Willingness to know oneself. Clearly, it is impossible, or nearly impossible, to develop an affinity for another group when one is unsure of oneself. Consequently, work with undervalued groups must be undertaken only when one is willing to examine one's own values, beliefs, and background. Much is learned about one's upbringing, for example, when initiating contact with those in a house of worship.

In essence, work within nontraditional settings results in the acquisition of new knowledge and skills, but also in the development of greater self-awareness. In many ways, the acquisition of new insights is probably more valuable than knowledge and skills related to engagement, assessment, etc. Conversely, self-awareness may be much more painful and have greater impact on a worker's life.

Communication skills. Staff must possess excellent communication skills. Communication does not necessarily refer to language; it also refers to an ability to converse in "everyday" language. Individuals working in nontraditional settings are not "professional social workers" who, as part of their socialization into the profession, have adopted the terminology associated with being a "professional." They converse in simple, straightforward language that is not meant to impress. It may seem obvious, but nevertheless needs repeating, that the ability to communicate in the primary language used in the nontraditional setting is a must. It does not mean, however, that some of the settings do not employ staff who are bilingual. Being bilingual, nevertheless, greatly expands the possibilities for collaboration.

Staff Embrace of Principles and Philosophy

Although it would be great to believe that it would be natural for all social workers to embrace work within nontraditional settings, it would be naive to do so. Some social workers would, on philosophical grounds, refuse to work within nontraditional settings, just as there are human service organizations that would not.

Workers and institutions may believe that these settings, at best, are engaging in misguided actions or, at worst, engaging in fraudulent practice. Consequently, having the right "disposition" is necessary for the job. Practice within nontraditional settings must be undertaken by those who share a vision for community involvement and the many forms it takes. Deploying staff to work within nontraditional settings when they have serious questions about the value of the practice is guaranteed to result in failure. In addition, it creates a climate of distrust within the community.

Supervision and Staff Development

The nature of work within nontraditional settings requires intensive means of supporting staff so they can carry out their responsibilities. This form of support transcends the usual staff supervision and obligatory attendance at professional development workshops. Social work practice within nontraditional settings requires intensive supervision and extraordinary efforts to provide relevant in-service training.

Supervision and other forms of support take on added significance because of the community-focused requirements of the job. Like outreach workers, staff will spend most of the work day out in the community. However, unlike outreach workers, staff will spend considerable time in particular nontraditional settings. As a result, they will be working in situations for which they have rarely, if ever, been fully prepared. Consequently, staff supervision must take these factors into consideration. "Situation-enhanced" skills serve better to equip staff and others in the organization for this problem. The author is reluctant to call this process "problem solving," because this is not a "problem" but a "situation" that creates opportunity.

Supervisors must be prepared to visit nontraditional settings with their staff, and they may even be expected to spend a considerable amount of time in the community. For supervisors to be able to supervise effectively, they too must be open to this type of practice, be flexible with their time (supervision may not always take place in an office), and possess excellent problem-solving skills. In essence, supervisors must be unconventional in carrying out their responsibilities. In so doing, they send an important message to their staff, to those in nontraditional settings, and to the community: flexibility is essential in this form of practice, and no one is exempt.

Most supervisors rely on workshops and conferences to help develop staff skills. However, this will not be possible regarding nontraditional settings. Unfortunately, there are few conferences and workshops on this topic, though I hope this will not be the case as we enter the next millennium. As a consequence, agency administrators must undertake special efforts to sponsor and offer workshops about nontraditional settings. In-service efforts, however, provide excellent opportunities to initiate innovative training projects and involve personnel from nontraditional settings.

Development of Internal Institutional Support

It would be unrealistic to expect that all personnel associated with a social agency, no matter how progressive an organization, would embrace practice within nontraditional settings. Consequently, internal institutional support cannot be taken for granted. Administrators must systematically develop this support. Internal support can be achieved through implementation of a three-prong strategy:

1. Informing and involving the board of directors in the case of private, nonprofit agencies and representatives from nontraditional settings. It is recommended that two advisory committees be established: one consisting of board members, administrators, senior staff, and other stakeholders; the other consisting of key representatives from non-traditional settings. These two advisory committees can provide guidance on how best to develop and maintain a partnership. Instead of one committee, two committees are recommended because each has a different vision of the relationship, agendas, and, in all likelihood, style of work. This does not mean that each committee cannot be kept abreast of what the other is doing; periodically they may come together during celebrations and other events.

2. Agency staff not involved in nontraditional settings must be kept informed of the project. This does not require major changes in agency function or a tremendous expenditure of time and energy. For example, project

staff may be asked to do short presentations on the nature of their work during regular staff and agency meetings. This activity not only serves to inform but also integrates project staff into the agency.

Agency staff working within nontraditional settings must be provided with periodic opportunities to do in-service training for the rest of the agency, discussing their work within nontraditional settings or with people of color. The goal of this training is to stimulate discussion among staff in other sections of an agency. This also serves to demystify the staff's actions, as the nature of their work will differ considerably from that of other staff.

Failure to integrate project staff into the organization may result in staff feeling marginalized, jeopardizing the success of any undertaking involving nontraditional settings. These feelings, in turn, can easily be transmitted to those in nontraditional settings, too.

3. Administrators must develop mechanisms that enable the benefits of the project to be shared with the rest of the agency. This can take various forms, from having project staff consult with other staff on how to access nontraditional settings to modifying intake forms to gather information on these settings. In essence, before work within nontraditional settings can be "accepted" by most, if not all, of an agency, all staff must see the value and benefits of such collaboration.

Development of External Support

Administrators would be wise to conceptualize support from two perspectives—internal and external sources. External sources of support are particularly critical if an agency undertaking work within nontraditional settings is to be taken seriously. There are three external sources that must be considered: (a) funding sources; (b) other social agencies, including those that are ethnic oriented; and (c) nontraditional settings not participating in collaboration.

Funding sources. This may seem obvious to any seasoned administrator. However, making sure that funding sources understand the goals of work within nontraditional settings and actively support these types of activities is no small feat. Most funding sources, although stressing the need for innovation, generally like conventional services and projects. Administrators, as a result, must actively involve and elicit advice from funding sources. As noted in various case studies, the funding source is a key variable in the development of partnerships within nontraditional settings.

Some funding sources may be more likely than others to be flexible and patient about how funds are utilized, particularly during the start-up phase of a project. Those that are not will require a considerable amount of documentation, including scholarly and research literature, and check-off, before work can commence or proceed. This "selling of a project" seriously limits the potential of partnerships.

Other agencies. The human service field is not devoid of competition and rivalries between agencies for funding, market share, and prestige. Consequently, the initiation of an innovative project can result in other agencies worrying about the implications for them. This is particularly the case when initiatives involve communities of color. Consequently, agencies undertaking work within nontraditional settings must also consider doing public relations with other agencies.

Although other agencies may have the option of working within nontraditional settings, they may not exercise this option. Nevertheless, this may not stop these agencies from sabotaging the work in the community. These agencies can raise concerns with funding sources, key stakeholders, etc. Consequently, administrators must undertake public relations campaigns with other agencies and explain the nature and importance of their work. There may be many agencies that simply do not care. However, it is important to minimize their concerns, should they have any.

Nontraditional settings. Just as there may be agencies that worry about the implications of collaborative activities within nontraditional settings, there may also be those in nontraditional settings who worry. This concern can be manifested in worries that they, too, will have to develop collaborative relationships to maintain their status within the community, to keep customers, etc. People in these settings may pressure participating nontraditional settings not to continue with partnership projects. This pressure may be manifested straightforwardly by direct requests not to participate, or indirectly through the spreading of rumors concerning the participating nontraditional setting.

Consequently, it is recommended that agencies, in partnership with participating nontraditional settings, undertake public relations efforts to minimize widespread concern. Partners may present at community events and celebrations or co-sponsor community educational workshops, fundraising, etc. Any publicity related to these events must make note of the partnership.

Schools of Social Work Collaborating with Community-Based Organizations and Nontraditional Settings

Several of the community-based projects that will be presented in this book represent collaborative efforts between schools of social work, community-based organizations, and nontraditional settings, and would not have been possible without such a relationship. The author of this book, for example, had a 5-year professional relationship with Centro Panamericano (Lawrence, Massachusetts) as a result of consultation and training on natural support systems. Centro had been in existence 20 years, and served as a Latino multiservice agency with a rich history of community involvement.

The pivotal role of Centro in the Latino community made accessibility to botanicas very easy; all botanicas were aware of this agency and its role in helping the community. The executive director of Centro is a doctoral-level sociologist (Puerto Rican male) with an interest in folk healing, botanicas, and HIV/AIDS. The field interviewer (Puerto Rican female) was not native to Lawrence, but had worked and lived in the city 5 years. The coming together of these factors enhanced the chances of success by minimizing potential sources of resistance to an "outsider" engaging in this form of work.

Nowhere are the potential benefits of collaboration greater than when they focus resources and attention on undervalued and underserved groups. The benefits are not restricted to service delivery, and can also be applied to research:

> Researchers who focus on Latinos' needs and issues must develop a research agenda in collaboration with community-based organizations. True partnerships with academic institutions should be demanded and pursued. This research agenda could include . . . (a) the protective role of culture in the promotion of risk-reduction behaviors; (b) the potential role of communities in changing Latinos/as' norms and beliefs about risky and safer sex; (c) well-designed and evaluative intervention studies to determine which empowering strategies work best for Latinas in negotiations with their partners regarding safer sex . . . Engage all sectors of the . . . Latino community in this endeavor as it is a problem that pertains to all of us. (Ortiz-Torres, 1994, pp. 113–114)

The Boston University School of Social Work-Centro Panamericano study of botanical shops did not focus just on developing a better and more "scientific" understanding of these establishments; it also served as a foundation for the development of a partnership between three key entities (university, community- based organization, and botanical shops). The initial assessment resulted in the development of a series of programmatic initiatives to prevent the spread of HIV and assist Latinos with AIDS.

The involvement of botanical shops in collaborative efforts can be viewed from a variety of perspectives: (1) community agency-botanical shop; (2) university-community agency-botanical shop; and (3) university-botanical shop. Clearly, the latter form of collaboration offers the least promising outcome due to the pivotal role trust plays in this effort. However, the first two, and more specifically the second form of involvement, hold the most promise for all parties.

Collaboration between researchers and community-based leaders and practitioners holds much promise. Urban-based universities must develop partnerships to fulfill their mission of service and research and restore vitality and health to neighborhoods. However, faculty will not be welcomed if they view the community as a laboratory for testing their preconceived hypotheses. To have meaning, research must have practical, immediate benefits, as well as scientific significance (Coulton, 1995b).

The Lawrence experience added botanical shops to the collaborative partnership. This addition, although offering many potential benefits, also made the process of collaboration more time-consuming and subject to testing. People in botanical shops are not used to having a great deal of attention paid to them and the way they interact with the community.

The goal of involving botanical shops in addressing HIV/AIDS in practice can best be achieved through the implementation of self-efficacy efforts. A number of self-efficacy techniques can be employed: (1) reliance on indigenous role models to demonstrate that self-efficacy can work; (2) developing and fostering positive networks to disseminate culture-specific health protection messages; (3) imparting skills that enable behavioral change; and (4) fostering community participation in all facets of health delivery and planning (Singer et al., 1994).

These techniques not only serve to address a "current" problem or need, but also to better prepare the community to meet future needs when they arise. When self-efficacy initiatives are applied to nontraditional settings, a form of capacity enhancement results, which benefits the entire community. This should also be a goal of any form of intervention, and not just those focused on nontraditional settings.

Impact of Lessons Learned

The lessons learned from implementing an agency–nontraditional settings project can serve as valuable tools to facilitate work with these important resources. Mistakes will undoubtedly be made, even in circumstances where there has been painstaking attention to details. However, the lessons and considerations discussed in this chapter will serve to minimize the frequency and severity of the negative consequences of these mistakes.

It is critical to remember that collaboration with people in nontraditional settings is a relatively new phenomenon for both parties. Initiatives in this arena will in all likelihood be undertaken by staff who have not received formal education and training in this area. The California case cited in this chapter required the agency to have a consultant travel 3,000 miles to provide technical assistance. Efforts at locating technical support in the immediate geographical area of the agency proved unsuccessful. As a result, expectations of the process and outcome must be tempered to account for these new relationships and the possible lack of "experts" in this area to aid in the process.

Nevertheless, it is recommended that agencies wishing to engage nontraditional settings fully embrace a set of principles to help guide them. It does not mean that projects such as the ones described in this book are possible only with the "right" technical support. True, this support can facilitate the development of partnerships. However, it is not necessary for nontraditional settings and agencies to engage in collaborative projects. The beauty of work within nontraditional settings is that these settings are everywhere around us, regardless of geographical area of the country. Not all non-traditional settings will be willing to engage in partnerships, as the author and others who have tried this form of initiative know. Nevertheless, an agency need develop only a few partnerships before it and the community reap the rewards.

Conclusion

Social work practice within nontraditional urban settings provides a context for the above approaches to come together as a unified and cohesive approach. Practice within nontraditional settings requires a dramatic shift in paradigms (service delivery can transpire in any setting, whether it is formal or informal); new strategies; and tools for assessing, engaging, and structuring delivery of social services.

There is a need for the development of innovative social service delivery strategies for communities of color. Service demands from communities of color are expected to increase in the future as these communities become more populous. Social service providers must be prepared to respond to the needs of these communities. A very dismal picture can develop if strategic steps are not undertaken. It is unlikely that nonethnic social service agencies will evolve into ethnic agencies; ethnic agencies, in turn, will likely not proliferate to meet all of the needs of communities of color (Iglehart & Becerra, 1995). Consequently, exploring services provided within nontraditional settings may represent a promising arena to meet the needs of these communities.

6

Nontraditional Settings:
Literature and Case Illustrations

It is safe to assume that people in most nontraditional settings in the United States go about the business of helping without any validation or support from human service agencies. In many ways, these two important forms of service delivery co-exist, as if in different dimensions. When it comes to undervalued groups, this parallel process is a luxury that many communities cannot afford.

Practice never takes place in a vacuum, and practice within nontraditional settings is no exception. This chapter's primary goal is to provide the reader with a brief review of the literature regarding various types of nontraditional settings. This review has been included to provide greater detail, where applicable, about how these nontraditional settings have been viewed by professionals and news media. In addition, cases will be used to illustrate the possibilities for various kinds of collaborative partnerships.

The demographic profiles presented in this chapter are not intended to provide an in-depth understanding of demographic trends and socioeconomic conditions, or to describe the most pressing social problems confronting a community. The goal is to place a case within a demographic context. Descriptive profiles are provided on those cases in which there was personal contact with key individuals in a social service organization (field visits or in-depth telephone interviews) or field-based interviews within nontraditional settings.

Literature Reviews and Case Illustrations

Literature reviews on various nontraditional settings and the needs they address within their respective communities will be presented whenever possible. Every effort was made to undertake extensive literature searches for all of the nontraditional settings covered in this book. These reviews covered scholarly printed sources, as well as the popular press. However, as might be expected, these reviews are severely limited by the paucity of material on the topic of nontraditional settings. Nevertheless, limited as they may be, the reviews still function to place nontraditional settings within regional and national contexts, extending the implications for social work education and practice beyond a specific place and issue.

Literature reviews were undertaken on nine nontraditional settings: (1) bath houses; (2) beauty parlors/barbershops; (3) botanical shops (Latino versions of pharmacies); (4) eating establishments; (5) ethnic businesses; (6) houses of worship (focused on African Americans and Latinos); (7) laundromats; (8) liquor establishments (bars and stores); and (9) single-room occupancy hotels. Case illustrations will be included whenever possible. The reader is advised that numerous case illustrations are presented throughout this chapter that are not attributed to a source; in those circumstances, the case material was derived from field-based research.

Bath Houses

The topic of bath houses conjures up visceral and very vivid images of gays, AIDS, San Francisco, unsafe sex, etc. There is a tremendous amount of controversy concerning the role bath houses had or continue to play in the spread of HIV/AIDS (Green, 1996; Reed, 1994; Seigel, 1994; Tuller, 1994; Vulliamy, 1994; Woodard, 1993). Nevertheless, these settings have appeal for an undervalued population with limited options in this society. Their popularity and eventual outlawing in San Francisco during the 1980s has been the subject of debate and has raised issues concerning the rights of consenting adults versus the state's need to combat the spread of HIV/AIDS.

There are tensions between those who favor and those who are against the return of bath houses: "A dramatic change in sexual practices, wrought by a mix of education and terror within the gay community, has taken hold in San Francisco. And the proposed re-entry of the bathhouse on the landscape of the city where almost anything goes is being greeted variously as a herald of better times in the wake of the storm or as crazed folly, a return to the days when bath houses were the symbol of sexual liberation or the transmission of death."

Seigel (1994, p. 22) places bath houses within a broader context: "In the epidemic's second decade, arguments revolve around whether bathhouses will encourage unsafe sex or slow the transmission of AIDS by providing on-site education about risky behavior already occurring elsewhere . . . 'Bathhouse' is still a loaded term in the city known as the heart of the gay-rights movement."

However, Vulliamy (1994, p. 24), in quoting a columnist of a local weekly gay and lesbian newspaper who is opposed to the opening of bath houses, captures the passion opponents have about this move: "Anyone brave enough to question whether (bathhouses) should re-infest—or is it reinfect—our streets will, again, be pegged an anti-sex Nazi. Let's cut through the crap and tell it like it is: men are sexually irresponsible. I don't want to hear the argument that a bathhouse is the best place for safe-sex education. It's nonsense."

The debate about opening bath houses has also touched the gay community of color. Young African American and Latino gays have been left out of the concerted efforts at getting the message out on safe sex (Vulliamy, 1994, p. 24): "Among those aged 18 to 22, and among black and Hispanic men . . . we are finding increasing levels of infection—among them there is a certain resignation, an idea from the stereotypes that we will all die of AIDS. Or else [there is] a sense of immortality, people who say: 'We are sorry about those who died, but we want to live our lives too.' "

The city of Berkeley is located next to San Francisco. Although its reputation is based on its renowned university, the city is also well known for its street soothsayers, political activism, and social iconoclasm. Located in northern California, the city's total population is approximately 103,000. Of this population, 19 percent (19,300) is African American, 15 percent (15,200) is Asian, and 10 percent (9,900) is Latino. The largest segment of the population, 62 percent (64,000), is white.

Steamworks is a bath house located in Berkeley. This nontraditional setting has been open since 1987. The site of the bath house is a small building on a side street in a fairly industrial part of the city; it is open 24 hours a day. Steamworks employs the full-time services of a health educator. This educator develops and coordinates ten services that fall into seven categories: (1) in-house education; (2) HIV and STD testing; (3) counseling; (4) advocacy and referral; (5) community education and information dissemination; (6) community outreach; and (7) financial and condom donations.

The health education office is funded entirely by the profits made by Steamworks. It is estimated that the cost of running this office, not including rent, heat, air conditioning, etc., is approximately $40,000 to $50,000 per year. There are, in addition, many one-time costs (e.g., curtains for HIV and STD testing).

(1) In-house education. The provision of educational services within Steamworks is multifaceted and multi-goal directed:

> Condoms are distributed without limit throughout Steamworks. If specific sizes or types are desired, they are for sale at the front desk. The health educator makes presentations/demonstrations covering a wide range of safer sex topics to the patrons of the house. Typically, there is an open discussion period following each presentation. The educator believes that the open discussion, which allows the customers to set their own agenda, allows more room for personal discovery and growth. These sessions are co-led with the assistance of outside facilitators, some of whom are bilingual (American Sign Language, Chinese, Mandarin, Spanish and Tagalog). Workshops, in turn, are less verbal and more participatory than the presentations. Examples in-

clude: "Swedish Massage," "Food Sex," "Body Electric," and "Tribal Play." Workshop topics are chosen by their potential to attract participants. Facilitators for these workshops are found throughout the community and are described as "positive and humorous people." These workshops offer "alternatives to unsafe and unimaginative sex." They are designed to build self-esteem, improve body image, build trust, support limit-setting, and foster a sense of community. It is believed that after the workshop experience, participants have a "greater repertoire of truly useful safer sex options and methods to use outside the bath house environment." All workshops are free of charge to customers in an effort to encourage participation.

(2) HIV and STD testing. The importance of testing for HIV and STDs cannot be overestimated. Consequently, it becomes essential to facilitate access to this service at Steamworks:

> A local gay health collective offers, through "Steamworks," bi-monthly, in-house HIV and STD testing and pre-testing counseling. Over 195 people are tested each year and the number, according to the health educator, is increasing on a yearly basis. The testing is free and if an individual is coming to Steamworks only to be tested, the entrance fee is not charged. There is a one week turnaround for test results.

(3) Counseling and (4) advocacy and referral. These services represent an important dimension to the health educator's role within Steamworks.

> The health educator is available to speak with any customer for general counseling sessions. In addition, all employees are expected to spend one hour with the educator to obtain in-service training regarding HIV-related issues. The goal is to have all employees respond to the customers in a positive and supportive manner. The health educator, either during general counseling sessions or other times of interaction, offers referrals and advocacy for all customers.

(5) Community education and information dissemination. There is an active community education service provided by Steamworks that is related to recruiting potential customers to the bath house:

> Tables are often set up in the main lobby outside agencies and offer brochures, condoms, lubricants, resource referrals and other safer sex information by participating community based organizations in conjunction with the Steamworks Health Education Program. Each table's staff has previously met with the health educator to ensure that the appropriate messages are being imparted. In addition, the method of information dissemination is discussed. Currently, there is a trend to offer an enticement as a way of getting an audience. Once the men approach the table, information is offered. There are tables at all hours of the day in an attempt

to reach the various populations served by Steamworks. The schedule is set by the health educator. Because clients may represent diverse ethnic and socioeconomic backgrounds, the educator tries to invite organizations with this background. In the past, there have been as many as eleven outside agencies involved with this program; currently, eight agencies table Steamwork's materials. There is a particular approach that Steamworks uses in the distribution of educational materials. As a new customer enters the bath house he is given a packet which contains a short message about safer sex, along with two condoms and some lubricant. Education and prevention materials are available throughout the house: the hallways, congregation areas, and bathrooms. Every room has a notice posting safer sex practices and the house rules regarding this. Across from the Health Education Office there is a large bulletin board with many sheets of information, both social and informative. Across from that there is a smaller area which has pamphlets available. The topics within these materials include: safe sex messages, HIV/STD site locations and issues, medical information on STDs, HIV treatment options, condom usage, substance abuse intervention information, and counseling information. The materials, in turn, are "designed to reach different ethnic and socio-economic groups." In addition, there are safe sex messages on the public announcement system repeated throughout the day. Condoms are available throughout the house in well-marked containers. The health educator has also started to write a monthly newsletter which is available at the front desk.

(6) Community outreach. Steamworks has also made a concerted effort to reach out to other agencies and interested parties:

> Steamworks, through previous and current health educators, goes into the community (City of Berkeley and County of Alameda) to participate in outreach events. Examples of some of the past events include: a health education fair, a yearly safer sex party, network of HIV service providers, and an informal coalition for providers to promote safer sex information.

(7) Financial and condom donations. Steamworks donates funds and condoms to various Bay Area organizations. It is estimated that it donated 20,000 condoms during the 1995 calendar year.

It becomes very evident that Steamworks is a highly unusual nontraditional setting. The controversial nature of the organization, however, has severely limited the type and number of collaborative partnerships it has established. As a result, the potential for collaborative activities with more "mainstream" social service organizations has yet to be tapped.

The opening of bath houses and the inclusion of various services that can be considered educational is predicated on a "harm reduction" philosophy that seeks to minimize the deleterious consequences associated with risky behavior (Buning, Brussel, & Santen, 1992; Stimson, 1992; Stover & Schuller, 1992). Nevertheless, public sentiment, gay and nongay, is very divided on this topic.

Beauty Parlors/Barbershops

Beauty parlors and barbershops are often not thought of as providing anything but cosmetic services. However, these nontraditional settings lend themselves to work with women and men, particularly those who do not feel comfortable using formal agencies. As one HIV/AIDS outreach/community educator noted (Bryant, 1994a, p. 1): "Almost every man and woman in America goes to a beauty parlor or barbershop." In these nontraditional settings, beauticians or barbers may speak with customers about various human service topics.

Three case examples will be used to illustrate the importance of these nontraditional settings. The first example is based in Columbia, South Carolina, and examines how an African American beauty parlor has sought to have an impact on HIV/AIDS in that community. The additional two examples come from Lawrence, Massachusetts, and examine how gender plays a role in service delivery. One is a beauty parlor and the other a barbershop.

Columbia was established as the capital of South Carolina in 1786; it is also the state's largest city. Columbia is the home of many historic sights dating back to the colonial and Civil War periods. The overall population is almost 98,000, of which 54 percent (52,600) is white. African Americans represent the second largest segment of the population with 44 percent (42,900), followed by Latinos with 10 percent (1,900).

The case of DiAna DiAna in Columbia, South Carolina, is inspirational. The case illustrates how an African American woman single-handedly developed a highly complex approach toward educating her community because of the paucity of efforts on the part of human service organizations to address the epidemic of HIV/AIDS. In addition, it highlights the potential of nontraditional settings in the communities they serve.

DiAna has almost single-handedly been responsible for the use of beauty parlors as key nontraditional settings in HIV/AIDS outreach and education to communities of color across the United States. She has received numerous accolades and support for her endeavors. This acknowledgment and encouragement resulted in her creation of the South Carolina AIDS Education Network, Inc. (SCAEN). Although this commitment to HIV/AIDS education has expanded over the years, she has still maintained her beauty parlor. The organization is run out of her home (third floor), with the first floor being the beauty parlor, and the second floor her living quarters.

This establishment caters to the African American community, but also serves a small number of white customers. DiAna and Dr. Bambi Gaddist have directed most of their attention and energy to the prevention of HIV and STDs within the community. DiAna is a most exceptional human being who easily could have been a social worker, health educator, or counselor, because of her talents. Being a beautician, however, provided her with an opportunity to fulfill all of these and other roles, and to do so in a nonthreatening way.

Her interest in HIV/AIDS developed by chance one evening:

DiAna became interested in HIV/AIDS and other STDs one evening when she was cleaning up her beauty parlor at the end of the day. She came across a magazine someone left behind and noticed a story on HIV/AIDS. She decided to take a break from cleaning and read the article. She, as a result, became alarmed about HIV/AIDS and its impact on the African American community. DiAna decided to photocopy the article and make it available to her customers free of charge. She found, much to her surprise, customers taking copies of the article home with them.

This interest in HIV/AIDS prevention encouraged DiAna to take community education to another, more active, level:

She decided to buy condoms and distribute them free of charge in her beauty parlor as a community service. However, she experienced a less than receptive attitude when purchasing condoms at a local store. She decided that her negative experience would no doubt discourage other African Americans from purchasing condoms. As a result, she decided to purchase a large quantity of condoms from a chain store. Initially, she put the condoms out in her shop for customers to take. However, there was a reluctance to do so. Consequently, DiAna decided to wrap the condoms up in gift wrap as a means of destigmatizing the process. This change had immediate and immense success. Customers did not hesitate to avail themselves of this product.

DiAna and her colleague, Dr. Gaddist, have taken community education on HIV/AIDS to new levels through the development of materials targeting the African American community (SCAEN, 1995, p.1):

To date, the South Carolina AIDS Education Network, Inc., provides a variety of services to the community . . . AIDS videos are shown daily at DiAna's Hair Ego Salon. AIDS pamphlets and materials are available along with mini-sessions during the day. A variety of condoms, contraceptives, and safer sex information is available to clients and their visitors. Educational and training materials developed by teen peer educators [trained and supervised by DiAna and Dr. Gaddist] are free for individuals with children or persons with low/or little reading ability . . . As of March, 1990, SCAEN's **Home Safer Sex "Tupperware"** program has been expanded to include the participation of an audience in larger settings. Community leaders and HIV/AIDS educators have invited DiAna and Bambi to conduct parties in a game show format . . . a producer created "DiAna's Hair Ego: AIDS Info Upfront" video [an educational video targeting health educators and other providers] . . . DiAna recently created a board game which will ultimately become part of the total educational package.

In addition, DiAna has written and produced several plays on the topic of HIV/AIDS. Her rationale for writing these plays as educational vehicles and for providing safer alternatives to unprotected sex provides an insight into her thinking on the topic:

> The things that I have chosen to write about in my plays are things that I know exist and see as a barrier to doing AIDS education in the community . . . I am aware that all these issues are "real," and they do reflect the problems in the community. I was hoping to make more people aware of the dangers that they are putting themselves in by not practicing "safer sex," or by not just saying "No." I had incorporated the "basic AIDS 101" information into each of the plays I wrote. I call that "getting people accidently educated." (Sort of slipping one in on them.) We performed my first play over a dozen times throughout the two years, and went to various parties in the state [South Carolina] to put on the plays. Sometimes in the first years of my trying to teach kids about AIDS and the dangers, they came to me and said they wanted to know more about "Sex" and what they could do since I told them all of the things that they could not do. I went home that night after hearing this request several times and came up with an idea. I made up a "Safer Sex Game."

DiAna created a health corner in her beauty parlor as a means of facilitating the education of her customers:

> The Health Corner was created as a means of providing a wide range of information on HIV/AIDs and STDs for customers and visitors. This section of the salon is easily accessible and facilitates the distribution of materials, condoms, and the showing of videos on HIV/AIDS to customers as they wait their turn. This section, in addition, conveys to the customers the importance of having knowledge on HIV/AIDS. In addition, there are materials written for and by teens so that children have the benefit of this information. HIV/AIDS impacts families and not just individuals. Thus, information must be made available to all age groups in order to succeed in reaching the community.

Lawrence, Massachusetts, the site of two case illustrations, is located approximately 40 miles north of Boston. It is the second largest city in Massachusetts in absolute numbers and has the highest proportion of Latinos in the total population (Gaston Institute, 1992). The Latino community increased 184 percent between 1980 and 1990, from 10,300 to 29,300. This population primarily consists of Puerto Ricans (14,700) and Dominicans (13,900), with other Latino groups accounting for approximately 700, or 2.2 percent, of the Latino population (Gaston Institute, 1992). The Latino community can be classified as economically poor or working class, and has a disproportionate number of school dropouts, percentage of families living below the poverty level, and other "problems" associated with poverty or a near-poverty existence (Gaston Institute, 1994).

The Lawrence study of Latina beauty parlors (Delgado, in press c) raises the importance of not lumping all nontraditional settings together because each is very unique:

> Not all of the respondents indicated having an awareness of alcohol-related problems. Only two beauty parlors . . . indicated knowing customers who had alcohol problems—either themselves or their relatives. Most beauty parlors, however, did not have any knowledge of this or other social problems impacting on their customers. Beauty parlor willingness to collaborate with agencies differed by level and type of involvement. Some beauty parlors were willing to distribute information, i.e., pamphlets, provide advice (counseling), and facilitate lectures/discussions. The two owners . . . who indicated not having very much knowledge on the topic, were the most willing to provide an extensive range of services. Not all beauty parlors are alike, even when owners share the same ethnic background and the shops are located in the same geographical area. Even when there is agreement to collaborate with human service agencies, collaboration is operationalized in a variety of ways. The Lawrence study highlights the need for AODA [alcohol, and other drug abuse] organizations to undertake community based assessments of these establishments, and not taking cooperation and awareness of alcohol-related problems for granted. Although all beauty parlors indicated that they had not been approached by human service agencies to engage in collaboration or assist in the delivery of services, and all were willing to collaborate in some fashion, there were still major differences between them. Owners who indicated not having knowledge of customers with alcohol problems showed the greatest willingness to engage in multiple collaborative activities. This willingness reinforces the need for AODA organizations to reach out to these establishments and offer some form of education on the signs of alcoholism and the options available to customers and their families. The Lawrence study raised the possibility of a number of collaborative ventures between AODA agencies and beauty parlors. The impact of alcohol on Latinos does not allow the field of alcoholism the luxury of not seeking partners in addressing the problem. Consequently, beauty parlors have tremendous potential in this and other fields.

Beauty parlors have recently been the subject of increased attention as settings for outreach and education for women on a variety of topics, HIV/AIDS being prominent among them (Chan, 1992; Hutzler, 1991; Mangaliman, 1994; Pina, 1995; Sengupta, 1996). These nontraditional settings are accessible to the community, provide an atmosphere that is culture-bound, and women can feel free, and have the time, to discuss personal concerns without fearing stigma or being misunderstood.

Evans and Boyte (1986) specifically touch on barbershops as examples of "free spaces" within communities, where customers can exchange ideas, relate experiences with social injustices, and can be accepted with dignity and self-respect. As a result barbershops, like their beauty parlor counterparts, are excellent nontraditional settings for outreach, community education, and engaging men in the community. Barbershops are community gathering places that are ideal locations for people to discuss sexually transmitted diseases, HIV and safer sex, and other "sensitive" topics. Barbers are in an excellent position to talk to people about various topics. People sit there getting their hair cut, and the barbers can make presentations about HIV (Bryant, 1994a).

The Lawrence study of Latino barbershops (Delgado & Santiago, in press b), illustrates the role of gender in service provision by nontraditional settings:

> The four barbershops in the Lawrence study catered almost exclusively to men, with the exception of one shop. That shop employed a female barber, thus having a small (10) percentage of female customers. Customers, however, ranged in age from young boys to senior citizens, and consisted of working and nonworking groups. All four shops expressed concerns about various issues and needs in the Latino community. All four shops, unlike their female counterparts, sponsored sporting leagues and teams. The nature of service delivery, however, was not as extensive as those of beauty parlors. Three of the shops (the exception being one shop where the owner did not want to be involved with human service agencies and did not specify why), indicated a willingness to collaborate with human service agencies. These barbershops were generally willing to distribute materials related to HIV/AIDS, alcoholism, and family violence. In addition, they were willing to make referrals for services when appropriate and show public education videos followed by staff led discussions.

Botanical Shops

The topic of botanical shops is rarely addressed in the field of social work, although these institutions can be found in virtually every community of color in the United States and can play a role in addressing HIV/AIDS. Although the case example addresses two Latino subgroups (Dominicans and Puerto Ricans), the reader should not associate these nontraditional settings just with these groups.

Local initiatives utilizing natural support systems as means of addressing HIV/AIDS are critical (Drucker, 1994). Unfortunately, the professional literature on Latinos has largely eschewed examining botanical shops and other forms of natural support systems, although these and other nontraditional settings represent an important aspect of community (Crocker, 1994; Delgado & Santiago, in press, a, f).

Santiago (1995) comments on how staff overlooks this resource:

> Every day, squads of outreach workers, casemanagers, and prevention specialists go out into the Latino community in an effort to reach those at risk of contracting HIV, as well as those already sick from the virus. Gallant efforts are made by . . . dedicated workers to reach the sick . . . at-risk . . . the families . . . . Still these very same workers ignore a key institution that

can help them reach more of their target population, and provide much needed information and assistance to the Latino community: the local "Botanicas."

The popular press has identified these establishments as vital indigenous resources that are owned, operated, and patronized by the community (Carr & Perez, 1993; Delgado, 1996c). These culturally indigenous institutions can play a significant and active role in addressing HIV and AIDS within the Latino community and, more specifically, help residents who either mistrust health settings or who, for a variety of other reasons, have not accessed formal services.

Botanical shops are defined as community-based establishments with an extensive history of meeting a variety of community informational, expressive, and instrumental needs in the physical, spiritual, and religious world within a Puerto Rican cultural context. These storefront institutions represent outlets of important Puerto Rican cultural traditions pertaining to healing/spirituality, and are places where customers can socialize with others who share similar beliefs (Delgado, 1996c; Delgado & Santiago, in press c; Harwood, 1977).

The following case example is based on research undertaken in Lawrence, Massachusetts. Fetherston's (1992, p. 32) description of a New York botanical shop provides a vivid picture of the range of products that are for sale in these stores:

> Santos Variety is a slightly misleading name for the store, since the variety is confined to four groups of products; the greeting cards in Spanish and English on the rack at the center of the sales floor, the music on cassettes in the center case, the cotton crochet yarn in a rack at the back, and the paraphernalia of Santeria that lines the walls and dominates the scene. This concentration is duly noted on the front window, upon which is painted, in yellow and cherry red paint, the word, "Botanica."

Valdes (1994, p. 78), in conducting an inventory of a botanical shops in Boston, focuses specifically on healing and identifies four major types of medicinal-related products:

> The Botanica San Expidito . . . Boston, is typical of the more than two dozen area stores that sell items used in the Santeria religion . . . A sample of available products: Cleansers for the house and bathroom . . . Air Fresheners . . . Perfumes . . . Oils . . .

Delgado and Santiago (in press c) studied how Latino botanical shops in Lawrence, Massachusetts, addressed the problem of HIV/AIDS in the community, and provided an overview of the types of services offered and how certain botanical shops played a greater or less significant role in this area.

Virtually all of the botanical shops, with the exception of one, provided some form of emotional counseling, comfort and advice to patrons who have AIDS or to their loved ones. The nature of this counseling could be described as "supportive." However, two shops have provided customers with information on HIV/AIDS. This information, verbal in nature, focused on women having "safer sex" and on detection of symptoms associated with AIDS. One shop did not provide information or counseling. Two shops prescribed herbs to help patrons deal with AIDS-related symptoms. One botanical shop owner prescribed an herb that "thins the blood" to reduce the severity of the symptoms; another prescribed an ointment to help reduce body aches, discomfort of sores, and tremors. Only one shop owner indicated there was a cure for AIDS. However, the plant used for this cure was located deep in the jungles of Peru and not readily accessible. Last, none of the botanical shops made an effort to refer patrons with AIDS for health and social services. None of the owners had ever been approached by human service organizations to collaborate on a project reaching out to the Latino community. However, several owners (N = 3) noted that they had been approached by individuals who worked in the field of human services either to seek assistance for themselves or to learn more about how botanicas functioned. All five of the botanicas participating in the assessment indicated a willingness and a desire to be part of a collaborative venture with Centro Panamericano (community-based organization). This partnership venture would involve reaching out to and educating the community concerning HIV/AIDS.

Who are the owners of these botanical shops? What is their demographic profile? Answers to these questions are important in designing any collaborative effort within this or any other type of nontraditional setting. Delgado and Santiago's findings (in press c) findings provided an often missing perspective:

The average botanical shop owner was 35 years old (range, 23 to 51) and had no previous experience owning an establishment, of this or any other type. Four out of five owners had achieved at least a high school diploma (one owner had a 7th grade education). Owners represented three Caribbean islands—Dominican Republic (N = 3), Cuba (N = 1), and Puerto Rico (N = 1). All of the owners were women, highly unusual in a Latino community. The botanical shops were relatively recently established in Lawrence, with the exception of one botanical shop.

Botanical shop owners represented mixed backgrounds in terms of country of origin. However, they all were women and fairly well educated by community standards. In short, they were a formidable group of providers. In addition, they all believed that their powers to heal were given to them by God (Delgado & Santiago, in press a):

All of the owners stated that they had "special healing powers," and this was definitely an asset in their business. All of the owners indicated that this "power" was a gift from God and that it had always been a part of their lives. Their mission in life was to care for the health and emotional needs of people. Botanical shops provided them with an acceptable way of carrying out God's wish for them to heal.

The continued spread of HIV throughout all sectors of communities of color challenges health practitioners and policy makers to develop bold and innovative prevention and early intervention initiatives. The devastating impact of AIDS on Latinos necessitates a comprehensive approach to preventing and aiding those who have the virus. A comprehensive approach, however, must actively involve nontraditional settings. Botanical shops represent a great potential for achieving maximum impact in a relatively short period of time.

Although botanical shops represent an untapped resource that is strategically located to reach out to the community, they are often overlooked by dominant as well as Latino social service organizations (Delgado & Santiago, in press a):

> The typical botanical shop had been in existence an average of approximately three years, ranging from less than one year (N = 2) to twelve years (N = 1). Botanicas were opened six days per week, Monday through Saturday, and an average of 9.5 hours per day, with a low of eight hours and a high of twelve hours. All of the botanical shops indicated that they provided a community service that went beyond what is usually associated with botanical shops. The average establishment provided 3.4 services with a range of one (N = 2) to a high of five (N = 1). The botanical shop that provided the most services had been in existence the longest, with twelve years. Providing counseling for customers with personal problems was mentioned by all of the owners. This type of counseling ranged from marital and interpersonal to health-related matters. Information and referral for social services was the second most frequently mentioned service (N = 4), followed by provision of financial assistance (N = 3) for those who were homeless or destitute and assistance with location of housing or provision of food (N = 3). With the exception of one botanical shop, which had the longest longevity, no establishment provided all five services. All five botanical shops indicated a willingness to collaborate with Centro Panamericano [a community-based organization] in prevention activities and in the outreach to customers with HIV/AIDS.

However, as found in Lawrence, past involvement of indigenous resources with HIV/AIDS is mixed, at best. Some botanical shops have taken a much more active and supportive role in addressing the needs of consumers with AIDS, while others have played a minimal role. Nevertheless, botanical shops, regardless of past roles, are willing to engage in collaboration with human service organizations. Much work needs to be done before involving this institution in any collaborative projects.

These healing institutions fulfill a multitude of roles in the community that can be classified as health or social services related, in addition to sharing cultural values. As addressed by Delgado (1979, 1996c), botanical shops very often represent the first and only effort on the part of Puerto Ricans/Latinos seeking medical attention.

Botanical shops generally carry a wide assortment of herbs and other healing paraphernalia, along with religious objects such as candles, prayer books, statues, and amulets (Fetherston, 1992). Some botanical shops carry more "commercial" products such as records/CDs, "novelas," tickets to local dances/events, etc. This is most common in communities where there are few Latino-owned businesses.

These nontraditional settings cannot be ignored by health and social service organizations because they represent an untapped cultural resource in the prevention and early intervention for HIV and AIDS among Latinos. However, very little is known about how botanical shops and folk healers have responded to HIV and AIDS in the Latino community.

Rivera (1990), in one of the few publications on this topic, studied AIDS and Mexican folk medicine, and noted that many of the symptoms associated with this disease can be confused with symptoms of other folk-related illnesses, masking the true nature of the presenting illness. This may result in individuals delaying or not seeking medical attention from health professionals. Consequently, formal organizations simply cannot ignore the existence of alternative approaches to treating AIDS.

The transmission of HIV in inner cities, particularly among Latinos and African Americans, has been closely linked to drugs through needle exchange. This further compounds the consequences of substance abuse on addicts, their families, and their communities (Bastian, 1995; Freudenberg, Israel, & Germain, 1994; Jackson, 1989; Levy & Rutter, 1992; Rivera, 1994; Vazquez, 1994).

The impact of HIV/AIDS on the Latino community in the United States has been well acknowledged in the health and social service field (Bletzer, 1995; Menendez, Blum, Singh, & Drucker, 1994; Singer et al., 1991; Zorrilla, Diaz, Romaguera, & Martin, 1994). Indications are that this disease has not slowed its spread in the Latino community (Diaz, Buehler, Castro, & Ward, 1993; Drucker, 1994; Singer et al., 1994), with very few Latino families not having experienced multiple losses as a result of this epidemic (Chachkes & Jennings, 1994; Sexton, 1995).

The prevention and early diagnosis of HIV among Latino groups continues to present serious challenges to the field of health and social services (Colon, Sahai, Robles, & Matos, 1995; Epstein, Dusenbury, Botvin, & Diaz, 1994; Kilbourne, Gwinn, Castro, & Oxtoby, 1994). Recent government (Centers for Disease Control and Prevention) acknowledgment that communities must be actively involved in the development and implementation of HIV prevention represents an important shift in national policy (Valdiserri, Aultman, & Curran, 1995). Botanical shops can prove to be viable settings for reaching out to and engaging Latinos who would otherwise not seek assistance from health and social service organizations.

Food Establishments

Unfortunately, the literature on retail establishments has primarily focused on grocery stores, known in Spanish as bodegas and cormados (Agins, 1985; Carmody, 1972; Howe, 1986; Vazquez, 1974). Botanical shops (Borrello & Mathias, 1977; Delgado, 1996c; Fisch, 1968; Spencer-Molloy, 1994) and restaurants (Hernandez, 1994; Raynor, 1991; Stout, 1988) have received superficial attention.

Bodegas and restaurants, like their religious counterparts, provide a variety of social support services that supplement the primary commercial interests of the establishment (Delgado, 1996b). These establishments provide at least seven key services to the Puerto Rican community in general, and elder population in particular: (1) counseling (Agins, 1985; Vazquez, 1974; (2) cultural connectedness to homeland (Raynor, 1991; Rierden, 1992; Rohter, 1985a; Vazquez, 1974); (3) assistance in filling out or interpreting government forms (Howe, 1986; Vazquez, 1974); (4) community-related news and information (Agins, 1985; Korrol, 1983; Terry, 1992); (5) information and referral to social service agencies (Howe, 1986; Vazquez, 1974); (6) credit (Agins, 1985; Fitzpatrick, 1987); and (7) banking—check cashing (Fitzpatrick, 1987; Howe, 1986).

Grocery stores are complex institutions that fulfill a multitude of functions within their respective communities (Valdes, 1997, p. B4):

> The dictionary definition of a bodega is "a store specializing in Hispanic groceries." But experience says it's much more. Here are some definitions of a bodega you won't find in a dictionary: * A place where you can go several times a day to hang out and talk to people from your home town in Puerto Rico or the Dominican Republic. * A place to buy Spanish-language newspapers. * An extension of the Latino social support network. * A place to find out about upcoming Latin music shows from bright yellow and pink flyers in the front window. * A place to buy calling cards on credit. * A place to buy everything, from pots and pans, baby socks, mojo for yucca, to sofrito and diet soda. * A place to eat fresh pineapple off a knife in the summer. * A place to learn a new joke [preferably about a well-known Latino politician] . . . * A place to watch your favorite Spanish soap opera or the "Cristina" show on the TV above the dairy case. * A place to listen to the new Toros Band CD if you don't already have it. * A place to get milk and coconut candy from Santo Domingo. * A place where no one will make fun of your accent.

The following example of one grocery store in Holyoke, Massachusetts, does an excellent job of highlighting the importance of this type of setting. Holyoke is located in the western part of the state, approximately 100 miles west of Boston and 60 miles north of Hartford, Connecticut. The city of Holyoke has an overall population of 44,000, of which approximately 28.9 percent are Puerto Rican (12,700); Puerto Ricans are the largest Latino subgroup, representing 93.5 percent of all Latinos (Gaston Institute, 1992b).

The Puerto Rican community is also the fastest growing population group in Holyoke, with an increase in representation from 5,760 in 1980 to 12,700 in 1990—a 120 percent increase in 10 years (Gaston, 1992, 1994). The Puerto Rican elder (over 65 years of age) population more than doubled (114.8 percent) over a 10-year period from 142 in 1980 to 305 in 1990 (Gaston Institute, 1992b). In 1990, their poverty rate was 35.1 percent (ages 65 to 74) and 27.3 percent (75 years and over), respectively, the highest of any ethnic group in Holyoke (Gaston Institute, 1994b).

Eating establishments are excellent settings for social interaction, lending themselves to provision of various kinds of services. The case example (Holyoke, Massachusetts) of Puerto Rican food establishments developed by Delgado (1996b, p. 70), provides a vivid picture of the kind of people who may own and operate such an establishment, and illustrates the potential for these settings to deliver services:

> Restaurant [Don Felipe] has been in existence three years . . . Both owners . . . (husband and wife) are also foster parents to a number of children. In order to become foster parents, they have had to take workshops that have increased their knowledge and skills. Consequently, they have a basis from which to provide information and make referrals to social service agencies. The restaurant has several bulletin boards that provide an agency or community group with the opportunity to post information of community interest and social services available within the community. This institution has a contract with a local senior agency and provides space and hot meals for Puerto Rican/Latino seniors in the community. This space is also utilized for workshops, festivals, and recreational activities such as dominoes. This restaurant also sponsors or co-sponsors recreational teams. Most Puerto Rican candidates for elective office use this setting to hold meetings, victory celebrations, and other events. Last, this restaurant has an excellent reputation for generosity by providing food/meals to the hungry, and donating food and money for community events. The leadership role provided by the owners has also resulted in their participation on community agency boards, advisory committees, and task forces.

Bodegas are much more than an establishment that caters to the nutritional needs of the Latino community (Valdes, 1997, pp. B1, B4): " 'For Latinos, the bodega is more than just a store, . . . It is part of what is called a natural support system in the Latino community. People may come in to the store like five times a day, just to have someone to talk to . . . Any time you have an immigrant population they feel estranged from the larger mainstream, and going into a bodega you feel at home. For most people it won't matter that they are paying 10 more cents for a can of beans' [when compared to a large supermarket]."

Grocery stores face increasing competition when large supermarkets open up in the community. However, those with a solid relationship with the community can weather economic competition (Nossiter, 1995; Valdes,

1997). In many instances, these nontraditional settings represent one of the few places within the community where residents can cash their checks, obtain small loans, or get credit for buying food. In addition, these establishments are an alternative to check-cashing places charging exorbitant fees (Hudson, 1996).

The following case (San Francisco) symbolizes the kind of dedication and willingness to help that can often be found in nontraditional settings. The case of Mr. Tom McKnight, Jr., illustrates the multifaceted services that can be delivered within nontraditional settings, social companionship being one of them (Cothran, 1996, p. 1–3):

> Tom McNight, Jr. used his various businesses to educate his children and counsel them in the doctrine of social obligation. Now his son must balance the demands of activism against the realities of commerce . . . His retirement imminent, he has passed the store to his second-oldest son . . . In doing so, he's carefully balancing the demands of community activism against the realities of entrepreneurship. He wants to improve his business and the neighborhood—complementary goals, to be sure—but he isn't sure how far he wants to express what friends say is his resonant sense of social obligation . . . What does it profit him if he improves the lives of the underclass only to lose his father's legacy in the process? Conversely, how can he make his business grow if the community remains the catch basin of San Francisco? . . . But the progress of his business is naturally linked to the surrounding community. And to succeed Ulan [son] will have to correlate his personal ambitions with the community's engrossing needs . . . He serves on the boards of the main nonprofit community groups in the area . . . Like a river, the neighborhood's eclectic population flows in and out of Tom's grocery . . . Ulan knows everyone on the street, their histories, their scams, their drug-habits, everything . . . Every new customer brings in a fresh story to feed the reciprocal exchange of news, gossip, and pleasantries. But on a street that's lost most or all of its social capital over the years—there used to be two black churches and two black barbershops many years ago—it falls to whomever and whatever is left to provide avenues of community. Tom's grocery is the most wholesome such outlet. The only other gathering points are bars and the sidewalk out in front of liquor stores.

The case of Tom McNight's store illustrates the important social roles nontraditional settings can play in the community. In addition, it reinforces how important it is for urban renewal efforts to view communities from a social rather than physical perspective. Housing can be built or rebuilt; grocery stores like McNight's cannot easily be replaced.

Finally, the following case, although not specifically focused on communities of color, illustrates the multifaceted role nontraditional settings can play within a community (Fisher, 1997, p. 23):

> The bulletin board about halfway into the bar was shingled with hundreds of personal ads . . . No one needed to convince Ms. X that it is hard to

meet a soulmate in New York and that was why she was there: at an up-scale bar and coffee house on the Upper West Side of Manhattan called Drip. Since August, Drip has encouraged its customers, most of them under 30, to fill out sheets with descriptions of themselves for blind dates that the staff arranges by telephone . . . By this week, with Valentine's Day around the corner, so many forms—nearly 2,400—had been filled in that they spilled off the bulletin board and into well-thumbed loose-leaf binders. By making mating its unabashed theme, the bar has managed to strip shame and stigma from taking out a personal ad. The service has become so pop-ular that the staff is often backed up several days before they can make calls.

The process of arranging meetings is systematized and must take place at Drip (Fisher, 1997, p. 27):

The way it works is, a customer picks through the personal ads on the board or in the loose-leaf binders—which include men seeking men and women seeking women—and selects a person or two, identified only by a num-bered code. A Drip employee . . . then calls the chosen with the informa-tion about the chooser. The chosen, of course, has the right to refuse, in which case it's back to the boards.

Although this establishment has specifically focused on providing a "so-cial" type of service, it does not preclude a nontraditional setting "broker-ing" other types of services that are more human service in nature.

Ethnic Businesses

Ethnic businesses are community-based institutions that provide, for profit, products and services within a cultural context; these establishments are owned, staffed, and patronized by the community (Gorov, 1997; Halter, 1995a,b). Some scholars note that the concentration of Latino businesses, applicable to other groups as well, also serves to heighten ethnic identity. The size of the ethnic community provides a market for services that would otherwise not be in sufficient demand (Padilla, 1993). In essence, group domination results in greater visibility of Latino products and services (Rohter, 1985b,c).

Hoffman (1994) notes that scholars traditionally had a tendency not to study neighborhood-based businesses. Sociologists have generally concen-trated on studying neighborhood social relations, institutions, and land uses. Urban economists studied city-scale economies, and industrial and residen-tial patterns, as a whole. Historians examined downtown merchants, large manufacturers, and the economic structure of entire cities. However, there has been a blatant disregard for the role of small, neighborhood-based busi-nesses.

Hoffman's (1994) study of the development of an urban neighborhood in Boston, Massachusetts, found that the importance of local businesses went far beyond the selling of a product or service and, instead, played a central role in neighborhood life for many ethnic groups. These establishments did much more than dispense goods to the community; they connected customers to the urban place in which they lived, and provided a neighborhood gathering place. The proprietors of local stores provided loans and goods on credit to their customers. Neighborhood salons also served as meeting places. Some of the proprietors of "respectable" local businesses emerged as community leaders.

Delgado's (in press d) study of merchant establishments in Holyoke, Massachusetts, specifically focused on Latino elders, and found these non-traditional settings fulfilling a service role in the community.

> There is no doubt that merchant establishments, like their religious and food establishment counterparts, are fulfilling multiple roles within the Puerto Rican community. The services they provide, however, are limited to just a few types. The average merchant establishment provided 2.83 types of services, from a low of two to a high of four, considerably lower than religious and food establishments. Three services (integration of the lonely, interpreter services, and community leadership) were cited by at least three-fourths of the establishments. The first two have great significance for elders. These services, incidentally, were also found to be frequently provided by religious and food establishments. Integration of the lonely ($N = 11$), the most frequently cited service, generally consisted of providing opportunities for community residents, particularly elders, to interact/connect with merchant personnel and other residents; these merchant settings facilitated Puerto Ricans meeting and socially interacting. Provision of interpreter services was cited by ten establishments. This service consisted of any one or all of the following activities: (1) assistance in reading and interpreting "official" government correspondence for those with limited or no English reading abilities; (2) assistance in filling out government forms; and (3) personnel, on occasion, will make telephone calls to government agencies and act as interpreters/advocates for customers. One institution noted that Puerto Rican elders were the group that most needed this service, since many either did not know how to read in English or Spanish. Several government/social agencies did mail elders letters in Spanish. However, elders were either reluctant (pride) or had great difficulty in conveying to these institutions that they were illiterate in both languages. Community leadership, the third most frequently cited service ($N = 9$), consisted of any or all of the following activities: (1) sponsoring of community events and festivals; (2) donations to other organizations that provide social services (money, supplies, services); (3) allowing community to use space to conduct meetings; (4) membership on agency boards and advisory committees; and (5) allowing community organizations to place posters or distribute information on services. The remaining five services the questionnaire sought information on played minimal or no support roles within the establishments. Only two institutions donated services or money to the "poor"; one provided emergency child care and one provided elders with information/referrals to social service agencies. Two services usually asso-

ciated with Puerto Rican establishments (provision of credit and counseling) were not mentioned by any merchant institution.

The lack of service provision by those in nontraditional settings must be closely examined and does not necessarily mean that they are not interested in doing so. The lack may be due to a series of factors other than lack of willingness (Delgado, in press d):

> The nature and extent of care giving support provided by Puerto Rican merchant establishments was not extensive—an average of 2.83 services (5 different types of services). Merchant establishments, in comparison with religious (Pentecostal) and food (grocery store and restaurants) establishments in the same geographical area, are playing a less significant support role. Pentecostal churches provided an average of 7.3 services (16 different types), and food establishments provided an average of 3.36 services (7 different types). However, this should not come as a surprise in light of the high representation of elders in Pentecostal churches and the prominent role of religion in their lives.

The very nature of some stores, and their longevity, may diminish their ability to provide assistance to customers (Delgado, in press d):

> The lesser caregiving role for merchant establishments may be the result of an interplay of several factors: (1) the relatively recent establishment of these businesses—merchant institutions had been in existence an average of 3.65 years (Pentecostal churches had been opened an average of 6.0 years and food establishments an average of 4.6 years); (2) the lack of counseling and information referral services (only one institution noted information-referral) may be due to a lack of familiarity with or lack of outreach by social agencies; (3) customers may not expect merchant institutions to play active caregiving roles; and (4) the nature of the service/product that is sold does not lend itself to frequent and sustained contact with customers—thus, merchant establishments are not frequented as often as food establishments or religious institutions. However, the limited role that merchant establishments play in the community highlights a potential for more active involvement in providing assistance, if they have the opportunity and appropriate resources. It is important to keep in mind that virtually all of these institutions provided a setting for the lonely to connect, served as interpreters for customers, and were involved in various community-wide events or activities.

There has been a transformation of businesses in inner cities. It is not unusual to find classical corner buildings, originally built as banks, serving as storefront churches. Former chain stores might sell used appliances, with hotels transformed into senior citizens' apartments. Nevertheless, the most common forms of businesses are small food and furniture stores, fast-food franchises, dry cleaners and laundromats, gas stations, beauty parlors, check-cashing places, liquor stores, and bars (Vergara, 1995). This transformation to small businesses has resulted in these establishments developing a more personalized approach to the selling of goods and services that is ethnically and racially sensitive.

Local businesses must cater to the needs of local residents. Retailers still in business tailor their products and services to poor, inner-city residents rather than, as before, to the more affluent population of the entire metropolitan area. Local stores often sell different goods from those sold in the more affluent neighborhoods, and the buildings themselves are decorated and defended differently, as well, to reflect local tastes (Levett, 1995; Vergara, 1995). This resident-driven approach invariably involves provision of services that can be classified as human service related.

Hoffman (1994) found that local businesses and residents were closely connected in the life of a neighborhood, to a greater extent than manufacturers. Community merchants were strongly identified with the public life of the district. Observers of twentieth-century urban neighborhoods have noted how retail businesses contribute to neighborhood identity and organization. Stores and restaurants functioned as communication centers and owners as caretakers of the neighborhood. In short, there is a mutually beneficial relationship.

The success or failure of ethnic businesses must be viewed quite broadly, and any measure of success must encompass rates of self-employment, number of co-ethnic employees, diversity of economic activity, and size. However, the social role these institutions have within the community must also be taken into account (Razin & Langlois, 1996). Nontraditional settings are not interchangeable in informal services they provide. Some settings lend themselves to certain gender and age groups; others are particularly well suited to certain needs and issues.

Houses of Worship (Focused on African Americans and Latinos)

The literature on religion as a support system is getting increased recognition by professionals. There are even a number of publications that specifically address collaboration between houses of worship and social agencies (Cohen, Mowbray, Gillette, & Thompson, 1992; Eng & Hatch, 1992; Malony, 1992; Maton & Pargament, 1992; Moore, 1992).

Henry Cisneros (1996, pp. 1–2), former Secretary of Housing and Urban Development, recognized the importance of faith in the lives of inner-city residents:

> Most Americans are now well aware of the devastating chain of circumstances that has undermined once robust inner-city communities over the past two decades . . . But this essay is not about pessimism. Quite the contrary, it is about the remarkable hope being rekindled in communities across America. Faith communities are at the center of this good work . . . When I say faith communities I mean churches, mosques, temples—religious

institutions of all faiths. Religious institutions have a unique potential to contribute to community rebuilding . . . My purpose is to celebrate the impressive accomplishments of religious institutions in our cities—accomplishments that far too few Americans have heard about—and to consider how those contributions can be sustained and enhanced.

Houses of worship fulfill multiple roles within communities of color (Caraballo, 1992; Gaiter, 1980; Shepard, 1997; Tye, 1996a–d). These institutions have at least seven significant functions: (1) providing a cohesive institutional structure within the community; (2) playing an influential role in developing indigenous leadership; (3) providing citizenship training and as a source for community social action; (4) undertaking educational and social roles; (5) serving as charitable institutions; (6) fostering the development of community-based businesses and ventures; and (7) serving as a barometer of social class (Blackwell, 1985).

According to Delgado and Rosati (in press), in their study of Pentecostal churches, the typical church provided at least eight services that could be classified as human services: (1) financial assistance; (2) friendship for the lonely; (3) interpreter; (4) food for the hungry; (5) advice/counseling; (6) community leadership; (7) information and referral to social services; and (8) child care. Meeting the needs of elders played a prominent role in the organizing and delivery of these services.

There is a paucity of material on religious institutions and prevention written by human service professionals. This resource is extremely important in many people's lives and should be a critical area in any prevention initiative. There are a number of reasons for considering religious centers as resources for prevention. A central principle of prevention is that preventive activities must be grounded in the settings, systems, and events most central to most community residents. Consequently, it is not unusual to develop prevention programs directed toward families, schools, work settings, neighborhoods, and larger communities, and at critical points in people's lives. Religion is a central part of many people's lives, and as such, must also be targeted by human service providers (Maton & Paragamont, 1992).

The strength derived from mutuality between minister and congregation, congregation member and member, and congregation and community, is a very powerful factor in attracting and maintaining members within a church (Roberts & Thorsheim, 1992). This bond is no doubt reinforced by shared life experiences and the quest for social justice in this society.

Cisneros (1996, pp. 6–7), in describing his assessment of the role of houses of worship in inner cities, focuses on their outreach and service provision:

While their commitment has always been a powerful force in American life, inner-city religious institutions have now fundamentally expanded the meaning and horizons of that commitment . . . .There has been no national census of church-based community outreach activities, but a study in Denver suggests that they are now widespread: 60 to 75 percent of the African American churches surveyed there provide at least one community service. Of 333 identified programs, nearly half (148) were targeted to adults and families, and commonly involved the distribution of food and clothing. The many programs for children (106) involved youth activities, tutoring services, scholarship assistance, drug and alcohol education, and before school and after school child care. Community development activities (59) included church-sponsored voter registration drives and candidate forums as well as the operation of credit unions and housing development.

Mormon outreach efforts in the South Bronx of New York City have succeeded in reaching Latinos, because of the Mormons' commitment, long hours, and willingness to meet residents on their own territory. The Mormon church's worldwide outreach program, with nearly 50,000 missionaries (400 of them in the New York metropolitan area), is one reason why it has grown in membership, from an estimated 90,000 in 1950 to almost nine million members today (Niebuhr, 1994). Much of that growth has come from Africa and Latin America. Mormons also have been particularly successful among disaffected Protestants and Catholics struggling to survive in communities (Deck & Nunez, 1982; Gonzalez, 1994).

The case studies presented in this section reflect the important work these institutions undertake in urban areas (Cox, 1995; Kostarelos, 1995). The cases focus primarily on Puerto Ricans, with the exceptions of a Korean Protestant church and an African American church's initiative to fight crime. However, there is no community in the United States, regardless of ethnic and racial composition, in which we cannot find a house of worship playing an instrumental role in meeting the expressive and instrumental needs of a congregation. The first case involves a Catholic church in Brooklyn, New York; the second case focuses on a Pentecostal church in Holyoke, Massachusetts; the third case addresses the Korean community in New York City.

The story of St. Barbara (Catholic Church) in the Bushwick section of Brooklyn, New York, is an excellent example of how an institution can change its routine to meet a community's needs, thereby playing a much more influential and caring role (Sexton, 1995, p. 43):

There were 245 funerals at St. Barbara's in 1994 . . . 181 of them for people who had died of AIDS. The funerals this year equal last year's total . . . The overwhelming majority of the dead are in their 20s and 30s.

St. Barbara's Church made an important institutional decision to respond to an AIDS crisis in the community by being flexible with its schedule (Sexton, 1995, pp. 43, 49):

"Typically, they will have been away from the Church since childhood, but the families come and ask for a Mass. At the Masses, there was never anyone there beyond the family, sometimes not even them." And so there has not been a traditional early morning Mass at St. Barbara's since 1990. Faced with all the funerals and limited money to pay for professional musicians, Monsignor Powis approached the roughly three dozen elderly loyalists who had been coming daily to the 8 A.M. Mass and asked if they would consider permanently canceling the early services so they could attend instead, five days a week, the 9:30 A.M. funeral Masses. He asked them to be there, to sing, and they agreed . . . "We are not a choir, we are voices . . . We sing, and the family feels the strength. I think our singing gives them more faith."

Through this action, St. Barbara's Church increased its connectedness to the community (Sexton, 1994, p. 49):

> St. Barbara's attracts the dead partly because it is willing to hold funeral Masses for people who seldom if ever came to church when alive. As a result, several nearby funeral homes know they can direct the truly poor there, including many of those who died of AIDS, even if they had lived beyond the boundaries of Bushwick. Infrequently, but occasionally, the AIDS dead are infants or toddlers. There have also been 18 funerals for young homicide victims at St. Barbara's this year.

The church's role in helping the families of victims and the community grieve, is well understood by those who sing at the masses (Sexton, 1995, p. 49):

> The singers and their pastor have no doubts about the dividends their presence has paid for the families of the victims. They measure them in smiles. Often the family will even join in the singing. Monsignor Powis said a couple of dozen of the families have found themselves brought back into the full parish life by their experiences at the funeral.

The case example of a Pentecostal church in Holyoke, Massachusetts, provides a different perspective on how a house of worship can provide a wide range of important social services to a congregation. In this instance, services are focused on those parishioners who are experiencing problems with alcohol and other drug abuse:

> The Nazareth Pentecostal Church (pseudonym) was established approximately fifteen years ago . . . The congregation numbers approximately 120 members, almost all being Puerto Rican. Rev. Perez identified drugs as a particularly critical need in the community. He stated "I, too, have fallen under the curse of drugs and known firsthand its destruction of the individual, family, and community." The church offered four types of ATOD [alcohol, tobacco, and other drugs] programs: (1) detoxification (five beds); (2) day treatment (counseling, rehabilitation, and recreation); (3) counseling for family members who had relatives abusing drugs; and (4) provision

of workshops for youths, families, and other interested participants (focus of workshops was on development of self-esteem, identification of the problem, and refusal skills).

Nazareth Pentecostal Church obtained funding for these services from a variety of community-based sources:

> Services are provided free of charge to members of the congregation. Funding for these and other services has been made available by donations from the congregation, local businesses, and volunteers (some of whom were graduates of the program). Rev. Perez stressed the importance of not receiving funds from government, foundations, etc. "These types of money always have strings attached that can compromise what we believe in."

The services provided by Nazareth existed in complete isolation from the social service network in the city. In fact, although willing, the church had not been approached to collaborate on substance abuse-related projects:

> When questioned about how these services interfaced with formal services in the Holyoke community, Rev. Perez noted there was no interchange. He had never been approached by a human service agency to share information or collaborate on projects, ATOD or other areas. He made no effort to self-initiate contact either. Rev. Perez expressed a tremendous amount of distrust toward formal providers, even though many members of his congregation worked in the field of human services. He expressed concern that formal authorities would work to close down his services . . ."It does not mean we [human service agency and church] cannot work together. It means that our focus on 'The Lord' must be respected."

Kim (1987, pp. 233–234) notes that Korean Protestant churches fulfill a variety of roles within the Korean community in New York City, and indirectly identifies a variety of possible collaboration activities with social service organizations wishing to reach out to this ethnic group:

> Korean churches are much more than sites for religious services. Because they serve multiple, secular functions they are central places for community activities and they have, in fact, opened up membership to all segments of the Korean population . . . Ministers in the churches perform numerous secular roles, and they are mainly judged by their congregations according to how well they do so. The ministers' extrachurch activities include: matchmaking, presiding over marriage ceremonies, visiting hospitalized members, assisting moving families, making congratulatory visits to families having a new baby, making airport pick-ups of newly arrived members, interpreting for 'non-English' members, administering job referral and housing services, and performing other similar personal services.

A recent national-based initiative involving African American churches provides an excellent example of how these institutions can play an expanded role within their communities (Boston Herald, 1997, p. 21):

> A national coalition of black ministers announced plans . . . to fight black-on-black crime and street drug-dealing by expanding a church-based program credited with helping to lower crime in Boston . . . "We must mobilize in defense of our own future.". . . The plan is to use black churches, often found within the nation's most crime-ridden areas, as around-the-clock sanctuaries for young people seeking refuge from street life . . . In addition, church volunteers act as missionaries to show drug dealers, gang members and other wayward youth that options exist . . . The notion of church-based projects to remodel urban America has picked up steam recently. In February, Christian Coalition leader Ralph Reed announced an urban outreach program called "The Samaritan Project." The plan would have volunteer families take up residence in poor urban areas to help people there.

This African American church-based campaign is known as "Operation 2006" (Shepard, 1997, A6):

> The campaign . . . will mobilize 1,000 churches in 40 of the country's most dangerous neighborhoods to start or expand anticrime programs . . . The first cities for expansion include Philadelphia; Louisville, Chester, Pa; and Tampa, Fla.

Houses of worship can and must respond to the needs of urban-based parishioners. These parishioners are very often poor, of color, marginal to society, and in the midst of incredible crises in their lives. A recent *U.S. News & World Report* article explored how houses of worship can and often do help parishioners (Shapiro & Wright, 1996).

Laundromats

Laundromats are excellent nontraditional settings to consider in the development of collaborative partnerships, particularly when the target population is poor or working class (Pina, 1995). Very few people of low economic status have the funds or the space to buy a washer and dryer for the home. The capital outlay is quite formidable, and the space and necessary plumbing puts a washer and dryer out of their reach. Laundromats are very often located within geographical (walking or public transportation) reach of many low-income communities. In addition, patronizing these businesses is not stigmatizing, and their hours of operation are quite extensive, increasing their accessibility.

Laundromats are excellent places to conduct outreach and community education. Most laundromats have space for small group meetings. In addition, these settings lend themselves to engaging customers in workshops. Individuals doing their laundry generally must wait around until the washing and drying are complete. Most laundromats in poor and working-class area of the city do not have entertaining activities for waiting patrons. Consequently, this "down time" can easily be filled if the right inducements are offered.

Liquor Establishments (Bars and Stores)

The impact of alcohol on communities of color in the United States is widely considered to be devastating (Watts & Wright, Jr., 1989). A number of publications have focused on how this industry has targeted communities of color in its marketing (Hacker, Collins, & Jacobson, 1987; Maxwell & Jacobson, 1989; Sims, 1992). There is perhaps no other inner-city business that has been as lucrative as liquor stores. Liquor stores have done so well in urban centers that before the spring riots, South Central Los Angeles, with a population of 500,000, had nearly three times as many outlets (728) as Rhode Island, which had 1.3 million people and 280 liquor stores (Sims, 1992).

The market for alcohol in communities of color is very large and expanding (Sims, 1992, p. 6):

> No one knows the exact size of the inner-city alcohol market, but everyone agrees that billions of dollars worth of beer, wine, and other spirits are sold there each year. For many critics of the industry, the core of the problem is the big slice of the market occupied by malt liquors and fortified wines, which are sold predominantly in urban centers. Nationally, these products accounted for $2 billion in sales last year, three-quarters of which came from malt liquor.

As a whole, liquor-related establishments market a product that has had a deleterious impact on communities of color. However, all of these establishments simply cannot be written off for possible collaboration. Some of these businesses may have concerns about alcoholism in the community and be willing to collaborate in some prevention or early intervention project. There has been a movement among bars to stop the sale of alcohol to customers who might drive while intoxicated. These efforts have been driven by the insurance industry as a way of preventing accidents resulting from intoxicated drivers, and thereby avoiding lawsuits.

Unfortunately, the literature rarely provides examples of collaborative efforts with liquor establishments (Bond et al., 1997). This absence of literature may be the result of one or a combination of the following reasons: (1) agencies have eschewed engaging these establishments in collaborative partnerships because of the stigma associated with these nontraditional settings; (2) collaborative projects do exist, but have not received media or scholarly attention; and (3) agency efforts at involving these institutions have been undertaken, but failed, thus creating a widely held negative impression.

Collins and Pancoast (1976) examine the impact of "tavern" culture on homeless men. Within this culture, bartenders invest a considerable amount of time and energy fulfilling multiple roles, including friend and counselor to patrons.

Night Clubs

Nontraditional settings such as night clubs are excellent places for conducting outreach, community education, and other forms of service delivery. It is not out of the ordinary to have night clubs catering to people of certain ethnic/racial groups, sexual orientation, socioeconomic class, and other identifiable characteristics. Consequently, agencies wishing to target certain populations can do so by engaging these nontraditional settings.

These settings have a considerable amount of space that can be used for meetings, workshops, or conferences, and that are rarely used during daytime hours. During the evenings they are usually crowded with patrons of various age groups, presenting unique opportunities for service delivery, particularly outreach and community education on AIDS prevention.

A night club in New York City, for example, pays for the services of a "monitor" to ensure that sex that might lead to the spread of HIV doesn't take place in the establishment (Woodard, 1993, p. 15):

> Jim Bolas crouched beside a slender young man who dropped to his knees beside his partner at a gay dance club. Bolas whispered that oral sex wasn't allowed. The man stood up and started kissing his partner instead. It was 12:30 A.M. and Bolas had just started a four-hour shift as a safe-sex monitor. He works at Meat, a club in the meat-packing district in the West Village . . . The club pays him $60 a night to stop sex that might spread HIV . . . Meat is a place where black leather meets L.L. Bean. The customers are a cross-section of the gay community and about a third of them, at some point in their evening, wander down to Meat's back room. It's actually a dark, somewhat dank basement corridor set aside for sex. It is here that Bolas keeps watch. "There is a conscious attempt to maintain a sexy, erotic atmosphere and keep it safe . . . It's not easy to do that these days."
> . . . These days means the age of AIDS, which has changed the sex-club scene in New York City forever. Sex clubs never disappeared, but they were on the wane for a few years after a 1985 city crackdown. Eight years later, places for public sex—heterosexual and homosexual—are proliferating again. There are now at least 50 clubs, bath houses, movie theaters and bookstores . . . their popularity "reflects the failure on all of our parts to recognize the long-term effort of HIV prevention." . . . Monitors see a way of catching up . . . "We don't see how a facility without monitors could comply . . ." If city officials have their way, monitors such as Bolas would be as ubiquitous as bartenders. About a dozen clubs have them now.

"It says that we care about our customers," said [the] club manager and deejay at Meat.

The above case example focuses on one undervalued group and the importance of instituting "safer sex" protections as part of the night club scene. However, night clubs reach other groups that are undervalued and can benefit from service programs.

Single-Room Occupancy Hotels

The role and importance of single-room occupancy (SRO) hotels in the lives of individuals and families with low income is well understood in society and among helping professionals (Killilea, 1976). These places very often represent the final stop in the lives of people who have faced numerous setbacks and challenges.

The trials and tribulations of life have taken their toll on residents who often have no family or close friends as part of their support system (Wagner, 1985, pp. 7–8):

> They typically have few people in their social networks and tend to rely heavily upon the informal or "natural helping network" of hotel managers, desk clerks, storekeepers, and other residents to meet their daily needs. The decision to live in the downtown area is one of choice . . . Although most SRO residents choose to handle their own problems, hotel staff are important. Desk clerks and managers "keep an eye" on older residents, screen visitors, offer credit, make loans, and give advice. Other caretakers (shopkeepers, waitresses, post office clerks, police) offer a structure for social relations. The downtown offers a variety of services (cheap restaurants providing balanced diets, secondhand clothing stores, discount drug stores, hotels with laundromats, nearby police and affordable transportation.

Killilea (1976, p. 53) cites the presence and importance of mutual help within SRO hotels: "Reams of altruism, love, help, wisdom and self-knowledge have emerged from deeply embittered and damaged people. The SRO is a survival culture where chronic crises apparently stimulate highly social behavior in many of its members." Collins and Pancoast (1976) discuss the importance of strong, influential women who are residents of these establishments, and the role they play in helping other residents feel less isolated. In essence, these women play a role of unpaid staff.

Wagner (1985, p. 11) does a very good job of summarizing the appeal of a program targeting SRO hotels and the reasons for its success: "The Hotel Alert program is tailored to San Diego, but has great potential for being developed in any urban area. It taps into and utilizes the natural helping network that exists throughout our society. It stresses the importance of the volunteer, a precious and valuable resource. Most of all, it is a personalized and humanistic approach that emphasizes the importance of allowing the elderly to maintain an independent lifestyle."

Conclusion

This chapter has provided the reader with a basic understanding of the process used in selecting cases, along with the limitations inherent in the process that was utilized. Brief information on sites that were selected, along with applicable literature reviews, was also provided to develop a context from which to examine case examples.

It should be reemphasized that some types of collaborative practice within nontraditional settings may not lend themselves to applicability in all urban areas. The availability of these nontraditional settings, combined with cultural considerations and local sentiments about the settings, will exert an influence on feasibility.

7

Framework for Practice

The following quote from Collins and Pancoast (1976, p. 55) serves as an excellent introduction to this chapter because it points out the importance of reaching out to community and seeking ways of developing new working partnerships: "If it is agreed that vital helping networks exist in areas that social workers are concerned about but seldom reach, then it becomes of major interest to discover a way to reach them." Purposeful practice is not possible without a systematic way of conceptualizing and operationalizing intervention goals (Googins, Capoccia, & Kaufman, 1983; Pearlman & Gurin, 1972). Simply stated, a framework serves as a guide for the practitioner to systematically gather and analyze information. The professional literature is replete with examples of various kinds of frameworks that can be applied to micro- and macro-practice. The use of a framework is not restricted to formal interventions; it is also necessary for intervention within nontraditional settings. People in these settings may not share similar ideology, paradigms, and language with social work professionals. Consequently, how a framework is applied to practice within nontraditional settings is very important.

There are at least five strategies for promoting effective partnerships between professionals and local self-help groups that have applicability for work within nontraditional settings: (1) educational (capacity enhancement through the acquisition of knowledge, skills, and attitudes); (2) credibility (efforts to reduce barriers that result from social distance); (3) role and goal clarification (minimize misunderstandings that result from lack of clarity about what is expected of each party); (4) trust building (purposeful efforts at increasing respect, openly sharing concerns, dependability); and (5) communication building (instituting more open and frequent chances for meetings and exchanges) (Stewart, Banks, Crossman, & Poel, 1994).

Delgado (1994) developed a framework for use in collaboration with Latino natural support systems, cultural constructs encompassing nontraditional settings, and other forms of indigenous resources. This framework can be modified and applied to broader categories of nontraditional settings: "It is essential to view collaboration with [nontraditional settings] from a developmental perspective, with each phase representing opportunities and barriers . . . failure to follow a developmental approach will increase the likelihood of failure in reaching and engaging this important community resource."

Delgado's framework (see Figure 2) consists of five interrelated stages and builds on the work of other social work scholars: (1) identification and assessment; (2) mapping nontraditional settings; (3) engagement and relationship building; (4) development of collaborative activities and projects; and (5) evaluation. Each stage provides practitioners with an opportunity to integrate theory with practice and takes into consideration interactional (political) factors.

Stages must be approached from a developmental perspective, with each stage systematically building on the previous stage and setting the foundation for the following stage. Skipping a stage seriously limits the overall ef-

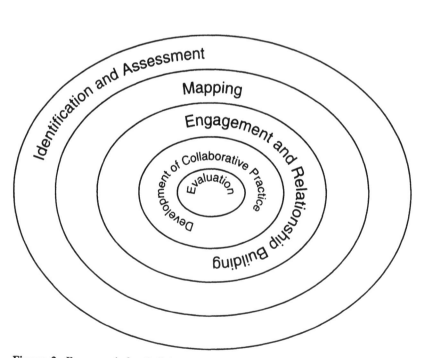

Figure 2. Framework for Collaborative Practice.

fectiveness of an intervention. Each stage varies according to time demands, resources needed, and degree of complexity regarding activities. The framework stages are interactive and highly dynamic. Movement along the stages is not linear; situations may arise requiring movement back to a previous stage before progress can occur. For example, an assessment activity may not have produced the necessary information to proceed to engagement, requiring a practitioner to re-initiate an assessment activity.

Identification and Assessment

There is a tremendous need for social workers to systematically gather information concerning nontraditional settings. Assessment is always the first step in a framework to inform the application of theory and analyze options. This phase, whether it is applied to micro- or macro-practice, is predicated on a paradigm (perspective). If the paradigm is based on principles of scarcity and pathology, the approach will be deficit driven. Conversely, if the paradigm is based on principles of resilience, coping, and strengths, then it will be asset driven.

It is important to note that using an asset approach to a client or community does not mean there are no needs to be addressed. It does mean that assessment of needs is viewed through an assets lens. In short, look first at assets so they can be incorporated into meeting needs.

Before an assessment can formally begin, it is necessary to take the initial, very important step of identifying nontraditional settings. Identification is complicated because it requires unlearning many years of teaching and experience about what a care giving resource is. Most social workers and other helping professionals have been socialized to think of care giving resources as being strictly formal; that for a resource to be "legitimate" it must have a series of initials over the front door of the institution, i.e., D.S.S. (Department of Social Services), D.M.H. (Department of Mental Health), H.S.S.C. (Health and Social Service Center), and so on.

The following example illustrates how this bias can easily translate into practice. The author was a consultant to a Latino community-based agency in a New England city. This agency was located in the heart of the Latino community. On the day the consultant was working with the agency's director, a group of student nurses were doing a community rotation assignment. This entailed visiting social service agencies in the community and obtaining answers to service delivery questions. The director of the Latino community-based agency welcomed this group and answered a series of questions concerning the nature of services provided, hours of operation, referral procedures, etc. The group of nurses then left the agency and stood outside the agency's door.

Next door to the agency was a botanical shop (cultural variation of a pharmacy). The student nurses formed a circle and looked at the botanical shop, talked among themselves, and continued to look at the botanical shop.

While this was happening, the director turned to the consultant and stated that the nurses would no doubt visit the shop and ask the owner the same questions they had asked him. The consultant, however, had doubts and shared these with the director. After a brief time, the group turned and walked away. The agency director was completely dumbfounded by their actions. The consultant, sadly, was not.

This group of nurses, who could easily have been social workers or any other helping professionals, needed to visit the botanical shop if they were to visit all health-related organizations in the neighborhood. This nontraditional setting provided a wide range of health services. The group's failure to enter the botanical shop could have been the result of the interplay of several factors: (1) fear of the unknown (not having the slightest clue as to what to expect); (2) not seeing the shop as an indigenous resource (How can a storefront with statues, healing paraphernalia, and candles be a health center?); (3) not having the knowledge or skills to engage the shop owner in an interview (clearly the group needed to modify or develop new questions); (4) fear of what their supervisor would say if they entered the shop (deviation from standard procedures can result in a reprimand or failing mark); or (5) not being bilingual, in this case Spanish speaking.

Needless to say, this example can be repeated countless times in urban-based practice. Identification of indigenous resources necessitates viewing the community through a different set of lenses and possessing the willingness to venture into uncharted territory. The process of identification is not restricted to a 9 A.M. to 5 P.M., Monday through Friday, schedule. In addition, as addressed in Chapter 5, indigenous resources do not subscribe to geographical catchment areas. Community, as already noted, is not restricted to one geographical area, and social workers may have to travel outside their usual territory to engage those resources. Although these factors are not insurmountable, they represent serious barriers to any form of service delivery system.

Process for Identifying and Assessing Nontraditional Settings

The question is not whether or not individuals or communities possess assets or strengths (Cowger, 1994). The proper question is what are they? It can safely be assumed that all communities contain a variety of skills, caring relationships, deep cultural traditions and values, and strong institutions. These assets form the basis for neighborhood stability, political empowerment, and economic development. Consequently, these assets form the basis of strategies and policies for building on local resources. To attract new resources and build on existing strengths, communities must identify their assets—resources that have helped people survive tough times and that bound them together in hope for the future. Community assets, as a result, cannot be determined from the outside (Boston Foundation, 1994).

Social work's challenge is to develop mechanisms for identifying and utilizing these assets (Hardcastle, Wenocur, & Powers, 1997). Assessment of nontraditional settings is one method, and it must accomplish three primary goals: (1) reveal how important the setting is in the life of the client and community; (2) determine the capacity of the setting to meet current or future needs; and (3) know the setting's potential for engaging in collaboration. These three goals must guide social workers as they set out to assess nontraditional settings.

A solution-focused approach is one such mechanism for developing an interview process (solution-focused) to identify and utilize client strengths in assessment and intervention that has relevance for work within nontraditional settings. This approach entails interviews based on well-formed goals and client strengths, which increases the likelihood of idenifying strengths most appropriate to a client's goals. Exception-finding questions entail determining a client's present and past successes in relation to the client's goals. These successes represent a critical element in building solutions (De Jong & Miller, 1995).

Six important concepts serve as a foundation for a solution focus to client strengths: (1) empowerment (importance of involving those who are most affected by the process); (2) membership (stressing the importance of belonging to cultural, geographic, and other groups); (3) regeneration and healing from within (focus on wellness and health promotion versus disease); (4) synergy (inner and outer human resources are expandable through meaningful interactions); (5) dialogue and collaboration (affirmation and working together in pursuit of common goals); and (6) suspension of disbelief (reaffirming client perceptions and statements rather than disbelieving them on impulse).

Delgado (1995d) developed a framework for identifying and assessing a client's strengths by focusing on the state of the client's natural support systems. Delgado's (1995d) research, based on African American, Latino (primarily Mexican American), and Southeast Asian (primarily Cambodian) clients in a large urban (Richmond) area of northern California, resulted in a framework for assessing the inability of natural support systems to provide assistance. This framework consists of five categories, each indicating a progressively more serious collapse of a support system. The results of an assessment inform the worker and agency of current issues and problems, and provide an inventory and status of key community helpers and nontraditional settings:

1. Temporary breakdown of supports (natural support system is in the midst of its own crisis and cannot be counted to assist others).

2. System is unable to respond to requests for assistance—this inability to assist may be due to two factors (a) the support system would like to assist, but the demands for help are beyond its current capacity (e.g., financial assistance, medical care for injury or illness), or (b) the support system has tried to assist but been unsuccessful in achieving results.

3. Support system refuses to provide assistance—this may be due to any one or a combination of the following reasons (a) a lack of a solid relationship (person seeking help no longer possesses the skills required to develop or maintain supportive relationships or participates in few social situations, thus restricting opportunities to develop necessary ties), (b) a history of negative experiences between the parties (e.g., disruptive influence on the helper), (c) the presenting problem is judged not to have high priority by the support system, (d) a history of not reciprocating when called on to help (the relationship is one-sided, without any dimension of mutuality).

4. Natural support system is nonexistent—the person in need of help must turn to formal systems for assistance. This barrier can be the result of either (a) a disintegration of the support system over time, (b) the support system has disappeared as a result of a major disaster such as a fire, flood, riots, etc., or (c) as is common with uprooted groups (i.e., refugees), the support system was left behind and has not been replaced in the new environment.

5. The needs are too sensitive to allow seeking help from a natural support system—issues related to substance abuse for women, HIV/AIDS, family violence, and child sexual abuse are very stigmatizing and not easily shared among friends and family; consequently, formal services may be the only viable alternative.

There are two basic approaches for identifying and assessing nontraditional settings: (1) personal contact that transpires during the process of providing services (individual-focused approach); contact may be made through the introduction of a "guide"; and (2) formal and systematic efforts at assessing these resources (asset assessments). Regardless of the method used, there are three key principles that should guide any effort during this stage of intervention:

1. Social workers must venture out into the community and develop a "cognitive map" of establishments that cater to residents. Most agencies have formal resources directories to assist them in making referrals to other agencies. However, there are no resource directories for nontraditional settings and other forms of indigenous resources. Consequently, this will require social workers to develop an in-depth understanding of where clients and residents go for help in the community. These informal settings must be identified first-hand by the worker. Identification can be facilitated by the client noting where and why they shop in particular establishments, and naming residents who play broker and helper roles in the community. This cognitive map may be developed by an individual worker and used in daily work activities.

2. Effort must be made to enter these settings and engage in dialogue with patrons, owners, etc. Eng and Hatch's (1992, pp. 312–313) advice for professionals wishing to collaborate with churches is also applicable to other nontraditional settings:

. . . health and human service providers need to consider modifying their frame of reference for "helping." This includes: not having to be in complete control; working with people who have different norms and approaches for helping; relating to colleagues who may not understand or value church-based network interventions; and not receiving immediate feedback or recognition from the lay system. Then it will be possible to recognize, learn from, and draw upon the lay expertise from the support system of the church.

Social workers making home visits can patronize local grocery stores. In the process of purchasing food items, they can speak with the owner or salesperson about the community. This visit does not entail a tremendous expenditure of time or money. If this visit is repeated several times, it may not be necessary to purchase food on future visits. Individuals who work in these settings will start to view the social worker in a different light, opening up the possibility of some form of collaborative partnership. Nevertheless, there is absolutely no substitute for personal contact.

3. Social workers must be prepared to be "tested" by being asked personal questions about their lives, work, and organizations, before they are accepted by those in nontraditional settings and other indigenous resources. It must be remembered that undervalued populations rarely go through a day without having someone in authority asking them personal questions. Thus for many of them, their lives are an open book, yet they may know nothing at all about the individuals asking the questions. A social worker's failure to be as open as possible will convey the message that the nonpofessional is not trusted severely limiting any potential for collaboration.

Micro-focused approaches. Social workers can work within nontraditional settings, even when their organizations do not subscribe to this approach. In fact, once social workers have established a relationship within these settings, contact may involve only a telephone call instead of an in-person request. The following illustrative example involves a grocery store.

A social worker in a private, nonprofit agency has a Latino client who has been seen for a few months concerning family problems. The client called the worker to seek assistance in replacing lost food stamps. She mentioned that the Department of Public Welfare was "giving her a hard time" and that it would take several days before they could reissue the missing stamps. The worker asked where the client shopped for groceries. The worker had a good relationship with the owner of the grocery store the client usually patronized. When questioned why she couldn't obtain credit until her food stamps were replaced, the client noted that she owed the grocer a considerable amount of money ($125.00), and he refused to give her further credit until the bill had been settled.

The worker then asked the client whether or not she felt comfortable having him call the grocer to explore the possibility of obtaining additional credit. The call was made and after a brief and friendly exchange, the worker asked the grocer whether or not he could give the client additional credit until the food stamps arrived. The grocer stated that he was reluctant to do so because it was like throwing "good money after bad." However, the worker convinced the owner that it was in his best interest to grant additional credit. The client worked out a repayment schedule and paid her debt. This example shows how a worker is in a position to broker resources from a nontraditional setting if there is knowledge of this resource and if the worker has a relationship that allows dialogue and a social exchange.

Institutional and staff bias against nontraditional settings, other indigenous forms of helping, and cultural beliefs, is reflected in all stages of clinical intervention, from the initial contact during an intake, when it is rare for a social worker to ask clients questions about their belief system and their informal efforts at seeking assistance, to the development of an intervention plan. It is very important to remember that in examining the intake process, the information gathered in this phase will form the cornerstone of an intervention plan.

This phase serves several critical purposes in a client-worker relationship: (1) the information is used to develop client-specific goals for intervention; (2) the questions asked convey to the client what the worker and organization consider to be important, and priorities for solving the presenting problem; (3) if handled properly, the answers given provide a worker with an opportunity to develop an in-depth understanding of the context the problem is given by the client; and (4) an intake provides a golden opportunity for a worker and client to establish a relationship based on mutual trust and respect.

The following intake example, from a public assistance office in a large New England city, illustrates how a cultural bias can translate into practice. The applicant, who was Puerto Rican, applied for public assistance. The applicant was monolingual in Spanish and brought an interpreter to the appointment. The worker, nonbilingual or bicultural, asked the applicant how many children she had. The interpreter translated this question into Spanish. The applicant paused before attempting to answer the question. The worker became visibly upset because the applicant was taking too long to answer what appeared to be a rather simple question. The impatience grew and the worker asked the applicant the question again, but this time there was an edge to her voice. The interpreter asked the question again but without the angry overtone. The applicant responded in Spanish: "Thank you for repeating the question. I did hear and understood you the first time you asked." The applicant proceeded to explain why it was so difficult to answer the question. She said she wasn't sure what information the worker wanted. She said that she had eight children, two of whom died shortly after birth. They were still her children. She left three children in Puerto Rico with her sister because she could not afford to bring all her children to the United States at once. They were still her children, even though they were in Puerto Rico.

She had two children with her who belonged to a sister, who, unfortunately passed away a few years ago. She "adopted" them, but this was not done "officially." That did not make them any less her children. At that point, the applicant started to cry because the question elicited many painful memories about the tragedies in her life.

The hesitating response to what appeared to be a straightforward question was interpreted by the worker to mean "fraud." Why else would anyone not know the answer to such a simple question? The applicant, in turn, was very dissatisfied with the process because she interpreted the worker's initial reactions as unkind and insensitive. A broader perspective on this example would have at least required an expanded view of "children," as well as the gathering of information on other aspects of the applicant's life. The process, unavoidably, would have taken longer. However, the information obtained would have met the three intake goals outlined earlier in this section.

Macro-focused approaches. Bias is not restricted to micro-practice. It can also be found in all aspects of macro-practice, from the initial needs assessment to the planning, implementation, and evaluation of a service or program. An example of this bias can be an agency implementing a key informant needs assessment. Invariably, these assessments involve interviewing community leaders, agency personnel, and other high-level stakeholders on their perceptions of community needs. However, they very rarely involve interviewing small business owners on their perceptions of community needs (Delgado, 1982).

Macro-practitioners usually view small businesses as centers for "profit maximization," thereby overlooking them as important nontraditional settings. It is rare for social work educators to talk about any form of business, let alone the role of ethnic businesses. These establishments are often misunderstood and overlooked in any discussion concerning communities of color.

These establishments are very often viewed from the same perspective that is applied to any mainstream business, small or large. In essence, a business's primary, and often only purpose, is to turn a profit. Ethnic businesses do this by catering to the needs of co-ethnics in the community. These establishments are attractive to residents because they are generally owned and operated by individuals who represent the ethnic background of the community. As a result, they provide goods and services that reflect awareness and respect for culture. In addition, in situations in which residents do not speak English as a primary language, they can communicate in their own language.

These settings are strategically positioned to know the issues, needs, challenges, dreams, and desires of a community. Thus, vital sources of information about a community are often overlooked in a macro-practice assessment. This bias, unfortunately, results in views of communities that are negative, and in services that are either noncomplimentary to those provided in nontraditional settings or actively undermine them.

The lack of an understanding of cultural values and the role of businesses in ethnic communities can result in an organization's failure to capitalize on a situation in which a relationship based on mutual trust and respect may develop. Thus, the organization dismisses potential resources in gathering information from nontraditional settings. Both the micro- and macro-examples could have had different outcomes had some thought, flexibility, and willingness not to jump to conclusions been applied during the critical assessment process. A willingness to take a broad view of resources will go a long way toward enhancing a community's abilities to help itself.

Community asset assessments represent the most systematic, economical, and sound method for organizations to identify, assess, and involve nontraditional settings in collaborative projects (Delgado, 1995c; Kreztmann & McKnight, 1993). The professional literature has started to produce case studies of asset assessments, particularly with undervalued communities (Boston Foundation, 1994; Delgado, 1994; Delgado & Rosati, forthcoming publication). Although asset assessments can be applied to any community, including those with privilege and resources, they take on added significance with undervalued communities.

Asset assessments, in addition, are an excellent method for involving residents in researching their own community, while enhancing their capacities in the process. Research design, for example, must reflect an understanding that those being studied have ultimate authority over their own lives and possess the prerequisite abilities (strengths) to express that authority. As a consequence, research must focus on eliciting, understanding, and developing these strengths (Holmes, 1992).

Asset assessments take on added significance when the process systematically and meaningfully involves communities. Involvement of a community can take on a variety of forms. Delgado (1995c), in an example related to youths undertaking asset assessments but also applicable to other age groups, stresses community involvement for the following reasons: (1) it provides people with a greater sense of control over their lives, families, and community; (2) it instills important research skills and knowledge that will serve participants and the community in future undertakings; (3) it provides the community with a perspective of participants that they can be, and are vital and contributing members of a community, thus counteracting pervasive views that are deficit based; and (4) it serves as a role model for other human service organizations to better utilize residents in service to their community.

Mapping Nontraditional Settings

The process of mapping a community's nontraditional settings is very important in the development of a broader understanding of these resources.

McKnight and Kretzmann (1990) first introduced the concept of an asset map, and further developed this concept in later work (Kretzmann & McKnight, 1993). Their map consists of three different types of assets: (1) local institutions (formal and informal); (2) citizens' associations (houses of worship, cultural groups, block clubs); and (3) "gifts of individuals" (residents with talent and a willingness to share).

The Center on Substance Abuse Prevention (Acosta & Hamel, 1995) utilized the framework developed by Delgado (1994, 1995a) to create a map of Latino natural support systems within a community. This asset map would then be used to assess the type and level of natural (informal) support that could be used in the development of substance abuse prevention initiatives.

The process for developing a community assets map is very similar to developing any other type of resource map. A geographical area of the city is delineated, and assets are placed within those geographical boundaries. A coding system is developed to reflect different types of assets, and pins reflecting those colors are placed on their corresponding map location. For example, houses of worship may be represented by the color green; recreational and social clubs may be yellow.

Once all of the nontraditional settings have been located on a map, it is then possible to study patterns of service availability and geographical access within the community, and to plan activities that take these assets into consideration. Assets, it must be emphasized, are dynamic; some settings may close, others may stop providing services, new settings may open. In short, a community asset map requires social workers to be vigilant and take into account community changes.

Engagement and Relationship Building

The process of engaging nontraditional settings is multifaceted and will prove challenging to a social worker. Engagement and relationship building are both ongoing processes, starting with the first contact during the identification and assessment phase through evaluation. Engagement and relationship building are sufficiently important to be considered a stage unto themselves.

Engagement with nontraditional settings is often very different from that of engaging formal organizations. Collaboration between houses of worship and social service agencies, for example, is not without potential barriers. Houses of worship usually provide social support from a spiritual point of reference, unlike health professionals who are usually motivated by self-care and direct service considerations. These differences must be clarified through a process of open exchange. Then and only then can the focus of the intervention be client centered. Consequently, agency staff must have the skills, attitudes, and values necessary to work through these significant differences (Eng & Hatch, 1992).

Social service agencies generally respond to more conventional factors such as the credentials of the worker (level and source of education), position of the worker within an organization (management versus line worker), reputation of the worker and agency within the social service network, political and financial gains to be made, and how collaboration would benefit the organization. It would not be unusal to start the engagement process with an initial telephone call, followed up by a letter. A meeting is set, at which time a decision is made about the nature of the collaboration and then eventually finalized. This finalization often results in a letter detailing procedures, staffing, client eligibility, and so on.

Nontraditional settings do not operate by the same rules as social workers. Consequently, social workers' motivation for undertaking collaborative work requires different strategies to achieve engagement. These strategies require social workers to be "tested," to share of themselves, and to have their patience "taxed." Challenges associated with engaging churches serve as excellent examples. An entry phase of a church-based intervention can be time consuming and is unlikely to be cost-effective in the short run. For the sponsoring health agencies or funding foundations, this can be problematic and a source of discouragement (Eng & Hatch, 1992).

Saleeby's (1996, p. 303) advice for social workers utilizing a strengths perspective is also applicable for work within nontraditional settings:

> They must engage individuals as equals. They must be willing to meet them eye to eye and to engage in dialogue and a mutual sharing of knowledge, tools, concerns, aspirations, and respect. The process of coming to know is a mutual and collaborative one. The individuals and groups the profession assists also must be able to "name" their circumstances, their struggles, their experience, themselves . . . The power to name oneself and one's situation is the beginning of real empowerment.

It is of critical importance to maintain open channels of communication between professional and informal providers through the maintenance of a dialogue and avoidance of "mutual estrangement" on the one hand or a "colonial takeover" on the other (Lavoie, Farquaharson, & Kennedy, 1994).

Development of Collaborative Practice

The development and implementation stage is probably the most exciting stage of any framework, as it often represents the first instance for "harvesting the fruits of labor." Mason's (1994, p. 7) words of advice concerning the development of culturally competent services are equally applicable to work within nontraditional settings: ". . . tasks should be identified as short-, medium-, or long-term in duration; divided into manageable incremental steps; and described in terms of whether personal or organizational resources are needed. The persons responsible for specific tasks should be identified and the methods for measuring programs [selected] . . . local community should be involved and empowered to have influence on a process which is ultimately for their benefit."

These words of advice should be heeded. The planning and implementation process requires active participation from those in nontraditional settings. Working together means laboring together. In short, social agencies cannot develop a plan and then "sell" it to nontraditional settings. It is not that agencies cannot have a vision or goal in mind before approaching nontraditional settings, but they must be flexible in modifying it or possibly adopting new goals based on the perception and needs of those in the settings. This shift in approach may prove unsettling for an agency. Nevertheless, a failure to do this will in all likelihood result in an unsuccessful effort at establishing a service.

Much can be learned from efforts to engage houses of worship in collaborating on service delivery. There are at least three key reasons why religious institutions should undertake collaborative ventures with social service organizations: (1) houses of worship can benefit from the experience and wisdom of human service providers; (2) houses of worship can use the additional instrumental resources available from social service organizations; and (3) both parties can complement each other's perspective and address needs from spiritual and physical realms (Anderson, Maton, & Ensor, 1992).

However, there are significant barriers that must be acknowledged and addressed if collaboration is to be successful (Anderson et al., 1992): (1) religious and human services represent significantly different world views, which are manifested in language usage; (2) both parties utilize different conceptualizations of problems, goals, and strategies; and (3) the presence of negative stereotypes of each other severely tests the development of trust and mutual respect. These barriers, incidentally, are not restricted to these types of institutions.

There is no doubt that religious institutions are an important resource in the lives of many undervalued groups, and represent excellent nontraditional settings for collaboration. There is little doubt that collaboration is desirable and likely to prove mutually beneficial for both religious and social service agencies. Nevertheless, both religious and human service workers must be cognizant of instances in which collaboration may not be feasible. Productive collaboration is possible and must be built on a realistic grasp of similarities and differences in perspective between the religious and human services domain (Anderson et al., 1992).

Joint activities can fall into five basic categories: (1) sharing resources; (2) knowledge building and consultation; (3) outreach; (4) community education; and (5) counseling/advice giving. These activities must be viewed developmentally, with each activity progressively requiring greater amounts of time and resources, and systematically building on the prior initiative.

Sharing resources. Collaborative activities involving the sharing of resources probably represent the "safest" form of partnership. This type of collaboration may be time limited and can serve to build a foundation that will ultimately involve more ambitious undertakings involving nontraditional sources. Resources must be broadly conceptualized and, in so doing, they expand the possibilities for this form of service delivery.

The use of space is one form of sharing resources. A local restaurant or house of worship may provide meeting space. These settings are located in the community and do not require provision of transportation for clients to receive services. There are numerous examples of self-help groups using such space. Provision of transportation, if needed, may be another form of sharing resources. Houses of worship invariably have vans to transport parishioners. These vehicles can also be used to transport clients. Agencies, in turn, may have vehicles that can be used to transport residents to community-sponsored events.

Knowledge building and consultation. A focus on knowledge building through training and consultation is one means of enhancing community and organizational capacities. Knowledge building, in addition, can be a short-term, not labor-intensive way to establish a collaborative relationship. The commitment to enhance knowledge capacity does not necessarily require a long-term working arrangement, allowing all parties an opportunity to terminate the partnership. This form of collaboration can also involve those in nontraditional settings who provide expertise to staff.

One form of partnership is called "collaborative consultation," which entails enlisting the advice of an individual or institution (nontraditional setting) that plays an active and supportive role in community life. This individual or institution, as the case may be, is then approached by someone from the agency for possible consultation or support in carrying out a helper role (Hawkins & Fraser, 1981). This form of consultation connects a community member to a provider, who then remains accessible as a consultant. Consultation sessions can be offered to network members as needed, thus building a strong network of social support with consultation backup (Hawkins & Fraser, 1981). This is only possible if the client and helper agree to be part of the process.

Delgado (1979–1980) proposes another approach for both providing and receiving consultation within natural or social support systems. Delgado proposes the development of a collaboration, in his example involving folk healers, whereby these community helpers could be scheduled periodically, or called on during a crisis, to provide consultation. The author goes on to recommend involving these helpers as trainers. They could come into an agency and hold training sessions on folk healing. These sessions could consist of one-time efforts or be part of an ongoing series, depending on the needs of the organization and the comfort level of the healer.

Outreach. Outreach, for the purposes of this book, is separated from other forms of service delivery. It is not unusual to have outreach closely tied to community education or counseling. However, this activity can have distinct goals and serve as a foundation for more intensive collaboration efforts. Outreach can be defined simply as a process of systematically contacting and engaging isolated people and linking them to services and financial programs for which they are believed to be eligible (Hardcastle et al., 1997).

There are three primary goals for outreach: (1) deploying agency resources to make them more accessible in the community; (2) increasing coverage of time periods to increase accessibility; and (3) brokering resources and consumers for more effective use of existing resources. These goals are clearly interrelated and highlight the close association between outreach and engagement of potential clients, the distribution of organizational resources, and the structuring of organizational support for this activity (Hardcastle et al., 1997).

Staff is dispatched into communities that are known to have high concentrations of needs. Staff members must have an ability to enter their target communities and establish relationships with residents. Staff members must have "street smarts," as they often must be acquainted with the rules of the streets (Fox, 1991).

Outreach collaborative efforts involving nontraditional settings can consist of simple distribution of information (pamphlets) informing the community of available services to more elaborate referral systems. The nature of this outreach would be dependent on the goals of the agency and the level of the working relationship staff has within nontraditional settings. Some people in nontraditional settings may be willing to distribute any or all types of information, show videos, and even entertain staff spending time in the setting meeting consumers. In other settings, owners may only be willing to display posters. Thus, it is important to conceptualize outreach actions as being multifacted, and to be aware that it is not an all or nothing proposition.

Community education. Community education can be used for multiple purposes. However, the primary goals are generally: (1) to increase public awareness of issues or problems that have particular impact on a community; (2) to serve as a vehicle to mobilize a community's ability to address common concerns through capacity enhancement; (3) to facilitate the identification of indigenous resources; and (4) to facilitate two or more parties coming together in common pursuit of nonlabor-intensive prevention and early intervention initiatives. In essence, community education goes beyond the transmission of knowledge, and includes resource identification, information gathering, and mobilization.

Community-based educational activities must be geographically based in the community to increase access. These activities can transpire in local parks, blocked off streets, houses of worship, beauty parlors, barbershops, bars, and other nontraditional settings that have sufficient space to allow attendance by groups (large and small).

Community education is just as "legitimate" in nontraditional settings as in classrooms. However, the setting will dictate the form of the educational activity, rather than the other way around. Thus, agencies must be flexible in designing a curriculum to allow modification in the field.

Counseling/advice giving. Delgado (1979–80), in describing possible collaborative activities between Latino folk healers and mental health providers, addressed an affiliation involving counseling or advice giving. According to the author, this form of partnership consists of a healer and formal provider "sharing" a client. Both parties would meet and discuss arenas and intervention approaches that were going to be used. Periodic meetings would then occur to provide updates, assess changes in intervention, and evaluate progress. Delgado (1979–80) cautions that this form of collaboration is probably the most difficult to institute of any partnership and is the most fraught with potential legal liability. This is also the most labor intensive of all forms of collaboration involving folk healers. Sharing clients requires a solid foundation based on mutual trust and respect, in addition to clear and open lines of communication.

In summary, collaborative activities represent the culmination of many hours of relationship building, "testing," and planning. As a result, the process for developing collaborative partnerships within nontraditional settings takes on greater importance because of the nature of the settings involved. Nevertheless, the benefits to be derived from these partnerships have far-reaching impact within a community, and can serve both short- and long-term goals.

Evaluation

The challenge of conducting an evaluation can be quite formidable. Accounting for and measuring the impact derived from the activities of natural helpers can be arduous. Establishing a fine balance between the need for reliable and valid data to evaluate effectiveness and the need not to undermine the functions of a nontraditional setting is a continual challenge (Eng & Hatch, 1992).

Evaluation lends itself to process, although outputs can and should be measured. The evaluation process, questions, and mechanism must be agreed on by both parties. In fact, it is strongly suggested that both parties develop them, though it is unrealistic to expect those in nontraditional settings to take the lead. Evaluation within nontraditional settings will present a unique set of challenges that can be viewed from four perspectives: (1) development of methods that do not scare off those in nontraditional settings and their customers; (2) data collection procedures that are not labor intensive; (3) getting staff to document their efforts; and (4) interpreting results within a cultural context.

Culturally relevant research, with program evaluation being a prime example, is of critical importance in the development of effective services in communities of color. The lack of culturally competent research seriously limits the development of appropriate services. Research must go beyond simplistic labels regarding outcome to provide an in-depth understanding of how, why, and in what situations a particular intervention works well. Domains measured must focus on community strengths and assets, as well as weaknesses and risks (Benjamin, 1994).

It is believed that culturally competent research cannot be accomplished without a team effort, with the community being a critical member of the team. In short, culturally competent research must be accomplished with the community rather than for the community (Benjamin, 1994).

The concept of partnership has been applied to a wide variety of contexts and situations. Recently, it has even been applied to the field of social work research (Hess, 1995). Social work practice and research must respond to growing demands for collaborative partnerships for the profession to better serve its clients; to improve its effectiveness; to demonstrate that it merits strong fiscal and moral support; and to improve its credibility and standing among consumers, policy makers, funding organizations, and other helping professionals (Feldman & Suskind, 1995).

Social work practice within nontraditional settings requires the development of culturally competent evaluation. Consequently, the same principles that are applied to practice must also be applied to research and evaluation: utilization of a strengths perspective, empowerment, and participation by those who will ultimately benefit from the service. Hynes' (1996, pp. 160–161) statement analyzing the challenges for evaluating urban gardens and their impact on the community is also applicable to nontraditional settings:

> With or without definitive academic proof . . . we ought to invest in and support them. Community gardens are one of our most participatory local civic institutions, and among the few living landscapes of our cities. Let us study them, with the eye and the heart as well as the calculator, primarily to protect and promote them. And let us listen to the gardeners whose stories may hold more strategic and political power than the rigor of quantitative data.

The complexity of the task must not deter agencies from accomplishing the goal; the challenge is in the development of methods that both capture gains but do not undermine or disrupt nontraditional settings in the process.

The recording of data can be accomplished through a variety of methods, all of which, as will be noted in subsequent chapters, also pose challenges. The use of field notes, or logs, are a popular way of gathering data and impressions that lend themselves to process evaluation. Field notes serve to document client contact and account for time spent. Staff can use notes to record information without having to return to the office, thus facilitating evaluation.

Conclusion

This chapter provided a framework that lends itself to establishing collaboration within nontraditional settings. This framework has analytical (theoretical) and interactional (political) dimensions, and takes into account the challenges that are inherent in any form of collaboration between social agencies and nontraditional settings. Viewing collaboration as developmental provides social agencies and nontraditional settings with sufficient time to allow the creation of trust and mutual respect. As addressed in Chapters 8 through 11, collaboration can vary according to time, energy, goals, and local circumstances. In essence, collaboration can take many shapes to fit local needs and opportunities, as well as the goals of the social agency initiating this form of practice.

The use of a framework by practitioners gives direction to a form of practice that is out of the ordinary. This framework is not carved in stone. Practitioners may develop their own frameworks with different analytical and interactional components. Neverthless, a framework is essential in facilitating development of collaborative initiatives involving nontraditional settings and other forms of indigenous resources.

III

APPLICATION OF FRAMEWORK TO CASES

Section III makes extensive use of case material to illustrate important practice considerations. These considerations can best be thought of as challenges that can be addressed successfully if anticipated, and if the practitioner if properly prepared. Key theoretical concepts will also be presented to aid the reader in making necessary connections with the literature, and recommendations are made to facilitate practice implementation.

Chapters 8 through 12 utilize case illustrations to bring to life the framework covered in the previous chapter. In addition, these chapters explore how concepts are applied, review the rewards and challenges for practice, and highlight key issues for practitioners. They also suggest approaches to surmounting these barriers. Chapter 13 (Reflections on Collaborative Practice) allows the author to share insights, in his own voice, for collaborative practice within nontraditional settings. Finally, the Epilogue raises for the reader unanswered questions and addresses the need for particular types of research to make this form of practice more informative to the practitioner and relevant to the community. In similar fashion to Chapter 6, case material derived from field-based research used in Chapters 8–12 will not be attributed to a source.

8

Identification and Assessment

This chapter applies the framework outlined in Chapter 7. It will draw on multiple case studies whenever possible to illustrate key practice principles and considerations for work within nontraditional settings. Each stage in the process, consists of a description of goals, a brief overview, challenges and rewards, and key practice concepts. In addition, each stage will have case illustrations and a discussion of key points and considerations. Particular attention has been paid to the Engagement Stage because of its critical nature. As a result, this stage is highlighted by the most case illustrations to provide the reader with a broad and detailed description, which may further appreciation of the multitude of perspectives and approaches to people in engaging nontraditional settings.

Goals

The identification and assessment phase plays a critical role in the successful involvement of nontraditional settings. This phase must accomplish four goals for it to set the foundation for the other phases of the framework: (1) identify the types and locations of nontraditional settings in a community; (2) list the types of services provided by these settings; (3) identify the days and hours of operation, including the best times to visit nontraditional settings; and (4) identify the best strategies for engaging the cooperation of people in nontraditional settings.

Accomplishing these four goals provides social workers with invaluable information concerning the rewards and challenges of collaborative practice within nontraditional settings. The amount of time, energy, and other resources needed during the execution of this phase will be determined by the agency's goals for service delivery—targeted versus broad based and time limited versus long-term or open-ended. Strategies for assessment, in turn, will be influenced by these considerations.

Brief Overview of Stage

Social service organizations need to become more cognizant of the operational characteristics of nontraditional settings to engage them meaningfully in collaborative activities (Delgado, 1996d, 1997b; Holmstrom, 1996a). In addition, agencies need to have a better understanding of the types of services provided by these institutions. Familiarity with their operations and service provision will enhance the likelihood that collaborative efforts succeed in reaching out to the community (Delgado, 1997c).

Data should be gathered on three operational dimensions of a nontraditional setting: (1) years in operation; (2) hours open; and (3) days of the week in operation. In addition, it becomes very important to determine the geographical location of the setting. A nontraditional setting may be centrally located, with relatively easy accessibility by foot and public transportation. It may be located in a cluster with other nontraditional settings, increasing the likelihood that community residents may use this and other settings on a typical day. All of this information can assist agencies in approaching nontraditional settings and in the planning of activities.

In the service delivery realm, data should be gathered on a minimum of seven factors that incorporate business as well as social services: (1) financial (provision of credit, loans, check cashing); (2) information and referral to social services; (3) integration of and outreach to the lonely and isolated (social relations); (4) interpreter services (reading of materials, letters, making telephone calls to social service and government offices); (5) provision of counseling (particularly crisis focused); (6) provision of food or money for those who are hungry; and (7) leadership role within the community (participation on committees, boards, task forces, sponsorship of events, etc.). Information about other social service-related areas may be necessary, depending on the mission of the organization sponsoring the assessment and its goals for collaboration.

Community asset assessments represent an initial and extremely critical step in systematically identifying nontraditional settings and the role they play in the life of a community. Four case examples based in Holyoke and Lawrence, Massachusetts, and San Diego, California, will be used to illustrate various approaches to asset assessments.

Challenges and Rewards of Phase

The author is very fond of telling graduate social work students in his Planning and Program Development classes that he is more likely to make a living as a professional bowler (110 average) than he is doing assessments, either needs or asset based. The moral of the story is that social service organizations rarely undertake systematic assessments before developing programs and services. Yet it is rare for a worker to develop an individual treatment plan without an assessment. One of the challenges for an agency is to undertake an assessment of the community.

The identification and assessment phase, if accomplished well, will ultimately influence all facets of any form of intervention involving nontraditional settings. A well-done assessment not only provides important service-related data, it also serves to develop a foundation for meaningful interpersonal interactions—namely, relationships built on mutual trust and respect. Consequently, this is not a phase to be undertaken without careful consideration. A well-executed assessment serves to inform both agency and nontraditional setting of needs and possibilities for collaborative practice.

A poor, or misguided assessment can create "hard" feelings on the part of people in nontraditional settings. These sentiments, in turn, can then be transmitted to community residents and other nontraditional settings, creating adverse reactions throughout a community. Further, they can create hard feelings on the part of the social service organization undertaking the assessment. Agency staff and management may resent the reception they receive, thereby setting back any initiatives for collaboration. Bad memories may, in fact, set back collaborative initiatives for many years.

Key Practice Concepts

The assessment phase affords an excellent illustration of many of the key theories and concepts addressed in previous chapters. Evans and Boyte's (1986) concept of free space plays out very well during this phase. Any asset-based assessment of a community will reveal spaces where residents congregate or come into contact with each other; where they feel comfortable and accepted. These settings can be gardens, barbershops, houses of worship, etc., and will undoubtedly vary according to local circumstances and resources. This is probably more true in communities whose residents are undervalued and, as a result, subject to oppression in this society.

Numerous examples will be presented, illustrating how some of these settings can be conceptualized as urban sanctuaries—places where residents can congregate or interact in a manner that reinforces their identities within an urban arena. Some of these settings can also be considered natural support systems because they are firmly anchored in cultural traditions and belief systems.

Nontraditional settings can be identified and assessed only from a strengths perspective. This paradigm provides the lens through which social workers and other helping professionals can actually see what was once invisible. A strengths perspective is not restricted to macro- or micro-forms of practice; consequently, the ramifications of this approach will be experienced in all aspects of practice.

Finally, the theoretical scholarship of Portes and Sensenbrener (bounded solidarity and social capital) will prove useful in examining ethnic groups, particularly those whose language and culture are distinctive, and who are residentially segregated. The role nontraditional settings play in brokering outside contact with a community must be taken into account during this phase of intervention. These settings may play a much more influential role within their communities by dictating the degree of outside influence on residents.

Case Examples

The first case (Holyoke, Massachusetts) involves the use of Puerto Rican adolescents in the planning and implementation of an asset assessment, and is an example of a broad approach to assessment. The second and third cases illustrate asset assessments focused on particular types of nontraditional settings—the Holyoke, Massachusetts case involves Pentecostal churches and the San Diego, California, case study targeted bars, single-room occupancy hotels, and mail carriers. The last case provides an example of a multi-stage assessment (Lawrence, Massachusetts) involving three different nontraditional settings—barbershops, beauty parlors, and botanical shops.

Delgado (1995c, 1996e) undertook an asset assessment of a forty-block area of Holyoke, Massachusetts, having a high concentration of Puerto Ricans. All nontraditional settings within this area were targeted for identification and assessment:

> The assessment consisted of two stages: (1) identification of all the Latino establishments within the geographical area of the study; and (2) interviews with the owners. Data were collected on five dimensions: (1) geographical location and category of resource (i.e., commercial, religious, recreational, etc.); (2) listing of key person and years in operation; (3) hours and days of operation; (4) type of informal or support services provided (i.e., referral, financial, information, etc.); and (5) general reactions of the interviewer to the receptivity of the setting for collaboration on community projects. The use of Puerto Rican youths (6 girls and 4 boys), aged 13–15, as interviewers made this asset assessment innovative.

The study focused on achieving four goals (Delgado, 1995c, p. 66):

> (1) provide a detailed description and location of Puerto Rican [nontraditional] settings with a specific focus on houses of worship and merchant/social clubs (grocery stores, botanical shops, etc.)—the study did not attempt to identify folk healers [Level 4 helpers] and significant community leaders (the former would be very difficult to access without a solid effort at relationship building; the latter because key community leaders had already been identified); (2) provide youth with a resiliency perspective on the community; (3) raise the consciousness of human service organizations and providers concerning the positive aspects of the Puerto Rican community; and (4) serve as a basis for [development of] a resource directory specifically focused on community assets.

Assessment, in this case study, went far beyond just identifying and listing services provided. The process raised community awareness of assets, provided adolescent interviewers with a more positive understanding of the community, increased possible collaboration between the social service community and non-traditional settings, and provided interviewers with skills that could be transferred to other arenas.

The asset assessment of Pentecostal churches in Holyoke, Massachusetts, resulted from a failure to assess these institutions in a prior community asset study (Delgado & Rosati, in press):

> The study of Pentecostal churches was a sub-study of a broader asset assessment undertaken by ten Puerto Rican adolescents [Delgado, in press]. This assessment gathered data on merchant/social clubs, in addition to houses of worship. Unfortunately, due to the hours and days of operation, the interviewers were not able to conduct interviews of Pentecostal ministers. Lack of data on religious institutions was considered a significant shortcoming of the original study and needed to be addressed with a study specifically focused on religious institutions. As a result, an adult interviewer (supervisor of the initial asset assessment) was hired to conduct the study . . . A total of eighteen religious institutions, all were Pentecostal, were identified . . . Field interviews lasting approximately one hour were conducted with eleven ministers—seven ministers refused to participate in the study. This asset assessment . . . focused on achieving three goals: (1) identify social service provision in general, and AOD [alcohol and other drugs] in particular; (2) identify factors that facilitate or hinder collaboration with religious institutions; and (3) the development of an asset inventory of religious institutions within a defined geographical area.

The findings of the asset assessment of Pentecostal churches in Holyoke, Massachusetts, highlighted the important role these nontraditional settings play in delivering various types of social services (Delgado & Rosati, in press).

> The average Pentecostal church provided approximately seven social/AOD services (X 7.3) with a range from a low of three (N = 1) to a high of ten (N = 1). Interestingly, the largest and second largest churches in terms of membership did not offer the most services. The Pentecostal church offering the most services only had a congregation membership of 80 and as only opened 9.5 hours and four days per week. However, it had the longest longevity of the churches established by Puerto Ricans (20 years). The fewest number of services were provided by the two newest churches, with three and four types respectively. Friendship for the lonely (social activities and a drop-in service) was the service provided by most (N = 10) of the churches . . . Surprisingly, home visiting for the frail and sick, and English classes were the least cited services by the churches.

The San Diego case illustrates how a senior citizens organization (Senior Community Centers of San Diego) focused on an age group and three distinct nontraditional settings. This elder-focused organization undertook an identification and assessment of all the bars, single-room occupancy hotels, and mail carriers located within a defined geographical area of the city.

Identification and assessment of nontraditional settings does not have to entail highly systematized plans and procedures. The identification and assessments (single-room occupancy hotels and bars) undertaken by Senior Community Centers of San Diego were based on very pragmatic considerations—namely, walking distance of the agency:

> The catchment area for the Senior Community Centers of San Diego in the downtown area of the city is located within a densely populated section with a high concentration of senior citizens. The area of San Diego is home to the highest percentage of low-income elderly with over 92 percent of the Center's clients reporting incomes at or below the poverty level. There are 35 SROs located downtown. The Center decided to deliver services within walking distance of the agency. A total of ten single-room occupancy hotels and four bars are actively collaborating with the Center in their Hotel Alert and Bar Alert programs. All of these nontraditional settings were within close geographical proximity to the Center, facilitating access for seniors residing or patronizing these institutions. The number of hotels and bars selected to participate in collaborative activities was based upon the number of institutions staff could comfortably work with.

The final example (Lawrence, Massachusetts) describes an assessment process that is sequential and that utilized the services of one adult (Latina) as an interviewer (Delgado, 1998c; Delgado & Santiago, in press a, b):

> A twenty-block area of Lawrence, Massachusetts, was selected due to its high concentration of Latino-owned businesses. A total of three studies were undertaken over an approximate one-year period. The first study focused on identifying and assessing botanical shops, of which eight were located and five consented to be interviewed. The second study focused on beauty parlors, of which seven were identified and all consented to be part of the study. The final study targeted barbershops, five of which were located and all were interviewed (one served Latinos but was not Latino-owned). A total seventeen nontraditional settings participated in the Lawrence asset assessments. The phasing in of settings was facilitated when a geographical area of the city was well defined and targeted. This phasing in allows social service organizations the option of not disrupting their services by utilizing a sizable number of staff to conduct interviews. In addition, it allows organizations to strategically focus on certain types of establishments that target specific subgroups. The focus of the botanical study was on Latinos (male and females) at high risk for HIV/AIDS. The beauty parlor study targeted Latinas; the barbershop study, in turn, targeted Latino males.

Acosta and Hamel (1995, pp. 23–24) utilize Green's (1995) concept of "cultural guide" to describe a simple, effective way to identify indigenous community resources in the Latino community (applicable to other communities of color):

> Drive or walk around the area where your program participants reside with a person familiar with the community. Take note of the businesses, housing, churches, recreational facilities, and public transportation. Also, consider the qualitative aspects of the community: How noisy is it? Are the streets well lit? Are the streets patrolled? Do youth congregate around street corners, arcades, and liquor stores? This inventory can reveal both the need for and impediments to prevention activities . . . Below is a list of common Hispanic/Latino gathering places. How many exist in your community? * Spanish markets and grocery stores (bodegas, tiendas, botanicas) * Music stores and concerts (salsa, mariachi, merengue, etc.) * Laundromats * Day labor pickup sites * Social clubs (billiard halls, dominoes tables, ice houses, coffee houses) * Health clinics and agencies and WIC offices * Travel agencies and places that arrange to send money to other countries, check lines in banks * Place of publication of Spanish language newspapers and magazines * Soccer games * English language programs (Berlitz, Sanz) * Spanish television, radio, newspaper, and consumer directories * Public squares * Ethnic and religious festivals * Street fairs and health fairs * Churches * Remedial and adult education programs * Advocacy agencies and other Hispanic/Latino community agencies (Legal Aid, La Raza) * Schools and day care centers with high Hispanic/Latino enrollment.

Acosta and Hamel's (1995) suggestion is not as systematized as some of the other case examples presented in this section. However, it is not labor intensive, nor does it require a major commitment from an agency to work within nontraditional settings. For some organizations and workers this may be the extent of their identification of nontraditional settings in a community. For others, it may represent the initial step before a formal identification and assessment process.

Key Points and Considerations

Social agencies wishing to undertake community-based asset assessments must take five factors into consideration: (1) the dynamic nature of community; (2) the influence of cultural factors; (3) operational and logistical factors; (4) development of an advisory committee; and (5) preparation and support of interviewers.

Dynamic Nature of Community

Asset assessments must be undertaken periodically because communities are quite dynamic with changing populations and the closing and opening of nontraditional settings. The case example of Cubans in a section of New York City serves to illustrate the dynamic interplay between population changes and the establishment of new nontraditional settings (Ojito, 1997, p. B1):

The neighborhood has changed . . . Not long ago, this stretch of Junction Boulevard and Roosevelt Avenue, the line that separates and connects Elmhurst, Corona and Jackson Heights, was dotted with Cuban businesses and familiar faces. Now, the old restaurant that served authentic Cuban dishes across the street is owned by a Mexican and tortillas are the main fare. The beauty parlor is a grocery store. And Mario's Jewelry, where Mr. Fiallo used to buy birthday presents for his wife and children, is a Peruvian-owned party-goods store.

The following example also involves a changing Latino community in New Jersey (McLane, 1991, pp. C1,C6):

Bergenline Avenue, which extends for 90 blocks through Union City and West New York, just across the Hudson from Manhattan, is a commercial hub for New Jersey's Latin American population, which according to the 1990 census, is increasing faster than any other ethnic group in the state. The strip, originally a beachhead for Cubans who fled the Castro revolution at the outset of the 1960s, is now a center for recent immigrants from all over the Latin Caribbean and Central and South America.

Dramatic demographic changes have far-reaching impact within a community, and also influence social service delivery. An upsurge in the number of undocumented individuals, for example, requires the development of new forms of outreach, engagement, and intervention. The New York City example can be replicated with other ethnic groups across the United States.

Influence of Cultural Factors

The influence of cultural factors is unavoidable in any form of social work intervention. However, the manner in which culture manifests itself within nontraditional settings may be unanticipated. The asset study of Pentecostal churches in Holyoke, Massachusetts, does a wonderful job of illustrating the impact of culture.

Maria (interviewer) is a Puerto Rican social worker who works and lives in Holyoke. Prior to this assignment, she had been employed in a variety of social service agencies and was very accomplished as a counselor, outreach worker, and community educator. Her research responsibilities on this project were to set up and conduct interviews with the Pentecostal ministers within a specific geographical area of the city. Initially, she dressed casually (slacks and blouse), and as was customary, she wore makeup. However, she quickly encountered ministers who were abrupt and refused to meet with her—either explicitly or implicitly (missed appointments). In her travels she had heard that Pentecostal ministers tended to be conservative and did not believe women should wear slacks and makeup. Consequently, she started to wear skirts and stopped wearing makeup. Once this change transpired, she was able to meet and interview ministers.

The change in Maria's appearance was necessary to effectively interview ministers. This cultural factor required the interviewer to choose between her beliefs concerning the right of women to express their individuality versus conforming to an orthodox view of women. Fortunately, Maria was flexible. Other interviewers, however, may not have been as flexible, seriously impacting the success of the project.

The gender and physical appearance of the interviewer are not the only considerations. Delgado (1995c, p. 72) found in the Holyoke, Massachusetts, study that age also factors into how culture influences an assessment:

> There are a variety of reasons why [people in nontraditional settings] were either hesitant or refused to participate in the study. The use of youth must be added to the list of reasons. The use of youth can convey a negative message to adults—namely, this is not an important activity, otherwise, adults would be conducting the interviews. Further, the idea of youth being in a position of "authority," of asking questions, may have been a barrier too great to overcome in certain instances.

There are numerous cultural factors that must be taken into consideration, such as matching ethnic backgrounds of interviewers with that of the community, place of birth (those born or raised in the United States or those born and raised in the country of origin), urban or rural experience, language skills (not just verbal but also nonverbal), religious background, etc.

Operational and Logistical Factors

It will not take an agency very long after initiation of an asset assessment to realize that nontraditional settings "march to the beat of a different drummer." Nontraditional settings very often have extensive hours and may even be open six or seven days per week. Finding these establishments closed may not be a problem. However, finding the right season, day, and time to conduct an interview may prove a challenge, as noted by Delgado (1995c, pp. 72–73):

> It is strongly recommended that assessments not be undertaken during the winter months or major holidays . . . Winter weather is not conducive to door-to-door surveys . . . Cold weather, in turn, also limited the amount of time interviewers could be in the field. In turning to busy holiday periods, several establishments did not want to be bothered during the most profitable time of the year [Christmas]. Consequently, fall/spring are perhaps the best seasons for asset assessments.

The asset assessment of Pentecostal churches, for example, was conducted during the late evening hours, generally after 10 P.M., when religious services were over, and the ministers were free to sit down and answer questions.

Delgado (in press d), in a sub-study of nontraditional settings (merchant establishments that were not restaurants, grocery stores, or religious institutions) in the Holyoke, Massachusetts, assessment, found that these settings have unusual days and hours of operation:

> The typical establishment had been opened three years, and almost half of the establishments (5 out of 12) had been opened one year or less and three-quarters (8 out of 12) had been opened under four years. These establishments, with one exception, were relatively new to the community. The typical establishment was open six days per week—only two were open seven days and one was open five days. Merchant establishments operated an average of 9.4 hours per day with a range of eight hours to twenty-four hours—the latter was a radio station. Most of the merchant establishments were opened Monday through Saturday, 9 A.M. to 6 P.M.

Delgado and Rosati (in press), found, as already noted, in their study of Pentecostal churches, that hours of operation severely limited who could conduct interviews and when they could take place:

> The original intent of the Holyoke, Massachusetts, asset assessment was to identify and assess all of the nontraditional settings within a select geographical area of the city. Using Puerto Rican adolescents presented a serious barrier to assessing Pentecostal churches. These institutions generally were opened during very restrictive times and dates. In order to interview the ministers, it was necessary to visit during the late evenings after services were completed. Consequently, using adolescents for these interviews was impossible. The adult interviewer would often conduct interviews around 10:30 P.M. Although the average time per interview was one hour, some interviews lasted until well past midnight.

Thus, the unusual hours and the community-based location of nontraditional settings require the establishment of a community base from which interviewers can be dispatched for interviews and reunite at the end of the day for debriefing. Consequently, researchers must be flexible in scheduling interviews, and allow for sufficient time for their completion. Thus, scheduling may be a challenge.

Development of an Advisory Committee

The need to involve many different sectors of a community is essential in the development and implementation of an asset assessment, with the community's well-being as a central goal. Use of advisory committees is not unusual in most human service organizations. However, their composition invariably consists of other social service providers, opinion makers, or key stakeholders. These committees provide important technical assistance, resources, and access to populations in greatest need.

An asset assessment advisory committee, however, requires membership that reflects the institutions and groups that are targeted. Nontraditional settings must have a prominent role in these committees. Delgado (1995c, p. 74) makes such a recommendation and outlines possible activities for a committee based on the experiences of the Holyoke, Massachusetts, studies:

> . . . it is strongly recommended that an advisory committee play an influential role in the planning and implementation of an asset assessment. This committee can help in the development of appropriate questions for the survey, gaining community access, disseminating publicity about the study, helping in the analysis of results and, most importantly, taking the results of the study and actively seeking to develop appropriate services. In essence, use of an advisory committee is an important form of empowerment for a community, in addition to making the asset assessment more culture specific.

In essence, an advisory committee can help with a multitude of functions that are essential if an asset assessment is to have meaning for all parties. It serves as a basis for the development of collaborative partnerships with nontraditional settings.

Preparation and Support of Interviewers

Any form of community-based research will prove labor intensive for an organization. However, an asset assessment will be much more demanding than a needs assessment. A focus on assets necessitates the development of questions and allowing sufficient time for the interviewee to answer them. Delgado (1995c, p. 71), based on the Holyoke, Massachusetts, studies, addresses this point:

> Field interviewers often had to spend significant amounts of time describing what an asset assessment was to individuals [nontraditional settings] with minimal or no awareness of the concept of assessment. It can be safely estimated that an asset-oriented question will require three times the length of time that a needs-focused question requires. Interviewers must be prepared to have various ways of asking a question in order to elicit an appropriate response. Human service providers are not trained to think about assets. Ordinary community residents, too, usually don't think in terms of community strengths. This shift in approach, in turn, requires interviewers to be skilled and patient in obtaining asset-related answers.

Once in the field, interviewers must have sites they can use to meet with each other, or a base from which to venture out to conduct interviews within nontraditional settings. This, according to Delgado (1995c, p. 73), takes on added importance if the assessment is conducted during the winter:

It is recommended that strategic sites be located and used as field bases for interviewers to meet and return to after completing the interviews. It was particularly important that [interviewers] have an opportunity at the end of the day to process the events that had transpired that day. These debriefing sessions, although time-consuming, are particularly important for helping [interviewers] put into context their experiences, both positive and negative, and help them problem-solve how to handle distressing situations.

Having an administrative office geographically located within a community serves to reassure residents of the legitimacy of the study, and it also provides them with access to information on the project. In addition, it reduces travel time for interviewers and provides a setting where they can go to meet and escape inclement weather.

9

Mapping

Mapping Nontraditional Settings

Goals

The goals of mapping are not ambitious, and usually consist of the following: (1) development of a systematic map of nontraditional settings; this map, at the very least, must consist of the key variables that are important to the social service organization; and (2) a map, to maintain its usefulness, must be easily updated and facilitate the adding and dropping of settings. Achievement of these two goals allows agencies to develop initiatives that are well planned and facilitate the implementation process.

Brief Overview of Stage

The process of mapping nontraditional settings is not complex. However, it requires social workers and other practitioners to develop a system for recording and updating new listings. The nature of this system is largely determined by the needs of the organization undertaking the mapping. The benefits of mapping far outweigh the limitations, as it is a mechanism for better understanding and conceptualizing the distribution and types of nontraditional settings within a community (Acosta & Hamel, 1995).

Challenges and Rewards

It is rare to find human service directories that include any form of nontraditional settings, including houses of worship. Consequently, most social service agencies must develop a mechanism for systematically developing some form of directory of these types of settings. A map serves this function by providing a visual representation of a community's assets. However, unlike a directory, a map is much easier to update to reflect the dynamic nature of nontraditional settings. Thus, a map of nontraditional settings serves as a critical planning tool in the development of collaborative partnerships.

One of the greatest challenges in using any map is ensuring that it is current and reflects the community. Consequently, any failure to update it will severely limit its usefulness. Communities are always changing in composition, with corresponding changes in the settings that serve them. One day a grocery store serving Puerto Ricans can change to one catering to Dominicans or Cubans. Although these groups all originate in the Caribbean, and the islands can be referred to as "sister" islands, there may be differences that distinguish on who patronizes the establishment.

Key Practice Concepts

The concept of mapping is certainly not new to human services, having roots in the social support literature. Identification of social support networks was used in the assessment and planning of interventions, both micro- and macro-based. The concept of mapping was also used in the natural support systems literature to identify various types of supports in communities of color (Delgado & Humm-Delgado, 1982). However, the degree of depth that is required in mapping nontraditional settings represents a departure from what has usually been the practice in the past.

Most of the literature on mapping social supports was not based on communities of color, and the maps generally focused on individuals, not taking into account nontraditional settings. A focus on communities and their nontraditional settings will raise issues of access for social service organizations, and require changing forms to elicit this type of information.

Case Examples

Mapping generally involves a two-step process using a local map and color-coded pins to stick into the map: (1) placing a color-coded pin on the geographical location of the nontraditional setting; and (2) placing in another identical map a set of color-coded pins covering various age groups. The Holyoke, Massachusetts, experience illustrates the simplicity of this stage and the implications it has for the development of collaborative activities:

> Staff, after the assessment process, placed an enlarged section of the geographic area covered on the wall. They then placed different colored pins, each color representing a type of nontraditional setting, on the map. Houses of worship, for example, were color-coded green; grocery stores were red; restaurants were blue; botanical shops, yellow; beauty parlors, purple, etc. Staff, after this initial process, examined how the pins clustered together and whether or not there were unusual patterns. For example, there were sections of the area that had no nontraditional settings; other areas had a disproportionate share. There were several blocks that had several houses

of worship. There was one section that had five grocery stores or restaurants. The absence or clustering of settings helps social workers plan for the development and location of community-based activities. The second phase involves using color-coded pins and a second, identical, map. This map, in turn, represents different age groups. Nontraditional settings with high percentages of elders, for example, were given the color brown. Settings that seem to target young and middle-aged adults were assigned white pins. Determination of age groups, whenever possible (some settings catered to all age groups), made it possible to plan activities with select nontraditional settings and specific age groups.

The use of mapping techniques for nontraditional settings is an excellent tool in helping to plan collaborative activities. In instances where an agency is actively involved with bars, for example, activities may vary according to location within a geographical area (select city blocks), type and intensity of involvement (type of outreach and information that is being made available for distribution), or even noting which bars refused to participate (necessitating the engagement of other types of nontraditional settings in that area as a means of overcoming this resistance).

Key Points and Considerations

The mapping of nontraditional settings lends itself to the use of a variety of perspectives in analyzing data. Two specific considerations in facilitating this process are: (1) mapping of age-specific information; and (2) mapping by years in existence.

Mapping of age-specific information. The gathering of age-specific information during the asset assessment process will prove very beneficial for the planning of collaborative projects. For example, the social service literature on Latino elders has increased in publications specifically focused on utilization of natural support systems, indigenous resources, and self-help approaches. However, not all nontraditional settings should automatically be considered as part of an elder's support system. Consequently, it is very important for practitioners to develop an in-depth understanding of what role nontraditional settings play with specific age groups.

The following case study serves as a good example of how age-specific information gathered during the assessment process lends itself to mapping (Delgado, in press d):

> The initial asset study conducted in Holyoke, Massachusetts, gathered information on a variety of topics, one of which was the characteristics of the population served by the nontraditional setting. When the analysis focused specifically on elders (65 years or older), the mapping process revealed interesting and important patterns related to nontraditional settings. In summary, most nontraditional settings that were not food-oriented (grocery stores and restaurants), and houses of worship, provided a considerably

lower number of social services when compared to food and religious non-traditional services. Elders did not constitute a high percentage of the customer base. This was particularly striking when this age group was compared with other age groups.

As the case in Holyoke with Puerto Rican elders showed, mapping lends itself to use with a multitude of factors, and allows for greater specificity in helping agencies determine which nontraditional settings are playing an important role in the life of sub-groups within the community and, as a result, should be involved in collaborative projects.

Mapping by years in existence. The number of years a nontraditional setting has been in existence is a very important way to map a community. The author's experience in working within nontraditional settings has shown that with some exceptions, the longer an establishment has been in existence, the higher the likelihood that the setting has been providing social services.

In addition, mapping the longevity of nontraditional settings provides important information concerning trends within a community. These data, unfortunately, are very often not collected or used in the development of social services. There may be sections of the community that have a long and distinguished history. Other sections may be much more transient and, as a result, less likely to yield results of extensive engagement because non-traditional settings have a very short life span.

10

Engagement of
Nontraditional Settings

Goals

The engagement and relationship building phase is undoubtedly the most challenging and arduous of all the phases. The goals for this phase vary in degree of difficulty according to the needs of the parties involved: (1) development of an in-depth understanding of how those in nontraditional settings view the community's assets and needs; (2) development of a relationship based on sufficient mutual trust and respect to withstand "tests" on the part of both parties; (3) development of an awareness of potential facilitating and hindering factors affecting a successful partnership; and (4) development of a successful relationship that can be carried over to other nontraditional settings as a result of a "positive" reputation. These goals stress the importance of communication, flexibility, and openness throughout all facets of this phase.

Brief Overview of Stage

The engagement of nontraditional settings entails learning about the other party, sharing information, and entering into a partnership in which all sides benefit. This is particularly critical in reaching out to persons who may be isolated and in great need. However, social workers must be aware that the engagement of one type of nontraditional setting can result in other nontraditional settings refusing to become involved with an agency.

A number of cases have been selected to provide a varied perspective on engagement. The first case (Holyoke, Massachusetts) shows how the process of assessment lends itself to engagement. The second case involves the author and his attempt to engage a local Pentecostal minister in providing space for groups. The third example describes how entry into nontraditional settings, in this case houses of worship, is possible if the worker is flexible. The fourth case (APRICHA, New York City) highlights the importance of the setting in influencing engagement.

Challenges and Rewards

As in any form of partnership, the creation of good will is an essential factor in ultimately determining the outcome of collaboration. The same principle applies to collaboration within nontraditional settings. A long and successful relationship will set a solid foundation for a social service agency within a community. Initially, the process of relationship building will prove labor intensive, with no guarantee of any returns on the investment of time and energy. However, every succeeding interaction will require less and less time and effort. A developmental perspective can be applied to this phase.

This phase is not without formidable challenges. Engagement will prove difficult, if not impossible, if the agency initiating a partnership has not done an adequate job of identifying and assessing the nontraditional setting. Resistance to engagement may be manifested in a variety of ways, none of them straightforward. Difficulty in assessing a nontraditional setting may be a good indicator of future challenges to engagement. People in a setting who do not have time to answer questions or who display a reluctance to answer questions in depth or in a straightforward manner, may indicate future resistance. Some persons in settings may ask interviewers numerous questions about the purpose of the assessment or project, who will have access to data, etc., and then refuse to answer more questions at that time, necessitating multiple return visits.

Agency personnel initiating the contact must feel comfortable in the setting, have a capacity to communicate in languages other than English, and use appropriate vocabulary. Lack of communication skills will often result in discomfort for the staff member; lack of comfort, in turn, can easily be conveyed and result in those in a nontraditional setting expressing reluctance to continue the engagement process.

Key Practice Concepts

There is little doubt that the ultimate success of engagement is contingent on the qualities of the staff undertaking the initiative. No ordinary social worker can work within nontraditional settings. As noted earlier in Chapter 5, social workers must be secure in their identities, have excellent communication skills, tolerate ambiguity, and have tremendous patience and persistence. It is not that social workers providing conventional services do not possess these qualities or are not called upon to use them. The intensity of the situation requires workers involved with nontraditional settings to be ever vigilant and to take advantage of opportunities that facilitate the process of engagement; these qualities, in turn, will often be necessary at a heightened level.

Further, social workers must be willing to be "tested" by those in nontraditional settings. Testing may involve listening to concerns expressed about the agency initiating the collaboration. It may also consist of requests for assistance, personal or for a patron, that clearly do not fall within the mandates of the agency. The testing process may extend over a long period of time and decrease in intensity as the people in the setting become increasingly comfortable with the worker.

Social workers must embrace the challenge of engagement during difficult circumstances. There are no private offices workers can use to discuss their goals; business is often discussed in a public arena with a constant flow of traffic. Some of the patrons may even join in the conversation. Workers must also be willing to discuss more of their personal lives than they are used to—a very unusual occurrence in our field. They may even be invited to attend celebrations or other major activities in the community, which generally do not fall within the realm of a more "typical" job description.

Social workers must be flexible in setting their goals for collaboration. Circumstances may dictate modified goals or the addition of another service, such as training or consultation, that was not part of the original plan for intervention. The time frame during which a project was to be developed may also be modified, with considerably more time devoted to engagement. Collaboration, be it formal or informal, may require marching to the "beat of a different drummer," requiring patience and flexibility.

Case Examples

Once engagement has occurred, it does not necessarily require further active and major collaborative efforts. Delgado (1996e, p. 173), in the following Holyoke, Massachusetts, case example, illustrates how the relationship established during an asset assessment can translate into a collaborative activity, in this instance the generation of funds:

> For example, the youths in the project wanted to raise money to pay for a trip. They decided on a car wash. However, unlike conventional car washes, where cars are charged a certain amount of money, the youths decided to ask Latino businesses [nontraditional settings] to sponsor each car they washed (amounts ranged from 5 cents to 25 cents per car). These establishments, in turn, would be given recognition by having their names listed on a billboard displayed at the car wash. Twenty-eight establishments agreed to sponsor the activity. Donations from washed cars were solicited but not required. The youths also decided to make a videotape of the activity to share with other youth agencies and to help other organizations generate funds. The car wash raised $575.00. The funds, although important, were not as important as how the event was planned and the community involved.

This community-based activity could not have been possible without the information gathered and the relationships built during the asset assessment undertaken by the youths. There are many different levels of engagement, depending on the complexity of the collaboration activity that is planned. The more complex and demanding the collaboration, the greater the importance of engagement.

The following description of the author's experience in developing a collaborative project involving a Pentecostal church brings to light the challenges social workers will invariably face as they seek to engage nontraditional settings:

> The worker visited a Pentecostal church where three of his clients worshiped. The worker was very interested in working out an agreement for use of space in the church. The church was strategically located within the community and had plenty of space for conducting groups and holding workshops. An appointment was made to meet with the minister. After the initial introductions, the minister asked Delgado about his religious affiliation. Delgado had been asked many questions throughout his career as a social worker; however, this was the first time anyone had questions about his religion. After an initial hesitation, he responded that he was an atheist. Delgado initially feared that once he gave his answer, the minister would refuse to discuss possible collaborative projects. Consequently, he was greatly relieved when the minister stated that he appreciated his candor. At the end of the initial meeting, as Delgado was walking out of the door with high hopes for an agreement, the minister asked Delgado to wait. He picked up some religious materials and asked Delgado to read them when he had an opportunity. At that moment, Delgado realized that the minister would question him about the readings at their next meeting. In essence, to engage in collaboration Delgado needed to engage in dialogue with the minister. Not to read the material meant the end of any possible collaboration.

Malony (1992, p. 290) provides another simple, but very realistic example of how engagement can transpire and the benefits to be derived, when telling the story of a new mental health worker moving into a community and engaging local houses of worship:

> For example, one psychologist moved into the city . . . without knowing anyone. He attended the ministerial association meetings and offered to provide the ministers a free workshop on clergy malpractice. He visited each church and became acquainted with the clergy leaders. He queried them about their needs and offered to teach classes in their church schools. Although he did not perceive his offers as being cost effective, he did see these as consultative opportunities which would result in referrals for service where he could charge regular fees. His plan worked. He is now firmly established as a reputable congregational resource and consultant in the area.

Men of Color AIDS Project (MOCAP), in Cleveland, Ohio, utilized a variety of methods, none of which were labor intensive, to identify and enlist the support of nontraditional settings (restaurant, bars, and barbershops):

The restaurant (men's support group) was selected because it was well located within the community, and the owner was a close friend of a member of the board of directors. The board member spoke with the owner and received permission to allow a support group. The bar that MOCAP uses to deliver prevention messages was selected because of its popularity within the gay and bisexual community of color and the help provided by a female impersonator who facilitated access to the owner of the bar. Last, barbershops were selected based upon their history of cooperating with other social service organizations; their track record of cooperation, and location within the community, were the two criteria for participation in the project.

The following case, based in New York City, reflects the necessity for strategic decisions in selecting nontraditional settings and the importance of using a variety of engagement techniques. New York is the most populated city in the United States, with approximately 8 million residents. The city consists of five boroughs (Bronx, Brooklyn, Manhattan, Queens, and Staten Island). New York City has a rich history of being home to numerous racial and ethnic groups. The borough of Staten Island has the lowest percentage of people of color (20.1), followed by Manhattan (51.1), Queens (51.9), Brooklyn (59.1), and the Bronx (77.3) (Roberts, 1994). According to the 1990 U.S. Census Bureau, there were approximately 1,840,000 African Americans (25.2 percent), 525,000 Asians (7.2 percent), and 1,800,000 Latinos (24.4 percent) in the city. New York City's communities of color have increased significantly over the past 30 years, from 37 percent in 1970, to 57.3 percent in 1990, and are estimated to be 65 percent by the year 2000 (Roberts, 1995).

> Engaging nontraditional settings in Asian and Pacific Islander communities must be well planned. APRICHA (Asian and Pacific Islander Coalition on HIV/AIDS) maintains an active and extensive outreach and education program. Nontraditional settings such as beauty parlors, restaurants, food markets, and other places have been targeted because of: (1) their high volume of customers; (2) their relatively easy accessibility for outreach workers to enter; (3) an atmosphere that allows and even encourages conversation; and (4) the activity or purpose of the setting provides sufficient time for a conversation to transpire.

Actual engagement in these settings necessitates the use of multiple techniques (Mangaliman, 1994, p. A12):

> For the past year and a half, Resurrection (HIV/AIDS outreach/educator) has been diligently coming here [Thai Beauty Salon]—first to get a haircut, then every week for a few months to get a manicure—getting to know Annie [owner] and her workers and customers, becoming a part of the scene. "It took six months to win the trust of people," Resurreccion said, "because they were not initially receptive to the idea. I have a lot in com-

mon with the immigrant women I work with," she said. "The talking comes naturally."

Engagement of nontraditional settings can often require staff to be persistent and creative, to give of themselves, and to be challenged, as experienced by APRICHA staff:

Engagement of nontraditional settings will often require staff to develop a bag of "tricks" to succeed in their work. One worker at APRICHA has developed a series of techniques that allows her to outreach in markets, grocery stores, and restaurants. The worker will shop in a setting and while shopping actively engage in outreach and distribution of condoms and educational pamphlets. If ordered to stop by the owner or manager of the establishment, she simply informs him/her that she is shopping and well within her rights to be in the store. Sometimes it may take up to an hour and one half in a setting before moving on to another nontraditional setting. This worker may spend up to $20.00 of her own money in a store in order to reach a large number of customers. In other settings, most notably nail salons and beauty parlors, the worker may approach employees about her activities. She may give them sample materials to be shown to the owner or manager of a store. These employees, in turn, act as "brokers" between the outreach worker and the owner or manager. She has found that employees often have the time to listen to her message about HIV/AIDS. Owners and managers, however, often are not on the premises, are very suspicious of outsiders, or do not have the time to listen to lengthy rationales for outreach activities. Employees have also been known to discourage an outreach worker from even bothering with approaching an owner or manager because of his/her attitude on a topic such as HIV/AIDS.

Outreach does not have to be very labor intensive, costly, or have very ambitious goals. One agency in Kansas City, Missouri, has taken a highly visible, but low labor-intensive approach toward outreaching to the Latino community (Bavley, 1995, p. A1):

"You have to meet people where they're at. That involves culture, economic status, everything that affects their life." In the past year, the Gadalupe Center has distributed more than 9,000 paper sacks to restaurants, beauty salons, groceries and hardware and liquor stores in the city's West Side and Northeast areas. Printed on the sacks are an AIDS message and telephone numbers for obtaining more information. "It's a subtle message to make you aware, but we've gotten a lot of response."

Another outreach initiative, this one involving two agencies coming together, makes outreach targeting nontraditional settings serving people of color that much easier to develop (Jackson, 1992, p. 1Y):

"Knowledge is empowerment . . . What will work in the gay community may not work in the community of color, and we need to be sensitive to the needs of the communities. AIDS is an illness, and education is life" . . . Volunteers will distribute fliers to liquor stores, beauty shops, clubs, and other social areas . . . Officials said the campaign will include special worship services, radio and television programs.

The Bar Alert and Mail Alert programs of the Senior Centers of San Diego are also examples of low labor-intensive efforts. The city of San Diego is located in southern California, 25 miles from the Mexican border. San Diego consists of eight counties (North Country, East Country, La Jolla, Mission Valley, Mission Bay, Point Loma, Downtown Coronado, and South Bay). The city has a population totaling approximately 1.1 million. Latinos (primarily Mexican Americans) and African Americans account for 230,000 (21%) and 104,000 (10%) of the population, respectively, with Asian and Pacific Islanders representing 131,000 (11.8%), and white, non-Latinos making up the largest sector with 745,000 (67%).

The Bar Alert program consists of four bars located within a short walking distance of the Center. In fact, one of the bars is located across the street from the agency. The program consists of staff visiting these bars and enlisting the support of owners, managers, or bartenders. These individuals are provided with food menus for meals served at the Center. Bar personnel, in turn, distribute menus to senior citizens who are customers. These customers are then encouraged to take advantage of this service. The Mail Alert program is even less labor intensive than Bar Alert. The program focuses on two zip codes within the Center's catchment area. Seniors who elect to participate get a red-dot sticker for their mail-box. Postal carriers see a red-dot and know to watch out for problems. If the mail begins to accumulate (2 days), then the postal carrier alerts the Postmaster, who then calls the Center. The Center, in turn, sends out a worker to check on the senior.

In contrast, the Center's Hotel Alert program is much more ambitious and, therefore, more labor intensive than Bar or Mail Alert:

A total of ten single-room occupancy hotels currently participate in this program. This program acknowledges the critical role hotel managers play in the lives of residents, and can facilitate staff access to residents. Managers were selected as the primary point of entry because they know the residents and, if trusted, are in a position to get seniors to seek services. Most managers understand that residents have a multitude of social and health needs that must be addressed. A senior resident who has an active and supportive social network would be a resident who is more likely to be cooperative with managers, and be good neighbors to other residents, thus making life easier for managers. Managers set the tone for staff. Once managers are educated, they can teach staff (clerks, etc.).

The engagement of laundromats and beauty parlors in Central Falls/Pawtucket, Rhode Island, provides a good example of how engagement does not necessarily have to be labor intensive and highly sensitive to local politics if the "right" community-based organization is involved. The cities of Central Falls (population of 7,600) and Pawtucket (population of 72,600), Rhode Island, border each other and are located approximately 3 miles from Providence. Both of these cities have very similar population characteristics. The two have the same percentage of African Americans (4%), and Asians and Native Americans (less than 1%). The white, non-Latino population of Central Falls and Pawtucket is the largest segment, with 77 percent (13,700) and 89 percent (64,800) of the population, respectively. The two cities differ in the percent of Latino residents, with Central Falls having 29 percent (5,100) and Pawtucket having 7 percent (5,200).

> Progreso Latino is one of Rhode Island's oldest Latino community-based organizations. This social service agency provides a wide range of services within the Latino community and has an excellent reputation for advocating for Latino issues. As a result, it has a high name recognition in the community. Progreso Latino's approach to engaging laundromats and beauty parlors consisted of a four stage process: (1) mailing a letter to these non-traditional settings explaining the impact of AIDS on the Latino community and the importance of offering educational workshops on prevention, and soliciting the cooperation of the owners; (2) setting up a meeting with the owners of these establishments to explain in person how the workshops would be offered and the value to the establishments of collaborating with this project; (3) if necessary, a follow-up meeting with individual owners to answer any questions or address any concerns; and (4) participating institutions would either receive a stipend ($25.00 in the case of laundromats) or complimentary cosmetics (provided by a major cosmetic company).

The process of engagement used by the Senior Centers of San Diego for their Hotel Alert program is similar to that of Progreso Latino:

> A letter is sent to the owners of the hotels targeted to participate in the program. This letter introduces the agency and social worker and explains what the program entails and why it is so important for both the owner and the resident. A request is made to set up an individual meeting with the owner to discuss further the details of the program and to answer any questions they may have. Very often, however, owners agree to participate and refer staff to the hotel managers to work out the details.

The payment of a small stipend can serve as a financial inducement to facilitate the engagement process, as experienced by the Progreso Latino (Central Falls/Pawtucket, Rhode Island) in its "Tupperware Parties":

> The experience in getting low-income residents to host "Tupperware" type parties on HIV/AIDS has been very successful. The agency has managed

almost to double the number of parties over the course of two years. The $25 offered to a hostess to have the party and invite around six participants has helped. That is a lot of money for someone with a very low income. The availability of food has also served as an excellent recruitment mechanism.

Meaningful engagement necessitates persistence, creativity, exchange of resources, and possible self-sacrifice. In what may pose a problem for many social workers, engagement does not necessarily require positive acceptance on the part of those in nontraditional settings to achieve the objectives of outreach and education.

As already noted, not all people in all nontraditional settings can be expected to engage in dialogue without tension and disagreement. Delgado found this out through his experiences with community-based studies. In a key informant study involving Puerto Rican elders and botanical shops, there was no unanimous support for developing collaborative activities between these nontraditional settings and social service agencies (Delgado, 1996c, p. 75):

Some elders believe that the proprietor is working with "evil" intents; . . . Elders who are "overly Catholic" and "fundamentalist Protestants"; Elders who consider that botanicas are places for evil things. "Pentecostal elders," for example, may not like to visit a botanica.

Delgado (1979–80, p. 8) found in another study involving folk healers that they, too, could prove to be very controversial:

Established religious groups also will no doubt raise a voice of dissent at any formal attempt to incorporate folk healers. The fact that most religious leaders in Hispanic communities feel that folk healers are either devil worshipers or, at best, charlatans, will present an obstacle to planners and administrators interested in developing formal relationships with healers . . . Pentecostal sects and the Catholic Church will probably be the most significant religious groups opposing spiritist [folk healer] affiliations with mental health settings.

The author's experience as a consultant to a social service center in the Boston area, although repeated in various forms in other cities across the United States, illustrates how nontraditional settings are often overlooked in the development of services, in this case alcoholism related, because of institutional and staff bias (Delgado, 1989, pp. 86–87):

The consultant was brought into the center to consult on program development focused on Hispanics who were alcoholic. Unfortunately, several major outreach efforts had failed to significantly increase the number of Hispanics utilizing the center's services. At the initial meeting, senior staff present outlined their efforts. At the end of the presentation, the consultant asked the staff what efforts, if any, had been undertaken with . . . bars, liquor stores . . . After a few minutes, no response was forthcoming, at which time the consultant rephrased the initial question by noting the number of each institution within a five-block radius of the center. After a brief period, the executive director noted that the idea of approaching these institutions was never contemplated.

Overlooking bars, liquor stores, and other nontraditional settings may be the result of professional bias toward these institutions:

After the consultant raised the importance of these institutions, the discussion raised a series of concerns on the part of center staff. One staff member said "bars and liquor stores are the source of the problem in the community." At which point, the consultant responded "where are your data?" Unfortunately, no data were forthcoming. One staff member raised concerns that these establishments do not have a vested interest in stopping the sale of alcohol, regardless of the consequences of excessive drinking. The consultant responded that unless these establishments are approached, there is no way of really telling this for a fact. It might be that all bars and liquor stores would resist engagement in outreach and community education collaborative activities. However, there may be a few that would entertain some effort at distributing materials on alcoholism, or even make an effort to refer a customer to the center. At the end of the morning's discussion, one of the outreach workers approached the consultant and said "To be quite honest, I do not feel comfortable going into bars or liquor stores to do outreach." The consultant did not have an opportunity to further question the worker on the reasons for this reluctance. However, outreach cannot be restricted to those institutions and areas where a staff member feels comfortable visiting. Nontraditional settings, in this case bars and liquor stores, are often not considered vital institutions in efforts to outreach to undervalued communities.

Reluctance to engage nontraditional settings such as bars and liquor stores very often results in these institutions not playing an active role in delivery of services:

After much discussion about how to engage bars and liquor stores, the sentiments of the executive director and senior staff was not to approach these nontraditional settings. This decision was ostensibly due to the following: (1) the concerns of the "message" being sent to the community that it was "important" to involve bars and liquor stores in the center's programs; and (2) concern on the part of outreach staff that these establishments would prove too difficult to engage and thereby waste valuable time and resources that could be better directed to other initiatives.

Key Points and Considerations

The following are major considerations when enaging nontraditional settings: (1) willingness to engage; (2) cultural competence of staff; (3) legitimacy of nontraditional setting; and (4) importance of certain staff qualities.

Willingness to Engage

Any shift in a paradigm that views communities as problem-ridden to possessing strengths and resources, necessitates an expansive view of community. However, it is important to understand that not all people in all nontraditional settings may be interested in collaboration, just as not all agencies may be interested in this type of relationship. It becomes particularly critical during an asset assessment to ascertain the willingness and ability of the setting to engage in collaboration. In addition, a willingness to engage should not be construed as willingness to receive and not give back—the concept of mutuality will undoubtedly manifest itself, as shown in the following story (Roberts & Thorsheim, 1992, pp. 261–262):

> In the affluent suburbs of a city, several white women wanted to do something to help the black women in the inner-city who seemed to be struggling so hard to care for their families. The suburban women gathered used clothes, gave money, and helped with providing food for these inner-city women. At first this helping hand was appreciated. But soon the women in the inner-city developed a need to reciprocate the help. The suburban women were urged to talk with the inner-city women, to learn ways that the inner-city women could do something for them in return. Could the inner-city women teach them something? Could they give advice about how to create community? Could they share experiences about what it is like to raise small children? However, the suburban women could not think of anything they had to learn from the inner-city women and refused to accept suggestions. As the inner-city women began to understand that the suburban women were not interested in really getting to know them and to care about what was going on in their lives, they felt diminished. Any sense of dignity that may have been developing because of the first show of support was eroded. The inner-city women felt that they were seen as second-class citizens by the suburban women—not as equals.

DiAna (1995, p. 93), the owner of an African American beauty parlor and an activist in HIV/AIDS education, expresses concerns about how professionals have addressed the subject of HIV/AIDS in communities of color, and what needs to be taken into consideration during an engagement phase:

> Doing AIDS education "should not have to be this hard" and I resent the fact that some people still look at AIDS as "being a business." There are too many people who are in the business of doing AIDS education and prevention that have too much to lose if a cure is found "too soon." Some people want to "retire" with the jobs that they currently maintain, and if the epidemic slows down too quickly they could be layed off, or lose their jobs altogether. The "currency" used in this epidemic has become that of

"human lives." Deals are made and negotiated in some cases with very lit-tle regard for the people affected by their decisions. There is still a need for some people to control others, and some people are willing to do that "by any means necessary," and although that is my favorite saying, some-times it is not "acceptable," not when the "trade off is a body count."

Some nontraditional settings may not be willing to address certain com-munity needs such as HIV/AIDS, thus avoiding entering into any form of collaboration with agencies. The following two examples involve clergy in African American and Latino communities who may be willing to engage in collaborative activities with agencies on certain needs. However, when it comes to the topic of AIDS, they may be resistant.

The first example focuses on African American churches (Ribadeneira, 1997, pp. B1, B7):

> The black church has historically been the bedrock of the African-American community, the place where many struggles, especially against racial injus-tice, have been launched. But as AIDS continues its devastating and dis-proportionate onslaught on African-Americans, many black clergy acknowledge that their churches have been woefully absent . . . While in-dividual black churches in the Boston area have taken initiatives to address the AIDS epidemic, too many African-American congregations still resist dealing with an issue many blacks regard as taboo . . . The reluctance of many black churches to deal with AIDS has been the product of the the-ological conservatism of most African-American congregations, especially on issues of sexuality. Black churches generally promote abstinence as the proper sexual conduct outside marriage. And many black churches, basing their views on Biblical readings, consider homosexuality a sin. "People are so afraid of being ostracized in church by the stigma of AIDS."

The second example occurred in a section of Boston with a large Latino population and illustrates an unsuccessful effort at reaching certain types of clergy:

> A social worker who tried to involve priests, ministers and nuns in educa-tion on HIV protection met with a great deal of anger from the priests in attendance. The ministers and nuns, however, were willing to be involved in community education and expressed a need for this type of service for the community. However, due to the unwillingness of the priests to coop-erate, the outreach effort ended in discussion without action.

Some people in nontraditional settings may be overwhelmed by the number of requests they get from human service organizations, severely lim-iting the process of engagement (Navarro, 1989, p. B4):

> Some of those whose support is now being courted also say that AIDS is competing with other pressing problems, like housing and education.

"We're asked to help with education, to help with the infrastructure, to help with children's programs," said one businessman who requested anonymity. "Now we're asked to educate workers on AIDS. Every now and then we'd like to show a profit."

Those in nontraditional settings may also avoid entering into collaborative relationships because of their fear of the implications these partnerships have for business:

Progreso Latino, in Rhode Island, experienced minimal resistance from beauty parlors and laundromats engaging in HIV/AIDS workshops. One beauty parlor refused to participate because of fears that customers would be adverse to hearing about this topic and, as a result, would stop patronizing the business and go elsewhere. One laundromat refused to collaborate because of expressed concerns that saying yes to Progreso would result in countless other social service agencies approaching them for cooperation on other social needs.

Resistance to engagement because of lack of time may not be too unusual. Progreso Latino in Central Falls/Pawtucket has approached schools of cosmetology about integrating information related to HIV/AIDS, without success:

Progreso Latino has made a concerted effort to reach as many beauticians as possible. One possible source is to target where beauticians get their training. The hope has been to provide at least one hour of training on HIV/AIDS. However, we have been unsuccessful in achieving this goal. The primary reason why it has not been possible is because of curriculum crowding. There are too many topics and insufficient time to cover them without adding another topic.

A reluctance to engage in dialogue about collaboration may also be the result of more sinister factors. One hotel approached by the Senior Centers of San Diego Hotel Alert's staff refused to participate in the program:

Of course there is no way of knowing for sure why the hotel was so adamant in refusing to cooperate. However, speculation was that the hotel had a very high percentage of residents who were on parole and were suspicious of outsiders. In addition, rumors were that a host of illegal activities were being perpetrated in the hotel. Consequently, there was fear that social workers would come across these activities in serving senior residents, necessitating reporting them to the police. In order to avoid the consequences of such an action, it was best not to allow social service agencies into the hotel in the first place. This speculation is based on informal communication between staff and individuals with intimate knowledge of the hotel.

Engagement is a complex process that necessitates both parties agreeing on a need, both being willing to give and receive assistance, and in which professionals hear concerns about how a community may view them and their colleagues. The failure of social workers to understand the importance of reciprocity will seriously undermine any collaborative effort.

Cultural Competence of Staff

The assessment process cannot be accomplished without culturally competent staff. Bilingual, and preferably bicultural, staff who are very knowledgeable about and feel comfortable visiting communities are essential to facilitate the engagement process:

> A Boston-based social worker in a health setting began to realize that there was a tremendous need to develop a creative HIV/AIDS intervention to reach Latinos within their community. She targeted by forming relationships with small Latin-owned businesses. She focused on beauty parlors because of an awareness that for many women, this setting became a place to "gossip and build relationships." She believed that it was possible to utilize beauty salon owners as leaders in the community. Inviting the owners to a breakfast and then an "AIDS 101" training, she provided them with basic information and then asked them to make available pamphlets (in Spanish and English) and condoms that she provided. Her approach was to make the dissemination of the information and condoms as discreet as possible. She made it clear that the beauty parlor owners and workers were not there as experts, but rather as conduits of information.

The importance of language cannot be overemphasized in the case of various communities of color. Language, in this instance, is much more than an ability to converse; it also includes understanding symbols that reflect cultural background (Singer, 1991; Sufian et al., 1990). Language and style of communication take into account cultural background and assumptions/ beliefs of a community (Nelkin, 1987). Bracho de Carpio, Carpio-Cedraro, and Anderson (1990), provide an excellent illustration of the importance of culture in communication when they report on how storytelling and problemsolving played an instrumental role in educating Puerto Rican youngsters on HIV/AIDS.

Hiring staff who are also community residents further facilitates the engagement of the community. One project that actively reaches out to the community and those in nontraditional settings (Hackensack, New Jersey), strove to hire residents whenever possible:

> The director of the project and her staff live within the community that their office targets with their programming. The director and the staff are on numerous boards of directors of neighborhood organizations. They attend committee meetings and are at all major community events. Additionally, since the director lives in the community, she sees the pro-

ject's constituency in the supermarket and other "ordinary" places. This not only helps the community to keep tabs on her, but vice versa. Visibility within the community is critical in order to develop a better understanding of its assets and needs, establish the necessary contacts with nontraditional settings, and maintain community support for services.

Legitimacy of Nontraditional Setting

Collaboration with a nontraditional setting that has a reputation for unethical practices will be detrimental to an agency; conversely, collaborating with a nontraditional setting that has an impeccable reputation can prove extremely beneficial.

According to a staff member at the Senior Centers of San Diego Bar Alert program, there are people in many nontraditional settings who are more than willing to help. One such place is a coffee house not far from the agency:

> Some of the seniors encountered in bars do not wish to use to the services of the Center. However, they feel much more comfortable going to another setting. One of the local coffee shops located within walking distance in the neighborhood targets seniors and other people who have a drinking history. This shop makes space available for Alcoholics Anonymous meetings and sells coffee mugs with "one day at a time" slogans.

Involving nontraditional settings that are principal collaborators should be a considered seriously by social agencies and workers for use as bases for involving other nontraditional settings. Bar Alert's use of a coffee shop as a place to meet certain clients is an example of how relatively easy it is to open up numerous opportunities without having to undertake elaborate asset assessments, engage in lengthy negotiations, or make long-term commitments. Clients can often be an excellent source of information on the kinds of nontraditional settings that are accessible and willing to facilitate service delivery without entering into formal agreements.

Importance of Certain Staff Qualities

Successful work within nontraditional settings requires staff and social service organizations to have flexible roles and schedules. These settings have been successful in reaching the community for a variety of reasons, one of which is their flexibility in carrying out their roles. Social workers or organizations that are not prepared to change established procedures and services to reach an underserved population group, will experience great difficulty in collaborating with nontraditional settings.

There are numerous qualities that staff must possess to get nontraditional settings to collaborate. When social workers of the Hotel Alert program were asked to offer advice to help other social agencies engage single-room occupancy hotels, they said the following:

One way to get through to hotel managers and clerks is to do something which benefits them. Show them good results. You need to keep going back and establishing a presence. Build trust. You can't come in with a strong arm. They will reject you. Know the neighborhood, and be able to identify where residents are coming from. Go through the manager. The manager then presents the idea to the owner. Establish rapport with managers. Show then that you are competent. Show them what are the benefits to using the program and referring people. They see a problem solved, they will want you back. In terms of mapping out an area, what is reasonable to work with? How far can you walk? You need to balance what is realistic. You need to be a worker who is outgoing and adventurous. You must expect to spend little time in an office. Don't feel rejected when you are told to get out. Keep going back and take things slowly. Represent you ideas again and again.

There is no doubt that the process of engagement can be both time consuming and require workers to be "thick skinned." There are many different levels of engagement, and each will vary according to the goals for collaboration, the amount of time devoted to relationship building, and the willingness of workers to give of themselves.

The following story of an outreach worker, who wished to remain anonymous, serves to illustrate the demands, professional and personal, of the role:

> The outreach worker had been working in that capacity for approximately two years and truly loved her work. She had a deep desire to prevent the spread of AIDS in the community, and this manifested itself in all aspects of her personal and professional life. Even though she had to cover a great geographical area and innumerable nontraditional settings, the work was still challenging and fulfilling. Her gender did not interfere with outreach, even though her ethnic group did not approve of women entering bars, liquor stores, and other nontraditional settings catering to men. Her family back in her country of origin did not know the exact nature of the work she performed. This was purposeful because if they knew, they would prohibit her from working as an outreach worker. Consequently, she had to be very selective and careful about what she shared about the work she loved.

Social agencies wishing to collaborate with merchant institutions must first be prepared to spend a period of time becoming familiar with these establishments. It is essential that personal contact transpire so workers are made aware of the types of people they serve, how business is conducted, what kind of services they provide that are supportive, etc. In essence, it is necessary to enter a phase that can best be described as relationship building.

This phase will provide social service agencies with invaluable information concerning which establishments are interested in a collaborative relationship and have contact with a high number of residents. As already noted, not all people in all nontraditional settings may be interested in working with social workers or their agencies.

11

Delivery of Services

Goals

The goals of service delivery speak for themselves. This phase can easily be referred to as the "bottom line" in collaboration with nontraditional settings. The goals for this phase, like those of the other phases, will vary according to the complexity and labor intensity of the services being delivered. These goals are: (1) to provide the maximum number of services with the minimum amount of resources; (2) to ensure that the rights of clients are protected and that they are aware of the recourses available should they wish to use them; (3) to provide services that are intrinsically based on the cultural background of the consumer to ensure delivery of culturally competent services; and (4) to provide services with a minimal disruption of the daily activities of the nontraditional setting.

Brief Overview of Stage

Delivery of services is probably the primary and only goal of most agencies wishing to work within nontraditional settings. However, like any other stage in this framework, it becomes critical to have a clear sense of what type of service collaboration is sought. There are numerous ways of providing even the most basic type of social services; thus, clarity takes on additional importance during this phase.

Rewards and Challenges

The rewards to be derived from service delivery can be multifaceted, and they extend beyond the collaborative partnership. The agency as a whole benefits from connectedness to the community; services, as a result, increase in relevance. The agency is also able to reach out to underserved groups in a cost-efficient and culture-specific manner. These benefits can easily be translated into greater visibility for the agency, and may result in increased referrals and funding. Further, the agency may develop a reputation as a place where innovative and exciting work is taking place; this reputation can serve as a mechanism for recruiting staff interested in this type of practice.

The development of an agency's widespread reputation for innovative service delivery, including seeking community participation can be considered political capital in the advocacy for greater resources to targeting undervalued groups. This increases the influence of the agency within and without the community. In short, tangible benefits can be increased. But benefits can also be intangible, like easier access to population groups that are difficult for other agencies to engage.

Four key challenges face organizations undertaking partnerships with nontraditional settings. First, it is imperative that staff continually be assigned for as long as possible to nontraditional settings. These settings generally relate to individuals and not institutions, a common experience with groups of color. Consequently, having the same staff involved with a setting over all phases of the intervention will increase the chances that relationships develop and deepen over an extended period of time.

The author's experiences have shown that there is minimal turnover of staff in these types of settings. It is not unusual to have only family members working in nontraditional settings. Consequently, the workers develop relationships with families and not unrelated individuals. Such relationships ensure that continuity within nontraditional settings is maintained.

However, the vicissitudes of agency life invariably involve staff turnover. Such occurrences are often not thought about in program development because they are so prosaic. Frequent staff turnover will seriously undermine agency partnerships. The challenge for an agency is to assign the right staff, based not just on qualities and interest but also on the likelihood of longevity staff can expect to have in the agency. It is possible to involve social work students in these kinds of endeavors if they are paired with permanent staff, and those in nontraditional settings are informed of the status of the student, particularly the duration of their participation. Nontraditional settings can prove to be excellent learning centers if those working in them are properly prepared and supported.

A second major challenge is to maintain continuity in service delivery when funding is curtailed or terminated. There is no such thing as "hard" money that can be counted on during financially hard times or political changes. Nontraditional settings do not write grants to support the services they provide the community. They deliver services because of their commitment to the community, be it based on cultural traditions of caregiving or good business. Agencies, in turn, provide services as a result of their sense of mission and acquisition of funding. Termination of funding will more often than not result in closing down a service.

Funding sources may initially like funding nontraditional partnerships because they are "innovative" and actively involve a community. However, these services, even when proven effective, may become more commonplace, thus losing their "innovative" caché. Agencies must develop multiple methods for obtaining funds for this form of practice. Incidentally, we are not taking about huge expenditures of funds; sometimes needed funding may involve only part of a staff's salary and some additional, incidental costs.

Third, agencies must strive to make services involving nontraditional settings an integral part of the organization's structure and mission. Agencies with multifaceted community-based service delivery structures will find it easier to accomplish this goal. Agencies with singular missions, for example, counseling provided at the agency, and minimal community-based services, will experience greater difficulties.

Acceptance of nontraditional partnerships is enhanced when all agency staff are kept abreast of activities related to this form of service. This not only "legitimizes" the project, but also gives staff an opportunity to ask questions or just absorb information. In essence, there should be no mysteries concerning nontraditional settings. Staff working in nontraditional settings can be invited to attend functions at the agency and share their experiences whenever possible with staff. This two-way communication serves to break down stereotypes each party may have of the other.

Finally, agencies must restructure forms, particularly those related to intake, to gather information in the most responsive manner. This information must seek to develop a well-rounded profile of the client, whether an individual or community, to better plan collaborative partnerships within the appropriate nontraditional settings. This restructuring may not seem like a challenge. Nevertheless, one only has to speak with anyone who was ever been involved in changing agency forms to realize how difficult, time consuming, and politically charged such efforts can become. This effort takes on greater significance when the agency has to decide what information is important to gather and what information is nonessential. The decision-making process may entail numerous changes over an extended period of time. If conceptualized as a long-term project, these challenges become easier to accept.

Key Practice Concepts

The service delivery phase of collaboration lends itself to the use of multiple concepts, adding to the richness associated with intervention. Collaborative partnerships provide social workers with countless opportunities to use empowerment, participation, and capacity enhancement strategies. The degree and nature of operationalizing these concepts is dependent on the goals for service delivery and the capabilities of the social worker and agency. Any effort at enlisting community participation opens up opportunities to use empowerment techniques; any form of empowerment will result in capacity enhancement, an important concept in community work. Agencies enhance community capacities by providing residents with opportunities to maximize their potential.

Capacity enhancement principles can be easily translated to institutions and to the broader community. Nontraditional settings can be helped to make it easier for them to provide services, minimizing misdirection from their other activities. Communities, in turn, can be helped to plan, develop, and maintain gardens, murals, sculptures, playgrounds, and so on. These projects also serve to unify the community in pursuit of a common set of goals and also result in the creation of places where the entire community can benefit.

The concept of capacity enhancement takes on life during this phase of collaboration. Nontraditional settings not only are made stronger as organizations, people in them are also able to benefit personally. As most individuals who work in these settings also live in the community, their enhanced skills can be utilized to help friends, neighbors, other residents, members of churches, etc. A ripple effect is caused, with positive implications for an entire community.

Capacity enhancement, as a concept, is not restricted to knowledge and skill acquisition; it is also applicable to attitudes. Enhancement can serve to help focus natural helpers in their service roles by validating their abilities and providing them with a broader context from which to view the helping process. If they are willing and the opportunities present themselves, some of these helpers can pursue employment in the field of human services. This option may not be attractive for all helpers. However, this is another form of enhancing the capacity of communities.

The concept of capacity enhancement has tremendous potential for both the field of social work and communities. This concept is firmly anchored on the premise that the community has invaluable assets that can be built on. Enhancement strategies provide agencies with the ability to deliver much needed services and to engage in community building within a cultural context. This building remains after services are terminated.

Case Illustrations

The establishment of collaborative partnerships between social agencies and people in nontraditional settings is exciting, challenging, and very rewarding. Collaboration, as already addressed in previous chapters, can take many forms and shapes depending on the needs to be addressed, the capacities of both social agencies and nontraditional settings, and the level of trust and respect each party has for the other. Following the framework outlined in Chapter 7, collaboration can be of the following types: (1) sharing resources; (2) knowledge building and consultation; (3) outreach; (4) community education; and (5) counseling and advice giving.

Sharing Resources

The concept of resource encompasses a multitude of forms, ranging from distribution of materials, posting of notices, use of space for meetings, to provision of transportation, to list only a few. This form of collaboration can vary in labor intensity and commitment. Consequently, sharing resources can serve as an excellent stepping stone for more ambitious and labor-intensive collaborative activities. Two case studies are used to illustrate various forms of collaboration.

The following case lays out the possible parameters for establishing collaborative relationships within nontraditional settings that also fulfill business functions within communities:

> A restaurant located in a mid-sized New England city was approached by the author to help co-sponsor a community event and provide complementary food and space for an advisory committee. The restaurant was well known and respected within the community, and well located geographically. The business was owned and operated by a well-liked and respected family. The owners, in turn, were very interested in becoming foster parents because their children had grown up and moved out of the city. Consequently, their parenting needs were not being met. Unfortunately, they had very limited English language skills, a low level of formal education, and did not feel "comfortable" approaching the appropriate authorities to investigate how they could become foster parents. The author, in return for their contributions (resources), and use of space in their restaurant for meetings, workshops, etc., brokered getting them an appointment with the necessary personnel to start the process of becoming foster parents. The author attended the first meeting with them to facilitate the process. In addition, the author was able to get them in a specialized training group that catered to Spanish-speaking foster parents in another city.

The following case illustrates a process of resource sharing involving a house of worship, which entailed training of and consulting with staff for provision of space and use of facilities:

> The author approached a house of worship in a New England city about using space to conduct community-based workshops targeting local residents. The church was strategically located within the community. However, this church had a reputation for avoiding any form of relationship with social service agencies. This was due in part to a previous relationship that was terminated under less than ideal circumstances. Consequently, this experience made church officials reluctant to seek partnerships. The initial effort to enlist the support of the church involved sending a letter requesting a meeting with the author. Much to the surprise of the author, a church official agreed to the meeting. The church would be willing to make space and administrative support available for the workshops. However, the

church official wanted the author to consult with religious personnel on concerns they had about some parishioners. In addition, the church requested a series of three-hour workshops on crisis counseling, alcohol and other drug abuse, and cultural awareness.

Knowledge Building and Consultation

The provision of training and consultation as a means of enhancing each party's capacity to provide higher quality services offers tremendous potential for the field of social work. Knowledge enhancement can translate into multiple types of collaborative activities, ranging from increasing staff capacities to establishment of an open referral system between social agencies and nontraditional settings.

A number of case examples are presented to highlight the tremendous range of collaborative possibilities. The first example examines a collaborative effort between botanical shops, a Latino community-based agency, and a school of social work, and illustrates the potential benefits of collaboration (Delgado & Santiago, in press a). The following description highlights the provision of multiple services:

> The training of the two botanical shop owners consisted of eight hours of instruction provided on a Sunday when businesses were closed. This scheduling facilitated participation, as businesses did not have to be closed for the owners to receive training. Participants were each paid $250.00 for their time . . . training covered the following topics: (1) cause of HIV/AIDS; (2) methods for spreading the disease; (3) length of time before symptoms appear; (4) common symptoms; and (5) testing procedures. Owners were provided with posters, brochures, and other printed (Spanish) material related to HIV/AIDS. In addition, condoms and bleach for cleaning needles were also distributed. A three-month period (June-July-August 1996) following the initial training resulted in nine individuals (17% of the total number of referrals for that period) being referred for testing. All of those referred were at high risk for contracting HIV due to injection of drugs, and displayed symptoms commonly associated with AIDS.

Progreso Latino's training of beauty parlor owners is another example of knowledge building within nontraditional settings:

> Beauty parlor owners and workers are in unique positions to help their customers become better informed about HIV/AIDS. They, too, are in positions that can make them subject to risk. The training program consisted of 10 hours of basic information concerning transmission of HIV and the necessary precautions that beauticians must take to minimize spread through contact with infected blood. Participants were paid $75.00 and donations from a cosmetic company.

According to Progreso Latino staff, the program was very successful. The initial year involved five beauty parlors. The second year, the number increased to seven, with no concerted outreach:

> The program was so successful that word of mouth among beauty parlor owners resulted in an increased demand for training. Seven owners telephoned the agency and requested training for themselves and asked that available staff do workshops with customers. Owners, when questioned about their primary motivation for participating in this program, stated the following: (1) the importance of HIV/AIDS information for their own health; (2) concern about the spread of AIDS in the community; and (3) fear that if they did not participate, customers will leave them for parlors that offered this training—in short, it made good business sense.

The involvement of botanical shops in the prevention of AIDS has been accomplished in several cities, New York being one example (Navarro, 1989, p. B4):

> [The executive director of the] . . . Association for Drug Abuse Prevention and Treatment, which provides services for drug addicts, said she has recruited at least a dozen owners of shops known as botanicas to pass AIDS prevention messages to customers who are usually seeking an herbal cure or spiritual advice . . . [the executive director] said she would use botanicas as outreach posts because "you have to deal within the culture." Next month the agency will give the shopkeepers a workshop on "AIDS 101," . . . and supply them with literature, condoms and sterilization kits for needles used by intravenous drug users.

Outreach

The concept of outreach can be misleading if defined within very narrow parameters. Outreach is a complex concept that involves more than just "reaching out" to underserved populations. Outreach also entails provision of multiple services, not the least of which can involve coordination, networking, advocacy, counseling, to list a few. Cases are presented to highlight the possibilities for this form of service collaboration.

The concept of outreach is well operationalized by a Latino outreach worker who states (Pina, 1995, p. 1C):

> Hispanics, because of their culture, don't like to discuss sex, so they don't talk about AIDS, never mind go to a meeting. . . . We have to go to them and make it comfortable so they can talk about it . . . AIDS educators . . . took condoms and packets of AIDS information and started visiting a laundromat, beauty salons and people's homes to educate them about the dangers and prevention of AIDS . . . taking AIDS information into community settings has been effective because social agencies that know their community have participated in trying to solve the problem . . . It was absolutely

effective because we reached people who may not have a tendency to seek out information.

One project based in Philadelphia, Pennsylvania, focused on distributing HIV/AIDS-related printed materials in a host of nontraditional settings (Bond et al., 1997, p. 290):

> Role model stories are also distributed through more than 100 businesses and institutions in the target community that support the project by serving as media drop sites. These sites include bars, hair salons, fast food restaurants, health centers, the local library, a parole office, and check cashing centers. In most cases, these sites provide counter space for the materials; some, however, are more actively involved in distributing the materials to patrons. For instance, the owner of a neighborhood variety store regularly places the materials into customers' bags.

The following case example occurred in Richmond, California, which is located approximately 10 miles from San Francisco, next to Berkeley. The City of Richmond has a population of approximately 82,700 with a sizable racial/ethnic composition. African Americans account for the largest segment of the population with 44 percent (31,600), followed by Latinos with 15 percent (12,700), and Asian and Native Americans with 12 percent (10,300). The case involving a Cambodian family, an African American church, and a Buddhist temple, highlights how houses of worship can provide assistance across denominations, if asked to help (Delgado, 1995d, pp. 20–21):

> This family emigrated to the United States three years ago from a refugee camp in Cambodia . . . They live in a single-family house . . . [in a] racially mixed neighborhood . . . For over a year, the family had been the object of random violence perpetrated against them, both the parents and the children, as they went about their daily routines. The eldest daughter had been a member of [an after school group] for almost a year. Eventually she brought her family's plight to the attention [of the worker]. The caseworker made a house call . . . [and] learned that the mother was Buddhist and feeling a great spiritual void, in addition to the overwhelming emotions she was experiencing in trying to adapt to a new country. Taking this cue, the caseworker contacted the Buddhist Temple in Oakland and asked if they would assist in some way. She also enlisted the attention of the neighborhood African-American Christian church. The Buddhist monks arranged with the family to perform an ancient ritual around the house, which would banish the evil spirits and break the cycle of negativity. The family invited some of their friends and neighbors to join them in the ceremony. The caseworker extended an invitation to the African-American clergy leadership . . . Everyone showed up . . . The family has not experienced any harassment since this event . . . The parents are continuing their involvement with the Buddhist temple and they have, in a modest way, continued to initiate communication with their neighbors.

The Asian and Pacific Islander Coalition on HIV/AIDS (APRICHA), based in New York City, employed a worker to undertake outreach and community education in Asian and Pacific Islander nontraditional settings (Sengupta, 1996, p. 37):

> As an outreach worker . . . Ms. Li has made it her mission to convince Asians that AIDS is a real threat. To get their attention, she travels to corners of the city not traditionally visited by AIDS educators: massage parlors and church meetings, beauty salons and taxi stands . . . delivering AIDS prevention messages can be tedious . . . safe-sex wisdom isn't always enough for immigrants who may be more concerned about getting green cards than contracting HIV.

One program (Shop Talk) in Hackensack, New Jersey, targeted distribution of HIV/AIDS materials to grooming establishments (see section on Community Education below for a description of their educational component) (Hutzler, 1991, p. 2):

> The grooming specialists were urged to moderate the message according to their clientele and to do whatever they can to raise public awareness, whether it be putting up posters, handing out pamphlets, providing condoms, or just talking about it . . . "We try to put a human face on AIDS . . . AIDS is not a gay disease. It's not a homosexual disease. It affects us all."

Shop Talk focused on small nontraditional settings that catered to meeting the cosmetic needs of women and men (Annual Report, 1994, pp. 26–27):

> "Shop Talk" . . . educated area barbers, hairstylists, and salon employees . . . and made AIDS literature and referral information available to their clients. The worker visits the shops on a monthly basis (more often when presentation requests are made). Literature is distributed on HIV/AIDS, STDs, and drug and alcohol prevention for personnel and patrons. The owners of the establishments are very supportive of our outreach and have made it possible for the counselor to deliver their messages.

Like APRICHA, Life Force, a program based in Brooklyn, New York, targeted outreach to women of color, particularly those who were Latina and African American (Life Force, 1994, p. 1):

> . . . Brooklyn accounted for 31% of all AIDS cases diagnosed among women, the highest number for all five boroughs of New York City. Of these cases, 85% were reported in African-American and Latina women, indicating the extraordinary disproportionate impact of AIDS in women of color . . . In spite of these alarming statistics, few programs exist to edu-

cate women in disenfranchised communities of color about their risk of HIV infection and what women can do to protect themselves.

Life Force not only targets women of color who are residents, it also employs them in their programs (Life Force, 1994, p. 1):

> Located in . . . one of the areas of highest AIDS incidence in the United States, Life Force recruits, trains and supervises community women who have a passionate commitment to preventing the further spread of HIV/AIDS and assisting those already infected with the virus. Women involved in Life Force bring a unique perspective to this project, since they are all HIV positive themselves or care for loved ones who are infected. Life Force peer educators receive stipends . . . during training and $5.00 per hour for the community outreach that they do after they are trained. In addition, the women receive reimbursement for travel and are assisted with their child care expenses.

The philosophical basis for Life Force hiring community residents has saliency for other groups, as well (Life Force, 1994, p. 2):

> The Life Force peer education model is based on the premise that people will respond best to preventive health messages when this information is presented in their own language and vernacular by persons with whom they share characteristics, norms and concerns. The peer education model in AIDS prevention work has already proven effective in slowing the spread of HIV infection in largely middle-class, gay, and white male communities, but has been tried on a much more limited scale among women, people of color, and hard-to-serve groups such as substance abusers and prisoners.

Life Force outreach workers target nontraditional settings, including the homes of residents (Life Force, 1994, p. 3):

> Street and door-to-door outreach target those women who may not be using organized health or social services including substance abusers and alcoholics, homeless women and illegal [undocumented] aliens . . . Based on the Tupperware or lingerie party models, Safer Sex parties in people's homes have proved to be a highly successful mode of reaching women in a lively, comfortable and nonthreatening atmosphere, enabling more frank discussion of safer sex methods and barriers to using these methods. These parties are generally held in the evening or on a weekend, snacks or a meal is served, and small gifts are given to participants and the hostess. The atmosphere, which is convivial, relaxed and fun, promotes learning about what is otherwise a highly charged and difficult subject. The possibility for dialogue, lacking in many outreach settings, also allows for in-depth discussion and the potential for behavior change.

The case example of Hotel Alert does a wonderful job of showing how social workers can initiate and direct services involving nontraditional settings (Wagner, 1985, pp. 8–9):

Recognizing the inability of traditional social services to reach single room occupants, two social work students from San Diego State University developed an outreach program to locate and assist downtown SRO residents. This effort, known as Hotel Alert, was designed to link a social worker with the existing natural helpers in the SROs. The social worker . . . trained the managers and other hotel staff in the types of problems and concerns facing elderly residents, services available within the downtown, and how to utilize them effectively. A directory of social service agencies was provided to hotel managers, and police assigned to the downtown were oriented to the program to enlist their help in referring seniors in need of assistance. Hotel staff, residents and police were provided with a wallet-sized Hotel Alert card to call us directly or refer seniors. An answering machine takes after-hour calls, which are returned the following morning.

There are others ways organizations can undertake outreach that are not very labor intensive. For example, information related to an organization or service can be printed on grocery bags and distributed within the community. One organization (Northwest AIDS Foundation) in Seattle, Washington, did just that (Bartley, 1993, p. F1):

Another hallmark came a few years ago, when QFC printed on grocery bags information about the [fundraising] walk. If anyone would have told me back in '83 that a major grocery store would have the walk on their grocery bags, I wouldn't have believed it.

Su Salud (Your Health) is the final case illustration of community outreach. On the surface, the case of Su Salud, in Stockton, California, may not seem out of the ordinary. The city of Stockton, California is located in the northern central area of the state and is the seat of the San Joaquin county. Stockton was founded in the late 1840s and grew as a supply center during the California Gold Rush. It is an industrial port city and is the easternmost Pacific deep-water port on the West Coast. Stockton's population was 210,943 in 1990, an increase from close to 150,000 in 1980. According to the 1990 U.S. Census Bureau, three groups of color represent 58 percent of the total population: African Americans (10%), Latinos (25%; primarily Mexicans), and Asians (23%; primarily Filipinos).

Su Salud is a health organization that initiates and supports a community health fair. However, this is no ordinary organization (it is a dentistry group), and this is no ordinary health fair (the nation's largest volunteer health fair). In many ways a dentist's office can be considered a nontraditional setting if it initiates and undertakes services that go beyond the usual expectations associated with that setting.

The case example of Su Salud illustrates the possibilities of health and social service organizations going far beyond their usual mission to meet a community need, tapping indigenous resources, and being willing to engage in collaborative activities with other human service and nontraditional settings such as houses of worship.

After initial, unsuccessful, efforts at reaching out to migrants in local labor camps, the leadership of Su Salud enlisted the assistance of a local church in an effort to win the trust of migrant workers (Fiffer & Fiffer, 1994, p. 131):

> Frustrated by their inability to gain the trust of more laborers in the camp, the trio turned to the church—not for prayer, but for an endorsement and a pulpit. "Most of the workers are very religious . . . We went to their pastors and said, 'You take care of their souls. Please give us fifteen minutes at the end of your service and tell your congregation that if anyone leaves, they'll go directly to hell. Then let us talk about their bodies.'" The pastors agreed to cooperate, albeit using their own words, and the three doctors finally had a captive audience—literally. "Some of the padres locked the church doors so no one could escape while we talked about prevention [of illness]."

After this initial effort, which proved very successful, Su Salud took another approach (Fiffer & Fiffer, 1994, pp. 131–132):

> After this successful "mass marketing" effort, Guillermo sought a larger pulpit. He visited television and radio stations that served the Spanish-speaking community and asked for air time to spread his message of prevention. Most accommodated him . . . Guillermo might have continued along this path for the rest of his professional career, if not for a pastor who challenged him one Sunday in 1987. "Why don't you do more than just come to my church and talk about prevention?" the clergyman said. "Why don't you do screening?"

The outreach services provided by Su Salud through its annual fair are in direct response to an unmet need for health and social services (Su Salud, 1996, p. 1)

> The Central Valley of California, from Bakersfield to Sacramento, has the second highest concentration of medically uninsured people in the United States. There are 700,000 individuals in this area without medical insurance and 190,000 of these are children. In San Joaquin County alone, the medically indigent population is estimated to be 150,000. In the last nine years, Su Salud has screened, immunized, counseled and referred over 70,000 people free of charge and without commercialization or public funds. We have found that 90% of fair participants do not have health insurance, cannot afford to pay for regular health care and have no other choice but to wait until it becomes a medical emergency.

Su Salud has grown dramatically over the years (Su Salud, 1996, p. 2):

> Su Salud and its innovative approach to health care for the poor has put Stockton on the map. What a handful of Latino professionals started over 15 years ago with a one-day health clinic at an east Stockton church has become the annual, all-volunteer health and education fair, the nation's largest.

Su Salud, although involving volunteer professionals from a variety of disciplines, has taken a purposeful approach toward obtaining funding for the fair and related activities. When asked if Su Salud has avoided certain funding sources, the answer was yes! (Su Salud, 1996, p. 3):

> One of the first times I received a call from the State of California (Department of Public Health), they wanted to give money to help Su Salud, provided that I fill out forms the size of a phone book. I could not do it. The bureaucracy is so phenomenal when you deal with the government, both state and federal. We decided right then and there, no government. Many private companies want a trade [something in return for financial assistance]. We say, no conditions. Colgate gives us 20,000 toothbrushes, 500 T-Shirts, helps with promotion of the fair, vignettes on Spanish television, pays for dental students to be transported from the University of California at San Francisco. They do not ask for anything in return. They want nothing in return. We have established a wonderful relationship with them. When you have this kind of relationship, it is magnificent. We do have our rules, however. [We could have lots of donated items.] When they say they want to do this and that, we say no trade, no conditions. If you want to contribute, fine, but nothing in return.

In a separate interview, Dr. Guillermo Vacuna noted the importance of taking a stand with potential funders (Fiffer & Fiffer, 1994, pp. 132–133):

> As Su Salud's administrator, Guillermo is adamant that no strings be attached to any donations. Recently a beer company offered a $60,000 grant. In return, Guillermo was asked to post a banner with the company's logo. "I turned them down," he says. "How would it look for a health fair that counsels about alcohol and drug abuse to promote a beer company."

Funding, regardless of source, almost always has conditions attached to it. In the case of Su Salud, there is an effort to garner positive publicity. However, government funding is not without strings and excessive paperwork. Consequently, social service agencies must be very careful in obtaining funding for work with nontraditional settings so as not to compromise their mission and projects. Many people in nontraditional settings are very wary of agencies because they fear that cooperation on a project may cause undue hardships for their establishment and customers.

Su Salud utilizes a variety of methods for reaching out to the uninsured. However, word-of-mouth among agricultural workers over the years seems to have had the most positive results:

> There is no question that Su Salud's success is due to a multitude of factors. The involvement of the Catholic Church, due to the high percentage of migrant workers who were Catholic, played an instrumental role in getting Su Salud off the ground. However, the use of informal communication, in this case, word-of-mouth, played a tremendous role in getting the message out. Individuals who attended previous fairs spoke highly of their experiences to new workers. In addition, they would often be willing to accompany the new workers to the fair. This personal contact could only be achieved when previous attenders outreached and promoted the fair within their community. Word-of-mouth, although very effective, requires considerable expenditure of time. However, there is no substitute for this form of communication and validation, and it should not be dismissed as a method of disseminating information, particularly among groups who may not be accessible through "typical" means because of their documented status.

Community Education

The provision of community education is without question a valuable service for a variety of reasons: (1) it engages the community through an educational process that not only imparts information, but can also be empowering; (2) to be effective, it must transpire in the community to increase accessibility; and (3) if properly undertaken, it can lead to case finding and development of other important services. In short, community education lends itself very well to involving nontraditional settings.

The case example of APRICHA (Asian & Pacific Islander Coalition on HIV/AIDS) serves to illustrate the variety of ways community education can transpire within a cultural context (Chan, 1992, p. 17):

> An Asian AIDS education group is giving out safe sex fortune cookies with messages such as "New Chinese proverb says, "AIDS does not discriminate!" and "Live long and prosper, practice safer sex." We are trying to be innovative and to use cultural reference points that people are familiar with . . . the group's health educator said the cookies have been useful in promoting Chinese immigrants, who usually treat sex and AIDS as taboo, to ask questions about the disease and condoms . . . Each cookie is individually wrapped with the group's name and phone number printed outside . . . Among other messages in the cookies are "Be proud, always carry a condom" and "Love your children, talk to them about AIDS and safe sex."

APRICHA outreach and community education workers have also targeted a variety of nontraditional settings in their efforts to reach and educate the community on HIV/AIDS (Mangaliman, 1994, p. A12):

Resurrection [outreach/community educator] goes to nail salons and beauty parlors in immigrant communities in Queens and Manhattan. While they're having their cuticles soaked or their hair pinned in a French Twist, she talks to customers about the proper use of condoms, the risks of transmission of HIV in unprotected sex, or the advantages of HIV testing. "Is this your first time here?" the 46-year-old Filipino immigrant says, addressing a South Indian customer getting her "tips," or nails, repaired at the Thai Beauty Salon in Woodside, Queens. Before the customer can look up, Resurrection, smiling, is handing her a brochure on AIDS and giving her a spiel on the ever-increasing rate of HIV infection in Asia . . . The coalition [also] does outreach in other areas: the Cambodian market in Crown Heights in Brooklyn, the No. 7 subway to Flushing during school hours and so-called "tofu-parties" hosted by gay Asian men who get together to talk about safe sex.

APRICHA has targeted women because of their high-risk status and the paucity of prevention efforts focused on this group (Mangaliman, 1994, p. A12):

A lot of immigrant women have no access to health care, and the traditional focus [of HIV prevention] has been gay men and not women . . . Immigrant women go to nail salons,' Resurrection said. Indeed, the Thai Beauty Salon . . . has a polyglot customer base: Vietnamese, Thais, Filipinos, South Indians, Cambodians, Irish, Central Americans.

The same organization has developed innovative ways of distributing condoms. Condoms cannot be distributed without regard to cultural factors. Consequently, the more a condom is placed within a culture-specific context, the higher the likelihood that it will be used. The diversity of the Asian community, as a result, requires that condom distribution takes into account national origins. The following descriptions of five differently wrapped condoms illustrate this point (Sengupta, 1996, p. 37):

Chinese: Red rectangular pouch that is traditionally stuffed with money and given as a gift during Chinese New year; Filipino: Pale blue tube that resembles a sugar candy known as "pastillas;" Japanese: Red square wrapped in origami style; Cambodian: Green and blue crepe-paper flower wrapped in a traditional Cambodian style; and Thai: Red crepe-paper pyramids resembling traditional gift wrap.

A Boston, Massachusetts, organization called Men of Color Against Aids (MoCAA) has developed a variety of approaches for engaging men of color who have sex with other men.

The focus of the agency is on education/information delivery through entertainment (i.e., poetry, music, dance). Service delivery in this form is an effort to better communicate with the target population, which is African

American men. The agency is small (two staff). MoCAA holds several annual events. For instance, there is a New Year's Eve party, a boat cruise around the harbor and several community forums which encompass ongoing conversations, food, and music. Many of these events are held in various hotels, nightclubs, and bars. The organization makes a concerted effort to hold these events in settings which are easily accessible to public transportation and where participants can be relaxed and themselves. Information is provided to participants in a language/mode with which they could identify, understand and remember.

MoCAA's work in bars is an excellent example of using nontraditional settings in conducting community education and outreach.

MoCAA has taken a multifaceted and highly creative approach toward community education and bars:

The organization is currently in the process of expanding outreach and community education to more than gay, bisexual, and transgendered men of color. It is also seeking to reach gay, lesbian, bisexual, and transgendered youths. It is very important that activities targeting this community also seek to develop community in the process. People of color who are gay, lesbian, bisexual, and transgendered are very marginal in this society. They do not fit with their white counterparts. They do not fit within the straight communities of color. Consequently, there is a need for the development of a sense of community. The work with bars is part of the organization's efforts called "edumatainment" (educate and entertain) using an entertaining situation to educate the community on issues related to AIDS. MoCAA is currently working with one bar to provide education on HIV/AIDS and develop a sense of community in the process. The manager of a gay bar was approached about sponsoring a night devoted to AIDS prevention. Upon agreement, the organization provides staff for the function (no bartenders), Go-Go Dancers for entertainment, advertises in key community outlets, and issues invitations to members. The bar, as a result, can expect approximately 150 patrons to attend this function. Information and condoms, lubricants, etc., are provided in baskets that are placed throughout the establishment. Consequently, a bar benefits from positive publicity within the community and increased business from the event. MoCAA plans to train the Go-Go Dancers to also do education about "safer sex" as part of their performance.

One program called Men of Color Aids Project (MOCAP), in Cleveland, Ohio, has developed a multifaceted community education project targeting gay and bisexual men of color. Their program has focused primarily on three nontraditional settings:

MOCAP has focused on delivering prevention messages within three community-based settings: (1) restaurants; (2) barbershops; and (3) bars. These settings have been selected because they are located within communities of color, are conducive to holding talks, and have the space for workshops, support groups, etc. Approximately 15 participants attend a weekly two-hour support group. The restaurant is closed during this period to facilitate discussions. The bar was selected because on Friday nights a well-known female impersonator performs a show. This performer knows a staff member of MOCAP and was able to broker with the owner of the bar to allow the organization to set up a booth on HIV/AIDS. The booth is open from 11 P.M. to 2 A.M. during which time it is staffed. A number of "visuals" are displayed emphasizing "safer sex" methods. In addition, staff engage in a question and answer format involving participants. No formal presentation is made, thereby minimizing the disruption of business. Five barbershops participate in the prevention program. These establishments were selected by staff because of their history of participating with human service agencies on prior campaigns.

One AIDS/HIV research project based in Mississippi (Biloxi and Hattiesburg), and Louisiana (Monroe), focused on gay bars and the training of bartenders to help identify opinion leaders for specialized prevention training (Kelly et al., 1992, p. 1484):

> . . . each bartender in that city's gay clubs was trained to observe people in the club independently over a 1-week period and to identify individuals who were most popular with gay men . . . . Bartenders served as judges because they were familiar with club socialization patterns. Persons receiving nominations by more than one bartender were considered to be popular opinion leaders and were recruited for training. . . . Opinion leaders attended four weekly 90-minute sessions that taught them the social skills they needed to serve as risk reduction endorsers to their peers.

In Central Falls/Pawtucket, Rhode Island, a Latino community-based organization (Progreso Latino), the lead agency, has developed a multifaceted approach towards HIV/AIDS education (Spanish and English) targeting nontraditional settings:

> The overall project goal is to continue to provide AIDS/HIV information in nonthreatening, personalized settings, to foster open dialogue and encourage community participation and referrals . . . [through] three program components: (1) Laundromats; (2) Safety Net Parties; and (3) Hair Salons.

The laundromat component of the initiative also involved another community-based organization in the provision of child care during the workshops. This program targets certain parts of the city and enlists the support of laundromats in the provision of workshops on HIV/AIDS:

> Laundromats are ideal settings for dissemination of information on AIDS and other problems confronting the community. Customers often find

themselves wasting time waiting for their laundry to be cleaned and dried and there is very little for them to do for several hours while this process transpires. These settings are usually well lit and have space to conduct a workshop. Consequently, Progreso Latino has developed a program to do AIDS education. Information related to these workshops, days, time, and location, is distributed throughout the community. Participants are paid a small stipend to participate and take a pre- and post-test in Spanish. The program consists of a short lecture, showing a video, discussion, and a question and answer period.

In Hackensack, New Jersey, an education program targeted beauticians and sought to better prepare them to address the topic of HIV/AIDS with their customers (Hutzler, 1991, p. 2):

> AIDS was one topic Juanita Guzzone would never have discussed while gossiping with her customers at the Charm Salon and Skin Center . . . But since attending an Englewood, N.J., Health Department Seminar on Monday, Guzzone has been talking about the deadly disease non-stop with everybody. "It's not a disease you can put in the closet and forget about . . . You have to talk about it" . . . Guzzone was one of 79 hairdressers, manicurists and barbers . . . who went to the department's first "Shoptalk" seminar, an outreach program designed to spread information on AIDS in those places where sometimes, racy, but less threatening conversation usually reigns.

The last case involves a partnership between a house of worship and an agency. Project Spirit (Strength, Perseverance, Imagination, Responsibility, Integrity and Talent), is an initiative involving an African American church and a nonprofit organization in Washington, D.C. (Holmstrom, 1996b, pp. 7–8):

> Mr Terry is the sparkplug and tireless coordinator for Project Spirit, an after-school tutorial and life-skills program created by the Congress of National Black Churches (CNBC) for inner-city children ages 6 to 12. As drugs and violence have become more commonplace in cities over the last decade, many black churches—traditional cornerstones for black communities—have stepped forward to offer children a safe learning haven. About 45 churches in 12 American cities offer the CNBC program . . . CNBC, a voluntary, nonprofit organization, provides a Project Spirit curriculum and training for churches. Both are designed to help build self-esteem in children, provide cultural appreciation, and bolster a child's capacity to do well in life and in school . . . Churches are not traditionally structured to provide this level of service . . . so we help them to implement this program, We have learned that churches have to develop an infrastructure and resources to support their efforts.

Counseling/Advice Giving

The enhancement of counseling/advice giving on the part of those in nontraditional settings is one approach to collaborative activities. It would be simplistic and unfair to think that counseling or advice giving is not freely provided and expected in nontraditional settings. Most of this counseling can probably be classified as crisis intervention. However, it very often represents a service that consumers have learned to expect and value. Consequently, the development of collaborative activities that strengthen counseling is very much in order. However, capacity enhancement must be conceptualized as two-sided—namely, social workers and other helping professionals can learn from those in nontraditional settings about approaches, interviewing skills, relationship building, and so forth.

Delgado and Rosati (in press), based on their study of Pentecostal churches in Holyoke, Massachusetts, stress the importance of enhancing counseling capacity in nontraditional settings:

> The provision of training represents one method for maximizing limited resources. There is no question that ministers are important community impactors; consequently, it is necessary to assess their needs . . . and provide the necessary support through training and consultation. Increasing their competence . . . will represent an important step in the development of collaboration between churches and agencies. However, it would be a tremendous mistake to conceptualize training as strictly one-sided—namely, ministers and key church members can also serve to train . . . staff in the methods they use to reach and help their congregation. Training is generally not labor intensive and can serve as an excellent foundation for more ambitious projects once there is a relationship built on mutual trust.

Enhancement of counseling skills, in this case related to smoking cessation, was central among several activities undertaken with Boston-area African American churches (The Medical Foundation, 1995, p. 5):

> Churches Organized to Stop Tobacco (C.O.S.T.) is a collaborative project of TMF [The Medical Foundation] and churches in Dorchester, Roxbury, and Mattapan. C.O.S.T. is an innovative church-based smoking education, prevention, and cessation model to reduce the use of tobacco within communities of color. C.O.S.T. provides skills training to lay volunteers in smoking cessation counseling, delivers "Intervention Sunday" sermons to congregations, and organizes health fairs offering health promotion, information, and referrals to community agencies.

Churches were selected as the primary sites for this project because of their importance within the African American community (C.O.S.T., 1995, p. 1):

> Historically, the church is the most stable institution and the strongest voice within the African American community, and provides an excellent and effective channel for health promotion and intervention within communities of color . . . As the central message of the church is the proclamation of hope, the smoking cessation theme is consistent with the church's mission of healing.

The project's covenant stressed the impact of tobacco within the African American community (C.O.S.T., 1995, p. 1):

> We agree to work together as members of the C.O.S.T. project, toward the prevention and spread of tobacco consumption. We agree as Pastors and Lay people to speak publicly and privately about the costs to health and well-being of those who smoke. We agree to eliminate the addiction of nicotine, to support smoking cessation, and to educate the African American community about the dangers of tobacco.

All six participating churches agreed to undertake the following activities (C.O.S.T., 1995, p. 3):

> Recruit volunteers from the congregations to assist in the design of the program and materials. Provide skills training to lay volunteers in smoking cessation counseling. Provide space for counseling sessions, support groups, and other activities. Publicize C.O.S.T. activities in church publications. Identify and provide referral to treatment resources for people identified with health problems. Maintain confidentiality of all health information about participants in the program. Provide technical assistance and equipment for health fairs, sessions, and activities. Assist with the evaluation of the success of the program activities.

The success of coffeehouses, which are very popular in most, if not all, parts of the country, opens up possibilities for social agencies to develop collaborative projects within these nontraditional settings or to establish their own coffeehouse as a means of reaching out to undervalued groups. The case in Farmingdale, Long Island, is an example in which an agency receives funds from the state (AIDS Institute for HIV Prevention) to provide services to an underage and undervalued group, and has done so by establishing a coffeehouse (Lee, 1995, p. A18):

> The coffeehouse . . . is part of a nascent gay youth social scene on Long Island. It opened June 2 [1995] to provide an alcohol-free social environment for gay, lesbian and bisexual youth. "We wanted a coffeehouse to be a safe alternative to the bar scene . . . We wanted gay kids to develop socialization skills that other kids get, that they can't get at a bar because they are forced into a situation that they are not ready for. Kids benefit from an environment that does not emphasize sex and sexuality." . . . Experts say that the coffeehouse represents a social effort to combat the loneliness and isolation that gay teenagers often feel in a conservative suburban culture. "You feel like you're the only gay person in the area . . . You don't hear about other gay people." . . . On the coffeehouse's second floor, loud music is pumped through a stereo system. The walls are covered with a pastel seaside mural and strings of Christmas lights sparkle in the dim light . . . The table by the door is laden with safe-sex and HIV prevention pamphlets, boxes of condoms and issues of mainstream gay magazines . . . The

building is a 15-minute walk from the Farmingdale railroad station, making it accessible for many gay teens who lack a driver's license. The coffeehouse has reimbursed for the fares of the first trip.

Key Points and Considerations

The following are key points that must be considered: (1) agencies cannot easily disengage from collaboration with nontraditional settings once funding terminates for services; (2) nontraditional setting assistance must be validated; (3) collaborative activities are determined by the nature of the nontraditional setting; (4) hiring indigenous staff and retaining staff can prove labor intensive for an agency; (5) high turnover rates among nontraditional setting staff can prove to be a challenge; and (6) successfully initiating and establishing outreach services can serve as a basis for more formalized service delivery.

Agencies Cannot Easily Disengage from Collaboration with Nontraditional Settings Once Funding Terminates for Services

Delgado (1996f, p. 12), in summarizing the experiences, issues, challenges, and rewards related to the California case example, issues a word of warning to human service organizations used to a "business as usual" approach towards collaboration: involve community when seeking funding; ignore community when the money is allocated; terminate relationship when money is expended:

> . . . community-based organizations cannot easily disengage . . . once a project's funding is terminated; in short, engagement raises expectations that the relationship is long-term. The benefits for both parties . . . are very positive, with implications that are far reaching.

The original Hotel Alert program was established in the late 1970s and early 1980s, and operated until the mid-1980s, at which time funding was terminated and the program formally closed. Between that time and the time Hotel Alert was reestablished (1996), not much harm resulted from the closing of the program because of a set of unique circumstances:

> Although the program was formally closed, staff still maintained informal contact with several hotels, although not all (originally there were 35 hotels participating in the program). This informal contact served to facilitate reestablishment of the program approximately ten years later. High hotel staff turnover made it easier to reestablish contact with previously participating hotels and to develop new relationships without addressing the "hard" feelings associated with termination of services.

Not all nontraditional settings may have high staff turnover or lend themselves to informal levels of communication. It is important to take into account the nature of the setting before deciding whether or not the agency is willing to continue with some form of service delivery, although in limited form, before establishing a program. Highly stable staff in a nontraditional setting will not easily forget engagement and disengagement in future contacts.

Work within nontraditional settings must not be viewed as a novelty that can result in numerous funding proposals. Involvement of nontraditional settings should not be undertaken with getting funds as a central goal. These settings should not be used to "go after money" to provide services. As shown throughout this book, these settings are generally staffed by individuals who view helping not as a vocation, but as central to their lives and as a way of interacting with people. These settings cannot be engaged and disengaged at will. Consequently, this presents a formidable challenge for social workers and the agencies that employ them—namely, are they willing to be there for the "duration," or will they pull out when the money is no longer available? If the answer is yes to the former, then the time and effort invested in these settings will provide a countless number of opportunities for collaboration in the present and the future.

If the answer is yes to the latter, pulling out of a relationship would have tremendous implications for the agency and its employees throughout the community, making it nearly impossible for the community to trust the agency again. It is important to remember that staff invariably come and go; in many ways, that is the nature of being a professional. However, agencies tend to survive and change over time depending on environmental demands and circumstances. Thus, institutional investment in the community, in this case nontraditional settings, will serve to allow future staff to engage in collaborative activities. Relationships cannot be turned on and off like a water faucet. People in nontraditional settings tend to have very long memories!

Nontraditional Setting Assistance Must Be Validated

Social service organizations must find ways to publicly validate the work of those in nontraditional settings collaborating in service delivery. Senior Community Centers of San Diego developed an extensive system for rewarding participating nontraditional settings (Wagner, 1985, pp. 10–11):

> The role of the community is an important one for the success of Hotel Alert. Twice a year, a luncheon is held for managers and owners of hotels participating in the program. [The social worker] solicits their advice and comments on the program, and constantly tailors Hotel Alert to meet the changing needs of the older person. This is also an occasion to honor the managers for their continued support of the program. Certificates of appreciation are awarded, which are proudly displayed in hotel lobbies throughout the downtown.

Collaborative Activities Are Determined by the Nature of the Nontraditional Setting

It is important to note that not all nontraditional settings lend themselves equally to outreach or community education. This point is well borne out by APRICHA's experience with the Asian community.

> There are certain settings within the Asian community that lend themselves to outreach and community education on HIV/AIDS. Places such as beauty parlors and nail salons lend themselves to distribution of condoms. Condoms can be wrapped and placed in a strategic place within the setting, allowing customers to take them without undo attention. Restaurants, however, do not lend themselves to this method. One Chinese restaurant owner refused to allow an outreach worker to leave condoms in a bowl. The owner's rationale for not allowing this was that it would give a "negative" impression of his restaurant to customers and the public.

Involvement of nontraditional settings must be viewed strategically and take into account the nature of the activity, setting, and the implications it has for the general public. Some of these less than "conducive" settings may be willing only to distribute pamphlets or educational materials, but not, condoms, for example.

Criteria for selecting nontraditional settings must include the following: (1) high volume of traffic; (2) atmosphere conducive to engagement; and (3) time for dialogue. It is very important to identify and engage nontraditional settings where there is a high volume of community traffic. High volume, by itself is not the sole criterion for selection. A newspaper stand in a high-traffic intersection may have a high volume of resident contacts. However, the setting is not conducive to interactions of any depth because it lacks the atmosphere for in-depth conversation.

High volume of traffic. Nontraditional settings become increasingly attractive for collaboration when they set the stage for a constant flow of traffic. This flow of traffic increases the likelihood that any effort at reaching a community will result in a high number of encounters. High volume, however, should not be measured in unrealistic numbers. The setting will dictate the volume of traffic.

A beauty parlor or laundromat, for example, may have a relatively low turnover in patrons. However, they make up for this low number by providing customers with an opportunity to spend a considerable amount of time in the setting. Restaurants, for example, may have higher turnover when compared with beauty parlors, but the time available to engage and educate a customer may not be as great. Also, the activity of eating may interfere with service delivery.

Atmosphere conducive to engagement. There are numerous nontraditional settings that lend themselves to providing a place where community residents can come together in a relaxed and safe environment. For example, one of the reasons why "Tupperware"-type gatherings have been very successful is because they take place in people's homes (Pina, 1995, p. 1C):

> To teach people about AIDS . . . holds what she calls "Tupperware parties" at people's homes. But instead of Tupperware they get food—and information about AIDS. The meetings are comfortable because everyone knows each other and participants tend to be more at ease talking about delicate topics.

Places such as bars meet this criterion, although the busy nature of the setting may act as an impediment to engagement in dialogue. Patrons who generally go to bars have sufficient time to engage in conversation. If a bar has adequate space, a section of that setting can be used for demonstrations, videos, meetings, etc., and not disrupt that natural flow of traffic and business.

Time to allow dialogue. The availability of time to engage and discuss a topic of mutual interest is critical in selecting a setting. A beauty parlor owner stated it well when she said (Pina, 1995, p. 1C) "When you are cutting someone's hair, they are a captive audience." Consequently, nontraditional settings in which customers spend a significant amount of time have the greatest potential for facilitating the delivery of services. This does not mean that a setting in which consumers spend a short period of time cannot engage in collaboration. It does mean that the type of service provision must accommodate this time period. One setting may allow for extended dialogue and demonstration of videos, etc., another setting may not and, as a result, the best activity may be distribution of materials for the customers to take home and read at their leisure.

Hiring and Retaining Indigenous Staff Can Prove Labor Intensive for an Agency

There are tremendous advantages to hiring local residents as staff, particularly capacity enhancement. However, as experienced by Life Force in Brooklyn, New York, such a strategy can result in high staff turnover rates (Life Force, 1994, p. 2):

> It should be noted that there has been attrition among Life Force peer educators over the past four years. Since some of the women who join are HIV positive, there have been illnesses and deaths within the group. Other peer educators have had to leave Life Force to care for their ill family members. Also, several women have moved from Life Force to full-time jobs in other AIDS organizations.

The Shop Talk program in Hackensack, New Jersey, has also experienced its share of challenges in hiring and supporting community residents as outreach staff (Annual Report, 1994, p. 13):

No program can function free of obstacles and setbacks, and the . . . program has had its share. Problems encountered include: limited funds . . . attracted persons with limited [formal] education, training and skills . . . Due to inexperience, the outreach worker often had problems understanding the need to document all encounters and write reports. In addition, she also had to develop outreach skills to promote the program . . . Workers need more flexibility—to be available evenings, weekends, and holidays. The low salary and unusual demands caused many applicants to withdraw from the interviewing process, coupled with the need to be available for contacts outside the 9–5 day.

The nature of work within nontraditional settings not only necessitates staff members working unusual hours, but also requires them to spend an inordinate amount of time in the field and away from the agency. Staff must constantly move from setting to setting (particularly if undertaking outreach and community education), establishing and maintaining relationships, following up, and meeting residents on their own. This puts tremendous stress on workers. The case of former drug addicts working as outreach workers presents a clear example of how no two days are alike in their work within nontraditional settings (Wlazelek, 1995, p. B1):

On the streets . . . former drug addicts are making deals with heroin users. Recovered addicts go into "shooting galleries" and other drug hot spots offering heroin users bleach kits, condoms and advice on avoiding HIV infection. In exchange, the intravenous drug users are cleaning their needles and kicking their habits . . . Instead of sending just one person into a bar or shooting gallery, outreach workers hit the streets, bars, shooting galleries and any drug "hot spot" they can identify to give IV-drug users bleach kits and demonstrate their use. The workers go door- to-door in communities . . . to offer advice and condoms to drug users and their sexual partners . . . It helps, they add, to have walked in an addict's shoes. "I'm a former IV drug user" . . . it's important for people who do this work to understand the culture . . . especially of the IV drug user, who won't trust anybody.

Stress is heightened when the work they do is significantly different from that of other staff in their agency. They may find themselves constantly explaining to other staff the nature of their work, and, unless it is an exceptional agency, they may not get the support (administrative, funding, and political) they believe they need because the organization is geared toward more conventional forms of service delivery. The following case examples do not identify an agency or community because staff requested anonymity:

The work that we do is very important. Many people and community institutions value what we do as professionals and human beings. However, it seems like we spend so much time trying to convince staff and management at the organization that the work that we do is just as "valuable" as they work other, more "conventional," staff do. Nevertheless, it feels like we are always explaining what we do and why the organization must be patient and flexible with us. The fact that we are not in the agency does not mean that we are not working or taking time off. Also, the inservice training they offer has tremendous relevance for agency staff who do not work with houses of worship, bars, and other community-based institutions. However, it really does not have applicability to what we do on a day-to-day basis. We would love to have supervision out in the community instead of always coming back to the agency. Having supervisors in the community will open their eyes concerning the nature of our work, and hopefully serve to facilitate support back at the agency. In summary, the work we do would be most difficult even under the most ideal conditions. However, it is hard to image a more challenging situation than we now face—namely, little or no support from the source that should be supporting us!

The following case, from Boston, illustrates how agencies may undermine efforts at involving nontraditional settings, even when they approve the initiative:

When a social worker at a small health center in Boston brought her idea to use nontraditional settings such as beauty parlors for HIV/AIDS education and prevention to management, she met with an obstacle—namely, the answer was no! However, after effectively using the local media to place the center in the spotlight as a health organization with a "community conscience," the worker was given permission to schedule these outreach activities as part of her functions. Unfortunately, other than money for food at meetings, no funding or staff was provided to aid with the initiative. Working alone, the worker was unable to develop her efforts. After a few years of working on this time-demanding effort, and with lack of support, she eventually left her job.

Staff working within nontraining settings will often require consultation, training, and supervision tailored to the nature of their work. Staff support needs increase significantly when staff works within nontraditional settings. They also manifest themselves in a very different delivery of support. It must be remembered that most, if not all, of the staff's work within nontraditional settings takes place in the community. Consequently, consultation, training, and supervision must take community into account if a project targeting nontraditional services is to succeed. The Richmond, California, project highlights this quite well:

Staff in the Richmond, California, project faced numerous challenges in carrying out activities such as outreach, referral and counseling. Workers not only had to do most of their work in the community, but each ethnic/racial group (Latinos, primarily Mexican Americans; African Americans; and Indochinese, primarily Vietnamese) had only one worker assigned to them. Consequently, although all three workers carried out similar job responsibilities, their assigned groups did not share much in common, making staff support such as supervision that much more difficult. Their supervisor, as a result, was often called upon to attend various committee meetings and functions, taking them away from the office. Staff training for this project necessitated flying in a trainer from the east coast (author) to review project-related forms, etc. In essence, the project was very labor intensive from the point of view of staff support. Fortunately, staff was able to count on organizational support to carry out its job responsibilities.

High Turnover Rates among Nontraditional Setting Staff Can Prove Challenging

Social agencies not only have to contend with the possibility of high staff turnover within their organizations, they must also take into account staff turnover in nontraditional settings. According to one of the original staff members of the Senior Community Centers of San Diego's Hotel Alert program, work with single-room occupancy hotels will prove labor intensive because of hotel staff turnover:

> A considerable amount of time and energy must be devoted to recruiting and orienting hotel employees such as managers, desk clerks, and other key personnel. The experience of Hotel Alert was that hotel personnel are consistently turning over. Consequently, it is important to set aside a portion of time to reintroduce social workers and orient and answer questions of new hotel staff. In addition, it is very important not to enlist too many hotels because of high hotel turnover of staff.

Successfully Initiating and Establishing Outreach Services Can Serve as a Basis for More Formalized Service Delivery

Successful work within nontraditional settings can serve as a foundation from which to undertake more formalized and intensive service delivery. The example of Hotel Alert in San Diego, California, highlights this potential:

> Hotel Alert wishes to build upon its successful efforts at getting single-room occupancy hotel managers to work with social workers. Managers know their residents well and can serve to facilitate service delivery. Hotel Alert social workers, in turn, know the managers well. Consequently, Hotel Alert staff can broker with managers who, in turn, can broker with residents. The hope, depending upon funding, is to develop a team of service providers who can enter these single-room occupancy hotels for more extensive service delivery. Hotel Alert staff, as a result, will pave the way to facilitate team entry.

12

Evaluation

Goals

The goals for evaluation encompass those that are typically associated with any program evaluation effort, including additional ones specific to non-traditional settings: (1) assess the success or failure of service delivery and all its components; (2) determine who (consumers) benefited the most and least from the initiative, and why; (3) identify ways the partnership can be improved (cost and quality of services); (4) develop ways of eliciting the support of all parties in constructing research methods, questions, and instruments; and (5) disseminate results within the community. It is important to consider that no service initiative is perfect, be it formal or informal. Thus, goals for evaluation must not come from an "either or" mind set.

Brief Overview of Stage

Evaluating collaborative work within nontraditional settings is without question the weakest part of the framework presented in this book. There is no disputing the importance of this stage in any framework. However, the challenges associated with evaluation are further compounded when they involve nontraditional settings.

According to Owen (1993), the goals for program evaluation should be: (1) enlightenment (provision of information on program activities); (2) accountability (a means of monitoring promised results); (3) program improvement (provision of information on how to improve services); (4) program implementation (information on how to increase effectiveness); (5) program clarification (further explicate program goals); (6) program development (assist decision makers in developing appropriate forms of intervention); and (7) symbolic (provide an appearance of action or undertake public relations).

The application of these seven goals of collaboration within nontraditional settings may not be possible. Consequently, it is necessary to determine which goals are most applicable and can be measured most easily without causing undue disruptions to the agency and the nontraditional setting.

Challenges and Rewards

Program evaluation, like assessment, rarely gets the attention and resources it warrants. This phase, nevertheless, is still very important in work within nontraditional settings. Information obtained about what aspects of the partnership were successful, and why, will serve as a foundation for future endeavors. To have significance, evaluation must include information on process as well as output. Process evaluation should provide invaluable information about what factors helped the practitioner deliver services, how much effort (time and resources) was needed, how the process can be improved, and how the project can be more easily replicated. Output information, at a minimum, should specify who benefited (profile), who didn't, and why. Further, it should address how nontraditional settings benefited. Both process and output evaluation should inform agencies about how better to evaluate future collaborative partnerships. The lessons learned throughout all facets of collaboration will prove immensely helpful in the planning of future collaborations. In addition, agencies must never lose sight of outcomes—funders very often are interested only in results!

There are numerous challenges to the planning and implementation of evaluation of collaboration with nontraditional settings. A nontraditional setting's definition of success may not match that of agencies or funders. People in nontraditional settings, as evidenced in the case examples section of the chapter, are not interested in keeping records and gathering baseline data that have little meaning to them, though these are essential aspects of evaluation. Further, they may wish to remain as unintrusive as possible so as not to compromise their position within a community.

Agency staff, too, face considerable challenges in carrying out this phase. Record keeping and data gathering must be integrated into service provision. Rarely has the author encountered staff in "conventional" positions who like keeping records and responding to evaluation requirements. Thus, the challenges take on added significance for work within nontraditional settings. Staff must have "user friendly" methods that do not cause undue hardships on all parties involved in this endeavor. As a result, it is recommended that staff, like their nontraditional setting counterparts, play an integral role in the development of evaluation tools and methods; this will be a new role and experience for some staff.

In a rare evaluation effort of an intervention (HIV/AIDS education) in nontraditional settings (African American beauty parlors) in a large urban area (Detroit), the evaluators made several observations and recommendations (Witcher, Gallagher, & Perz, 1997): (1) all respondents agreed that they liked receiving HIV/AIDS information in this location, and almost all (95%) believed that others would also like to receive it there, too; (2) collaboration within nontraditional educational settings takes considerable time and resources; (3) education in nontraditional settings is subject to distractions (e.g., noise, movement through the area); (4) information gathering needs to be kept to a minimum, resulting in not obtaining important demographic data and other types of information; and (5) it is recommended that evaluations of educational initiatives use post-presentation surveys because of time limitations and to cause minimal disruption of business operations.

Key Practice Concepts

Program evaluation is influenced by various theories, concepts, and philosophical viewpoints. So too is evaluation of nontraditional setting partnerships. The challenges of evaluation involving nontraditional settings can best be met through the use of emerging perspectives regarding participation of those most affected by the interventions. It is critical that the individuals subject to intervention do not become the "subjects" of the evaluation. Evaluation must be informed and shaped by the needs of the community and those directly impacted by the intervention; in this case, nontraditional settings. Evaluation must encompass both quantitative and qualitative dimensions; input must be actively sought and recommendations incorporated into both perspectives. The nature of evaluation methodology necessitates taking into account organizational capacities, funding requirements, and local circumstances.

The evaluation phase of collaborative partnerships lends itself to the use of various concepts related to organizational development and research. Principles of continuous quality improvement, empowerment, capacity enhancement, and total quality management (TQM) can easily inform and be integrated into an evaluation methodology. These principles place evaluation within a context that stresses involvement of participants throughout all aspects of this phase. To be successful in answering key questions, evaluation must elicit input from participants (staff as well as those in nontraditional settings), to ensure their cooperation, tap their expertise, and facilitate the implementation of changes in service delivery.

The following two approaches to evaluation can provide the context, process, and tools to achieve the goals of this phase of the framework. Each of these approaches will guide practitioners in all aspects of a process that has important political ramifications and requires careful thought and consideration.

Empowerment evaluation has received increased attention in the human services field (Fetterman, Kaftarian, & Wandersman, 1996). This form of evaluation is based on a philosophical foundation stressing development of knowledge and change for the betterment of those who are oppressed. In addition to measuring the impact of change, it also serves to involve those most affected by the information that has been generated, and enhances their skills in the process. This form of evaluation lends itself to tapping organizational learning and alternative ways of knowing (Mulroy & Shay, 1997).

Capacity enhancement research evaluation, like empowerment evaluation, actively seeks to involve (often by hiring) local residents in carrying out key research and evaluation activities. Training and active supervision form the core of an approach that stresses process (skill, knowledge enhancement, and employment) as well as outcome (answers to key questions).

The above approaches are complementary. They share a set of principles that can inform evaluation of nontraditional settings and any other initiatives targeting indigenous community resources: (1) to have intrinsic meaning, evaluation must include the context in which intervention occurred; (2) participation of residents and involved personnel must not only be actively sought, but cherished; (3) evaluation results must be disseminated to a broad sector of the community and not be restricted to key stakeholders; (4) there is no one way of evaluating a program, there are multiple ways; thus a consensus decision-making process will result in the most feasible and efficient methods; and (5) evaluation must utilize methods that are nonintrusive or disruptive, and that undermine the partnerships.

Case Examples

Cases presented focus on evaluation processes and challenges facing evaluators. These case examples will illustrate the methodological and sociopolitical factors that must be taken into consideration. However, for those readers who are purists in terms of evaluation, these cases will cause distress because they stress the importance of flexibility and the need to compromise. Some of the case examples will be shared with the understanding that the source is anonymous. The first case will address data gathering methods and contextual considerations.

There is a need for cost-effective, culture-specific evaluation methods that focus on nontraditional settings. Any form of evaluation must utilize data gathering methods that are cost-effective and that gather information that will assist staff in better delivery of services to undervalued groups. Although the use of field notes as a method of recording data is unintrusive, because the recording may be done well after an intervention, it has its limitations.

The case example of Steamworks, the bath house located in Berkeley, California, highlights both the importance of evaluation and the challenges for making it work in a nontraditional setting. The services offered by Steamworks through its Health Education Program are generally well thought out and planned. However, when questioned about evaluation, the health educator stated:

> Steamworks does collect statistics. The educator counts the number of people who attend workshops and presentations and breaks these statistics down demographically. Other than these statistics, the health educator obtains verbal feedback from customers or participants. However, the idea of a substantive evaluation was "too large of an issue." He does not have the resources for it. Also, it is too difficult to conceptualize a substantive evaluation given staff turnover and other forums of information in the customer's lives.

Fox (1991, p. 237), in an analysis of the challenges of conducting community-based research with intravenous drug users (IDUs), raises important concerns, which are also applicable to work within nontraditional settings:

> Most outreach workers express anywhere from disdain to indifference regarding field notes: "I just hurry at the end of the week and just fill up the page. Who cares about the field notes? I write less and less all the time: Went to the park, passed out supplies, went home." Some workers complain that the field notes take time away from serving clients. Others are concerned about the possibility of their field notes being used for surveillance purposes by the Federal government [funding source] . . . Clearing the project has two separate agendas operating simultaneously, yet insofar as street work is a requisite for providing data for analysis, outreach work takes precedence over scientific research.

The inherent tensions that Fox describes pertaining to field notes in research and evaluation, address a fundamental point—namely, loyalty of workers to their clients versus their agencies and, indirectly, their funders (Fox, 1991, pp. 238–239):

> The lack of commitment on the part of workers to their field notes and the mission of research [evaluation] is at the core of many struggles that exemplify the polarized interests of the workers and administration . . . Tensions accumulate due to the competing demands of legitimization and funding. Justification . . . depends on outreach workers dedicating themselves to client contact as their first priority, while funding depends upon their willingness to establish need and to document their influence on the street.

Evaluation methods do not have to be built with tension or be labor intensive. The case of Hotel Alert in San Diego is a case in point. The program has historically relied on low labor-intensive and user-friendly methods for gathering data:

> Hotel Alert's data gathering methods have purposefully been streamlined to facilitate obtaining data and minimizing impositions on clients and

workers. Program-related data focus on the number of referrals from hotels, type, number, and time spent on contacts with hotel personnel, and the number of calls initiated by clients. These data allow program staff to monitor which hotels have been the most active in making referrals; data on staff contact with hotel personnel allows for a closer examination of the labor intensity of the program and helps to calculate the amount of time each contact necessitates. This information, in turn, allows for an analysis of how much effort is necessary to generate a set number of referrals. The forms used to record data are not very complicated, thus facilitating the recording of information. The nature of Hotel Alert, which requires staff to walk long distances and meeting in hotels, necessitates the use of data gathering tools that are not labor intensive or intrusive in the nature of information that is required for fulfilling funding source requirements.

Undertaking collaborative initiatives within nontraditional settings will require agencies to change forms to gather new types of information. Centro Panamericano's (Lawrence, Massachusetts) case example addresses this important point:

> The project involving botanical shops on HIV/AIDS was exciting from an organizational viewpoint. Nothing like this had ever been attempted in this organization, even though it was community based. The project was presented to the Board of Directors so that they could be informed of the initiative. The board did not raise any objections, although they did raise questions about the project. The development of the collaborative project, however, required that Centro change its intake form to gather information on utilization of botanical shops. Although the change was not enormous, it was still significant. A question was added on whether or not the applicant had been referred from a botanical shop. As a result, all individuals requesting service from Centro were asked this question.

There is no doubt that agencies actively wishing to develop collaborative projects involving nontraditional settings must undertake consciousness raising with funding sources. Funders rarely, if ever, have had to contend with the challenges associated with nontraditional settings. Consequently, their expectations very often do not take into consideration a whole host of factors. The following case, anonymously shared, brings this point to the forefront:

> We were delighted to enlist the services of a well-known community leader who is also an owner of a grocery store. This store is more than a store, it is a central meeting place for the Latino community. Don Gomez (pseudonym) agreed to work with the agency in co-sponsoring an HIV/AIDS workshop. The funder, however, raised serious concerns about our agency collaborating with a grocery store. Our proposal talked about community-based institutions but did not specify that some of these establishments were not social service agencies. Consequently, the individual

responsible for our grant refused to allow us to go through with the workshop. We explained the public relations disaster this would cause our program. However, he insisted in reviewing and approving all publicity related to our program prior to dissemination. We were able to get around this by having another Latino community-based organization take the lead on this event; we, in turn, provided all of the technical assistance, materials, etc., but could not get any "credit" for this work. Nevertheless, it still got done.

It becomes critical that social service agencies strategically think about the sources for funding for work within nontraditional settings. Usually there are exceptions: monies from local and state government have the greatest restrictions, and may not be the right source for collaboration. Foundations, corporations, and grass-roots fundraising efforts, on the other hand, generally have the greatest flexibility, and may approve work within nontraditional settings.

Pre- and post-tests are relatively easy to undertake in workshops conducted in nontraditional settings. These tests, however, must not take too long, must be in the primary language of the participants, and must not ask complicated questions. In addition, there should be some form of payment or stipend that can be offered to those individuals who complete them:

> Progreso Latino in Rhode Island has used pre- and post-tests in their work with beauty parlors and laundromats. They have found that this method of evaluation, although not ideal without combining with other methods, works well with nontraditional settings. Progreso, in the case of beauty parlors, pays participants with a bag of cosmetic supplies after the post-test. Participants in the laundromat program get paid $5.00 after the post-test, which then can be used to pay for the costs of doing laundry.

The following example of an agency actively involved with nontraditional settings highlights the limitations of pre- and post-tests when stipulated by the funding sources:

> The funder required the agency to administer a pre- and post-test to workshop participants. Unfortunately, the test was developed by someone without intimate knowledge of Latinos and their culture. Consequently, the test was considered offensive from a cultural standpoint. We, in turn, had to translate the test into Spanish. Nevertheless, we did not place too much importance on the results, so we did not encourage the participants to take too much time answering the questions. Staff, in turn, developed their own test, but the results were never shared with the funders and instead were used for internal purposes. We tried reasoning with the proper authorities but were ignored. Thus, we had to meet the requirements of the funders, but did so with meaningless data.

Key Points and Considerations

The following key points must be considered: (1) agreements must be reached with funding sources; (2) evaluation procedures and forms must have community input; and (3) utilization of both qualitative and quantitative methods must be used whenever possible.

Agreements with Funding Sources

It is essential that agencies work out the necessary agreements with funding sources prior to accepting funds. There are several reasons "business as usual" is not feasible when working with nontraditional settings: (a) the review and approval of all materials prior to dissemination may not be feasible; (b) many funders also want letters of support or formal agreement to be attached to proposals; (c) some funders fulfill active monitoring functions, often visiting community-based sites, and this may not be feasible without a great deal of preparatory work within nontraditional settings; and (d) some funders expect collaboration parties to attend regularly scheduled meetings, making it difficult, if not impossible, for those in nontraditional settings to participate, because many of these establishments need to be open long hours to make a profit.

Evaluation Procedures and Forms Must Have Community Input

The principle of involving those who may have to be evaluated in the development of forms and procedures is not new to the field of social work. Their insights and cooperation are essential if evaluation is to have meaning for them and the community. If people in nontraditional settings are to be part of any evaluation procedures, they must be involved in all aspects of the process. However, the following example highlights the barriers to this participation:

> When questioned concerning how the participating nontraditional settings were going to be involved in helping to influence the evaluation of the program, staff response was that they would not involve the settings in the design of the methods or forms. Staff expressed concern that such involvement may "turn off" these settings from participation and be construed as "monitoring." Staff went on to say that it would require a significant amount of time, concerns, and energy on everyone's part. In addition, the lack of awareness of evaluation methods on the part of nontraditional settings severely limited their participation. When questioned what would be wrong with asking for participation rather than assuming they would not want to participate, the response was "why open a potential can of worms?"

People in nontraditional settings may not wish to participate in helping to develop evaluation mechanisms, forms, etc. However, they must be provided with the opportunity to so, otherwise collaboration cannot be viewed as a process of empowerment and capacity enhancement. Participation may be limited to the wording of certain questions or the creation of questions that might be of interest to those in the setting. The option to participate, however, must never be taken out of the hands of those in nontraditional settings.

Utilization of Quantitative and Qualitative Methods Whenever Possible

This consideration should not come as a complete surprise to social workers. There is little debate in the field pertaining to the importance of these two approaches in the development of a better understanding and appreciation of individuals and communities. There is no doubt that the evaluation of collaborative activities with nontraditional settings lends itself to qualitative methods. Quantitative data without a contextual understanding serves to provide only a broad and, at times, superficial perspective on a community, and fails to generate culturally rich information for concept development.

Burton, Dilworth-Anderson, and Bengtson's (1992, p. 133) statement, although focused on elders of color, is applicable to all age groups: "[t]he predominant method for generating knowledge about ethnic minority elderly has been cross-sectional survey research . . . Although this research has been a rich source of descriptive data, it has not provided the conceptual foundation needed to develop culturally relevant theories of diversity and aging."

Qualitative data in combination with quantitative data provide a more holistic understanding of the extent of an issue, problem, concern, or intervention, and its social and cultural meaning to the group being studied. In addition, the use of qualitative methods in research helps workers gather data through understanding patterns of meaning, context, language, and culture. Henderson (1994) stresses that the value of qualitative data increases in importance when one tries to develop an understanding of ethnic and racial groups.

Conclusion

As illustrated in this chapter, involving nontraditional settings is exciting, frustrating, and time consuming, and it requires extensive thought, contemplation, and strategic thinking. It will test the values and patience of a social worker, and necessitate the stretching of what currently constitutes social work practice in urban areas with undervalued communities. The rewards, however, are equally as monumental as the challenges.

Hopefully, this application of a framework to case illustrations will serve to challenge and inspire social workers to venture out into "new worlds" in an effort to better assist and reach communities, and to further enhance their capacity to meet pressing needs.

The nontraditional settings presented in this chapter represent the "tip of the iceberg." Nontraditional settings such as dance halls, auto repair shops (they provide an opportunity for customers to sit and wait, often reading magazines), malls, arcades, public swimming pools, taxi cabs, etc., are all awaiting visits from social workers and other helping professionals willing to be creative and flexible in service delivery. The challenges for evaluation researchers, however, are quite formidable. Just as we ask practitioners to rise to the challenge through creativity, personal commitment, and energy, we also have to ask evaluators, social workers or others, to rise as well. Ultimately, all practitioners are evaluators of practice.

13

Reflections on Collaborative Practice

This chapter is intended to provide a synthesis of the material presented in this book. A variety of themes will be covered that convey to the reader the wonders and challenges of collaborating with nontraditional settings. This book represents the culmination of a journey I started as a first-year social work student; a journey that involved learning and unlearning material, challenging commonly accepted notions and knowledge, and reinforcing the importance of urban-based practice. Some of this chapter will be written in the first person—without citations, definitions, or lists interfering with the author's description of his experience in this field of practice.

Introduction

The increasing segregation of many urban-based undervalued groups in this society will require bold and innovative changes in how social work practice is conceptualized. These new forms of practice will utilize principles such as empowerment, capacity enhancement, participation, among others, to guide interventions. These interventions will necessitate changes in how agencies structure services and funders support these services. The complexity of the problems undervalued groups confront cannot be addressed just through formal interventions. Partnerships need to be developed that will systematically marshall both formal and informal sources of care giving. This book specifically addressed one form of helping.

A historic break from past thinking and behavior is necessary so that the profession may embrace the new paradigms that address the challenges of the twenty-first century. No one paradigm will allow us to achieve our goals, just as no one method can address all the needs of undervalued groups in this country. This renewal can occur only if we remember who we once were and how and where the profession started. Transitional periods are always painful and chaotic, and require significant soul searching. The nation is in need of a new vision for addressing groups whose population will significantly increase and be heavily concentrated in urban areas. The profession of social work can place itself strategically to provide this vision if we are prepared to do the necessary work in the next decade. A book of this type is intended to help the profession "rethink" established ways of viewing and working with undervalued communities, thus helping the profession to position itself to make a national contribution.

This book raises more questions than it actually answers, resulting in an "incomplete" sense of closure for me. These sentiments will also be experienced by practitioners doing the type of work proposed in this book. The model I proposed is not a panacea for all that is wrong with urban communities or the profession, nor for how society views undervalued groups. Nevertheless, the model is based on an extensive review of the literature, and its critique of the profession builds on the work of others, both from within and outside of social work. I hope that the publication of this book results in a healthy debate about the profession, urban communities, undervalued groups, urban-specific practice, and places like nontraditional settings.

Social Work Profession

There are few, if any, professions that are so willing to be as self-reflective as social work. This propensity for self-reflection opens professionals up to self-criticism and a search for making practice relevant, particularly for "socially undesirable" groups. However, few professions have made significant progress in developing practice within a multicultural context, nor have their goals been social and economic justice. One goal of social work is to view culture within a broad context that goes far beyond the usual factors associated with race and ethnicity. This cultural context requires a search for interventions that run smack into the most highly sensitive issues in society. This book criticizes the social work profession and its inability to embrace paradigms that address issues of social and economic justice; but instead, social work relies on scarcity and deficits as guiding principles for practice under the guise of helping those who are "unable" to help themselves.

The paradigm explored in this book can probably truly be practiced only by social workers, although other helping professions can incorporate key aspects of work within nontraditional settings. Although I wish it were possible, I do not expect social workers to practice collaborative partnerships with nontraditional settings exclusively. Funding realities necessitate some form of compromise concerning practice. Yet compromising does not mean we abandon key concepts such as strengths, empowerment, community participation, and capacity enhancement. Practice utilizing these concepts must never be put aside because of "funding realities."

I propose that social workers and agencies incorporate some form of collaborative work within nontraditional settings as part of their professional functions. This form of work will create benefits that can be transferred easily to the more "conventional" forms of practice.

Practice within nontraditional settings represents an attempt to anchor the profession within a geographical and population-specific context. Social workers who practice rural social work have long known the importance of context in the setting of intervention priorities and use of rural-specific techniques. My experience in Arizona serves to illustrate this point rather well.

I was contracted to provide a day of in-service training on multicultural-based practice by an agency located approximately mid-way between Phoenix and Tucson. I arrived a day early and was briefed about the organization's mission, client profile, and services. In the process of providing an overview, my host asked me whether or not I wished to visit an outreach office and talk with the staff. The idea sounded interesting, so I agreed. On leaving the agency, I asked the host whether it was possible to walk to the site, as it was a beautiful day. The host's reply caught me completely off guard—he said we could walk, but he strongly suggested we drive. He then said that the walk would take a couple of days, as the outreach office was located 40 miles away! I was used to having an outreach office located a few city blocks away from the sponsoring agency, and in all likelihood in a public housing development. The moral of the story is that the concept of outreach is very much dictated by the context in which it occurs—urban outreach is different from rural outreach!

I argue that social work by default has used techniques that are predominantly "nonrural" friendly—therefore they are thought to be "urban friendly." Unfortunately, these approaches are not necessarily urban-friendly either—at best, these approaches are generic in nature and must be modified for urban realities.

I am not proposing partnerships with nontraditional settings because they will make practice "easier" or "less expensive." On the contrary, collaboration will prove to be very demanding and time consuming, and, as a result, more expensive. No two nontraditional settings are identical, even when they serve a similar clientele, are located within a short distance of each other, and provide a similar type of service. Partnerships must be customized to reflect local circumstances and the unique factors particular to the setting. Then, practice within nontraditional settings will result in greater relevance for the profession and the organizations providing services to undervalued urban-based communities.

The model of practice advocated in this book represents only one approach. I hope that social workers will be willing to modify the model to make it more relevant to the communities they serve. New models will undoubtedly emerge in future years, and will be easier to implement and evaluate. Knowledge, after all, is the result of a systematic building process, as shown by this book's acknowledgment of the many scholars who laid the foundation.

The types of settings addressed in this book represent only a small fraction of the types that might lend themselves to collaboration. Taxi cabs, for example, have not been seriously explored for their potential to reach people. Information and materials related to local social services can be distributed in cabs. Car repair shops that have customers waiting can also have available reading materials, videos, and other kinds of information for customer use.

Access to and engagement of nontraditional settings is not predicated on the position of staff members seeking contact or the nature of their credentials (source of degree, years of field-based experience, or post-graduate training). Accessibility will be determined based on personal qualities that cannot be taught: sincerity, flexibility, willingness to share of themselves, showing respect, willingness to go beyond a typical job description, and caring. In essence, legitimacy is not the result of expertise and institutional sources, though these are typical criteria in the human service field. Legitimacy is personal in nature.

We too often integrate credentials into our identity as social workers. These formal credentials very often open doors of opportunity, particularly if the workers we are trying to engage studied at similar schools. Within nontraditional settings, degrees hold no "magic" power to open doors. In fact, they may close doors. An emphasis on personal qualities necessitates social service organizations to be very careful whom they select to get involved in collaborative ventures with nontraditional settings.

Assessment of Nontraditional Settings

Not all nontraditional settings provide assistance that warrants establishment of collaborative ventures. Some settings may be prone to provide poor advice, are almost totally unaware of local resources, or have no interest in providing personal services. Some nontraditional settings may be interested only in generating income at the expense of services. Consequently, I do not wish to paint a "romantic" picture of these settings. In fact, I was once accused of being "nothing but a romantic" at a lecture on the topic of nontraditional settings. At first I was indignant at being labeled that way. However after some thought, I did not mind it because I have been called much worse. Nontraditional settings must be carefully assessed to assure that collaborative practice is not reinforcing "poor" services to a community suffering hardships. Such a relationship will have serious, long-term consequences for an agency within the community.

The success of any model focused on collaborative partnerships with nontraditional settings will rest on the results of sound research. The development of research methodologies and techniques will no doubt involve quantitative and qualitative approaches for assessing the impact of collaboration on the community.

Funding sources and other key stakeholders must be educated concerning both the process and outcome of work within nontraditional settings. Many funding sources require that any collaborative venture, or proposed venture (as with research proposals), has a signed and detailed letter of agreement or a contract. People in nontraditional settings will rarely be willing to contract with unknown or little known agencies. The process of collaborative development, as already noted, can be time consuming and not easily placed within a specific time period, with clear markers of achievement. Thus, funding sources must be willing to be flexible in their requirements. Documentation may not be similar to that of conventional programs. Those in nontraditional settings may not allow funders to undertake site visits or interview them to determine their worthiness.

Finally, asset-based assessments, health enhancement, and capacity enhancement activities must receive serious consideration by stakeholders. Society seems enamored with deficits, social problems, and needs. Effort must be made to sponsor and encourage asset-based activities, and not just those associated with nontraditional settings.

Micro- and Macro-Methods

The model of collaborative practice proposed in this book has equal applicability to micro- and macro-practice with communities. I would argue that any measure of success within nontraditional settings requires both methods. These two methods are often conceptualized as polar opposites in the political continuum and in how communities are viewed. However, collaborative practice offers the potential for these two methods to be joined in pursuit of a common vision.

Micro- and macro-practice methods employ different vocabularies, perspectives, techniques, and arenas of practice. Nontraditional settings offer the profession the opportunity to narrow the differences and reduce any conflicts between the two methods. Narrowing this gap, whether it is perceived or actual, is necessary if the profession is to influence social welfare policy decisions at the national, state, and local levels. In addition, any effort at teaching generic, or multi-method practice, must be based on common visions of community, with each part, or unit, being interdependent and exerting influence on the other.

Urban Roots of the Profession

The profession needs to rediscover its urban roots and strategically define itself as having the capacity (vision, knowledge, and skills) to address major social problems within an urban context. To accomplish this goal, we must be prepared to have the courage to be innovative in all aspects of practice, including changing the social work curriculum to meet the emerging needs and issues of undervalued groups. I firmly believe that as we approach the twenty-first century, this change will come from the field of practice, requiring social work education to refocus its attention on urban areas.

The need for this chapter will be particularly acute for schools of social work located in major urban areas of the country. The schools that fail to respond to this challenge will fail to draw students, and will have graduates who will experience difficulty finding employment because they lack the necessary skills to practice in an urban context.

Indigenous Resources

The use of indigenous resources, nontraditional settings being one example, must never be viewed as an excuse not to develop culture-specific services or not to change social service organizations and make them more multicultural. Indigenous resources have developed over extended periods of time and have survived during very difficult times in undervalued communities. In fact, their success is often due to the lack of resources targeted for undervalued groups. Consequently, it is important that social agencies view indigenous resources as part of an ecosystem that must be protected and enhanced whenever possible.

Nontraditional settings must be conceptualized as part of an overall service delivery system that must be carefully and consistently assessed and evaluated; any change in approach must be weighed based on how it will affect the ecosystem. Agencies wishing to involve nontraditional settings must consider the commitment they are making to the setting and community. This commitment cannot rely solely on availability of funding; remember, nontraditional settings do not depend on grants. Agencies must endeavor to develop a broad base of financial support for nontraditional setting initiatives to avoid the consequences associated with funding cutbacks or shifting priorities.

Changes in Social Policy

The advent of "welfare reform" will have tremendous implications in undervalued communities, particularly those that are low-income. Many stores depend on customers' food stamps to prosper; cutbacks in food stamps and public assistance will no doubt have a severe impact on food-focused businesses. Consequently, any serious effort at "community development" must take into account these establishments, and develop ways of ensuring their survival. In many cases, these establishments are much more than businesses; they are also "mini-social service agencies." To be successful, initiatives that address urban issues and needs must address both "formal" and "informal" resources.

Community Reactions to Partnerships

Partnerships within nontraditional settings will elicit both positive and negative reactions from within and without the community. Agencies must be prepared for this reality. Involvement of a beauty parlor in some form of outreach, for example, may cause other beauty parlors to minimize or undermine such efforts because of fears that business may be lost to that "special" shop. Similar concerns will arise when involving houses of worship, with reactions from other churches within the same and other denominations. Involvement of folk healers may cause a reaction from houses of worship, as well as "ordinary" residents who believe these individuals engage in some form of "devil worship."

As noted in this book, the involvement of bath houses in any collaborative initiative will cause a prodigious degree of acrimony and debate, which can result in a divided community. However, agencies may be willing to tolerate the wrath of one sector of a community if the gains, in this case education about HIV, far outweigh the consequences. In essence, there will rarely be a partnership initiative that engenders nothing but good will throughout an entire community.

Negative reactions are not restricted to communities, and will undoubtedly arise within the organization as well. It is rare that an organizational change is embraced by an entire organization. Thus, it would be fair to expect negativity when initiating partnerships with nontraditional settings. Reactions may be clearly articulated, and thus easy to address or reactions may be subtle and covert, and hard to trace and address. Agencies must anticipate negative reactions, be prepared to undertake "damage control" within and without the agency, and consider these consequences as part of doing business in this arena.

Multiple Collaborations

Agencies wishing to develop partnerships with new groups in a community, particularly those who are starting to arrive in sizable numbers and speak languages that are rare in this country, can establish agreements involving several organizations, or pool resources and develop partnerships. These ventures may entail using part of a worker's time (hopefully someone who is bilingual and bicultural in the group's language and culture) in this project, and developing intake or outreach mechanisms that involve other agencies. Creative partnerships do not have to involve only one agency and one nontraditional setting; they can involve multiple agencies, each with particular needs and contributions. A cooperative approach among social service agencies can easily be transferred to the nontraditional setting, and it may derive unexpected benefits in other areas.

Cooperation, nevertheless, is not a "natural" occurrence in our field, or for that matter in other helping fields. Although we often talk about and extol the virtues of cooperation, too often it is nothing but talk. Cooperation must be assiduously worked at and not taken for granted, particularly when it involves nontraditional setting partnerships.

Knowledge Dissemination

Social workers actively involved in collaborative initiatives must be willing to write about their experiences in professional journals and books. The latter is difficult because the time and resources needed are often beyond most social workers in practice. However, the former is not. The experiences, lessons learned, and recommendations associated with nontraditional settings must be shared with the profession, other helping professions, and society. The profession can never tire of examples of community assets. A strengths paradigm has only recently appeared on the social work landscape, requiring considerably more thought, and operationalization, before its impact on practice can be fully felt. Examples of practice within nontraditional settings in undervalued communities will serve an important role in furthering acceptance of a strengths paradigm.

Academics write about nontraditional settings from a vantage point that is often considered "irrelevant" by practitioners. Practitioners have a vantage point that reflects the operative reality of everyday life in an agency and community. Those practitioners who do not have the time, or believe themselves not to have the ability, to write "scholarly" articles can seek partnerships with academics. It is rare for an academic not to be prepared to collaborate on an article with a practitioner. A publication venture of the kind being proposed allows many people to contribute throughout the entire writing process. Future scholarship in this area will be advanced through these writing partnerships.

Academics rarely have access to undervalued communities; practitioners, however, might have this access. Thus, the most critical and labor-intensive phase of the research process is often beyond the grasp of most academics. In addition, practitioners are in the best position to know what kind of information they need to carry out their job responsibilities. Including real-life experience makes an article more relevant, and increases the likelihood that it will be read and its contents translated into practice.

Change Is Unsettling

I am aware that any shift in paradigms results in an uneasy feeling for a social worker or any other helping professional. This uneasiness will lead to questioning past actions, possible guilt over why an old paradigm was not the most liberating and culturally competent way of helping undervalued communities, fear of what embracing a new paradigm will bring (politically, professionally, socially), and possibly concern that the new quest will result in a "dead end": in wasted time, energy, and "political capital."

Change is never possible without risk, both personal and professional. Personal growth results from change, and serves to prepare us for future challenges that require discarding old paradigms in favor of new ones. There may even be circumstances in which the worker must undertake a highly involved intervention without much or any, support from the agency. Such effort is based on a conviction that one must "take the road less traveled" if one is to be true to the mission of our profession. This quest can be quite liberating when it results in a change or is successful in reaching an undervalued group in tremendous need. When it results in failure, we must pick ourselves up and learn from our mistakes!

Work within nontraditional settings can be very personally rewarding for a worker. I have developed numerous relationships with owners and other staff who have facilitated my connection to a new city and community. There were many instances in which these individuals became a "family away from home" for me. These relationships made my work within nontraditional settings pleasurable and professionally beneficial, with the benefits spilling over into other arenas.

Benefits to Nontraditional Settings

Collaborative work with a nontraditional setting can prove very rewarding for the people who work there. Their capacities can be enhanced through training and consultation, sometimes resulting in some of them obtaining employment in human service agencies. The settings participating in partnerships can enhance their reputation within the community, thus generating increased service utilization, and profits where applicable. In addition, these settings can serve as role models within the community, resulting in other settings wishing to participate in joint ventures. Settings where services pale by comparison may lose business. Collaboration with nontraditional settings is a win-win situation for all parties, and most of all the community will benefit from capacity enhancement in the short and long run.

Only time will be the judge concerning the saliency of collaboration with nontraditional settings. This form of practice may become widely accepted and possibly occur in combination with other forms of urban-based practice yet to be developed; it may form a vital and vibrant part of the profession. Such an advance will require collaborative partnerships, in this case involving nontraditional settings, communities, practitioners, policy makers, and academics, to name but a few. Nevertheless, the potential for creatively bridging the gap between the "formal" and "informal" worlds of care giving will take a giant step forward.

Who Should Practice?

The qualities of people who would make "good" workers for involvement with nontraditional settings highlights the importance of matching staff with job functions. I seriously doubt that any one social worker, including myself, possesses all of the necessary qualities outlined in this book. However, if after examining these qualities (see Chapter 5), not one applies, then this form of practice is not advisable. This does not mean that applicants could not be "good" social workers; it means that this form of work is not for them. If I had to pick one quality that can be considered essential for this line of work, it would be the ability to tolerate ambiguity.

This quality is extremely important because no amount of academic training, attendance at workshops, and reading scholarly material can prepare a social worker for all that will happen in nontraditional settings and community practice. The very nature of the work, which I find exciting and intellectually challenging, necessitates being very comfortable with ambiguity. For some, ambiguity will represent a test that will be embraced enthusiastically; for others, it means procrastination. Thus I for one, tolerate ambiguity and realize that it is endemic to this form of practice. The tolerance for or embrace of ambiguity will serve social workers well in their quest to better serve urban-based undervalued groups.

It is possible that when mentioning the subject of this book to colleagues, they would say that they are currently doing work with nontraditional settings. In fact, the concept of outreach within these settings may be commonplace with staff who are working with communities. However on closer scrutiny, their practice and their concept of "involvement" may be superficial. Collaborative practice with nontraditional settings must be purposeful, with systematic assessment and planning of intervention, for it to be considered faithful to a model. Otherwise, social workers may "involve" nontraditional settings when they "feel" like it, even though there are no agency policies and procedures dictating the form of this practice.

Concluding Comments

It is fitting to end this chapter and this book on a hopeful note. An experience I had within a nontraditional setting (restaurant) in a Massachusetts city symbolizes what this form of practice is all about. I had approached a restaurant that was frequented by a large number of residents, and asked the owner to distribute information on a community forum focused on Latino elders. The owner of the setting said that he would be delighted to help. He then went on to offer, free of charge, to cater the meeting. When asked why he was so generous, he replied: "Our elders have paved the way to this country through their vision, hard work, sacrifices, and helpful ways; the least we can do is provide them with sustenance as a way of showing them that we appreciate all they have done and that we value them."

It was a very touching moment for me to see the interconnectedness of many generations and to note the importance of validating experiences within the community. People in nontraditional settings very often go the "extra mile" because of a deep and abiding concern for the people who make up their community. As social workers we, too, must make efforts to validate, support, and enhance undervalued communities whenever humanly possible. Joining forces with nontraditional settings in urban areas is just one way of ensuring our relevance and making our contributions felt.

Epilogue

The potential for increasing community involvement in all phases of service delivery is greatly enhanced when social service organizations are prepared to enter into a meaningful and co-equal collaborative process with people in nontraditional settings. However, the potential of collaborative work between social service agencies and nontraditional settings has been virtually untapped. This is not the result of a paucity of nontraditional settings in communities of color. It has arisen because social workers and other helping professionals have not taken advantage of this golden opportunity to establish community-based linkages. Because of lack of space, this book has limited itself to just a handful of nontraditional settings with which social workers can form alliances.

Hardcastle, Wenocur, and Powers (1997, p. 415) summarize how strengthening communities can result in significant benefits for all parties: "The more social workers can build community capacity, the more groups and families can obtain needed resources and supports, the more societal problems will be addressed. There is nothing mystical about the goal or endeavor of strengthening community. Social workers need to take planned, collaborative, and concrete steps, just as they would with individuals and families."

Bruzy and Segal (1996) suggest the development of academic assignments involving social work students in community-based research. This recommendation offers much promise for undertaking asset assessments (Bruzy & Segal, 1996, pp. 67–68):

> Another advantage is that students tend to conduct community research that otherwise would not be done. Agency budgets often do not allow for research, or topics are too controversial for paid professionals to feel comfortable researching . . . Educators are encouraged to experiment and find innovative ways to help students be involved directly with their communities. Research into uncharted areas such as the diversity of our social culture and marginalized groups can be accomplished through student projects.

This book presented a series of planned, collaborative, and concrete steps for involving nontraditional settings in urban communities. Social work partnerships with these settings will go a long way toward reaffirming the profession's mission of urban-based practice, and reconnecting with undervalued groups residing within these communities from a strengths perspective.

The experience of conducting asset assessments and interviewing key people in numerous nontraditional settings across the United States proved to be very validating, enlightening, and inspiring. Although carrying out research is qualitatively different from activities associated with service delivery in collaborative partnerships, there is an inevitable overlap.

Numerous questions arose during the writing of this book that went far beyond its original goals. These questions need to be raised to take this form of practice to a higher level of analysis and to inform future research in this area. Thus, this chapter raises three key questions regarding nontraditional settings: (1) What factors facilitate those in nontraditional settings going beyond minimal provision of services? (2) What factors hinder nontraditional settings in maximizing their resources? and (3) Do these settings follow a developmental path in serving their communities?

What Factors Facilitate Those in Nontraditional Settings Going Beyond Minimal Provision of Services?

The nature of this book, which relied on a variety of methods for gathering case studies and utilized a variety of funding mechanisms for gathering data, did not lend itself to a longitudinal study of nontraditional settings in an effort to develop a better understanding of the stages and issues they encounter in serving the needs of community residents.

It becomes painfully obvious that not all nontraditional settings actively seek to provide a multitude of services that address instrumental, informational, and expressive needs within the community. Some settings provide a very limited assortment of services, most of which are nonlabor intensive (sharing information, allowing posters, etc.). However other settings, like the ones showcased in this book, go far beyond no or minimal service provision and willingly accept the challenge and responsibility to view consumers from a holistic perspective. Why is this so?

What role do owners and staff play in fostering this expectation on the part of the community? What role does the community play in fostering this role within nontraditional settings? Do nontraditional settings go through a developmental period during which they increase their capacity to fulfill multiple helper roles within the community?

Are nontraditional settings that provide multiple types of services much more amenable to engaging in collaboration with social agencies? Do people in these types of settings experience a greater or lesser need to receive support, training, and other resources from social agencies?

How important is it to those in nontraditional settings to have an extensive array of social services staffed by culturally competent staff? Are communities with comprehensive culturally competent services more competitive or complementary of nontraditional settings?

What Factors Hinder Nontraditional Settings
From Maximizing Their Resources?

Undoubtedly, nontraditional settings face formidable challenges in carrying out a highly diverse mission within their communities. How is the "burden" of providing help experienced and manifested by the individuals charged with providing this help? Does gender play a critical role in how males and females conceptualize nontraditional settings? Are men limited to seeking assistance from certain nontraditional settings such as bars, liquor stores, and barbershops? Or do they feel comfortable seeking help from other types of settings?

Do These Settings Follow a Developmental Path
in Serving Their Communities?

Development of a better understanding and appreciation of the development history of nontraditional settings will prove invaluable for communities, nontraditional settings, and social work. This information is critical in better planning collaborative initiatives between these two worlds, and it increases the likelihood of success.

Are nontraditional settings that have been in existence a greater period of time, let's say 10 years, more or less willing and able to provide a range of services? Are settings that are just starting out more flexible in engaging in collaborative activities? Or, is the reverse true? Are they too consumed with "start-up" concerns to be able or willing to work with an agency? Is there a different developmental path that is influenced by the nature of the setting, ethnic/racial group it targets, or size and composition of the community? If, in fact, nontraditional settings do follow a developmental path in serving undervalued communities, what are the key "markers" that lend themselves to analysis, and inform the worker and the agency about how to proceed?

Conclusion

The questions rasied in this chapter illustrate the excitement and the frustration of getting to know nontraditional settings in a more systematized and, if you wish, scholarly manner. The nature of the questions posed in this chapter highlights how little we know about community-based resources that play critical roles in the lives of countless numbers of undervalued groups in the United States.

It is very hard to summarize the experience of working within nontraditional settings. Writing this book was an attempt to give an overview. Issuing a challenge to the profession to recognize and enlist the support of nontraditional settings is another way of trying to give something back to the community and to the hard-working individuals who tirelessly give of themselves to help others. In essence, the profession of social work cannot succeed at urban-based practice without embracing a strengths perspective and a willingness to seek out and engage people in nontraditional settings.

References

Abrahamson, M. (1996). *Urban enclaves: Identity and place in America*. New York: St. Martin's Press.

Acosta, A., & Hamel, V. (1995). *CSAP implementation guide: Hispanic/Latino natural support systems*. SAMHSA. Rockville, MD: Center for Substance Abuse Prevention.

Agins, T. (1985, March 15). To Hispanics in U.S., a bodega, or grocery, is a vital part of life. *The Wall Street Journal*, 1, 6, 13.

Albrecht, T. L. (1994). Epilogue: Social support and community: A historical account of the rescue networks in Denmark. In B. R. Burleson, T. L. Albrecht, & I. G. Sarason (Eds.), *Communication of social support: Messages, interactions, relationships, and community* (pp. 267–279). Newbury Park, CA: Sage Publications.

Aldrich, H. E., & Waldinger, R. (1990). Ethnicity and entrepreneurship. *Annual Review of Sociology, 16*, 111–135.

Allen, R. L., & Allen, J. A. (1987). A sense of community, a shared vision and a positive culture: Core enabling factors in successful culture based health promotion. *American Journal of Health Promotion, 1*, 1–10.

Allen-Meares, P., & Lane, B. (1990). Social work practice: Integrating qualitative and quantitative data collection techniques. *Social Work, 35*, 451–458.

Alvarez, L. (1997, January 27). A once-hidden faith leaps out into the open. *New York Times*, B1, B3.

Anderson, Jr., R. W., Maton, K. I., & Ensor, B. E. (1992). Prevention theory and action from the religious perspective. In K. I. Pargament, K. I. Maton, & R. E. Hess (Eds.), *Religion and prevention in mental health* (pp. 195–214). New York: Haworth Press.

Applewhite, S. L. (1995). Curanderismo: Demystifying the health beliefs and practices of elderly Mexican Americans. *Health & Social Work, 20*, 247–253.

Atherton, C. R., & Bolland, K. A. (1997). The multiculturalism debate and social work education: A response to Dorothy Van Soest. *Journal of Social Work Education, 33*, 143–150.

Bacon, K. H. (1993, January 19). Inner-city capitalists push to start a bank of their own. *The Wall Street Journal*, 1.

Badshah, A. A. (1996). *Our urban future: New paradigms for equity and sustainability*. New York: Oxford UniversityPress.

Baker, F. (1976). The interface between professional and natural support systems. *Clinical Social Work Journal, 5*, 139–148.

Barrera, Jr., M., & Reese, F. (1993). Natural support systems and Hispanic substance abuse. In R. S. Mayers, B. L. Kail, & T. D. Watts (Eds.), *Hispanic substance abuse* (pp. 115–130). Springfield, IL: Charles C. Thomas.

Barringer, F. (1991, March 11). Census shows profound change in racial makeup of the nation. *The New York Times*, A1, B8.

Barringer, F. (1993, June 6). Minorities on the move, often unpredictably. *The New York Times*, E4.

Bartley, N. (1993, September 24). Miracle in motion—Northwest AIDS foundation helped movement take giant strides in 10 years. *The Seattle Times*, F1.

Bastien, A. (1995). HIV in the inner cities: Epidemiologic trends and their influence on policy-making decisions. *Journal of Community Health, 20*, 177–181.

Bavley, A. (1995, December 22). Face of AIDS changes among minorities in KC, number of cases has increased steadily. *The Kansas City Star*, A1.

Becerra, R. M., & Iglehart, A. P. (1995). Folk medicine use: Diverse populations in a metropolitan area. *Social Work in Health Care, 21*, 37–58.

Belluck, P. (1997, April 27). Urban volunteers strain to reach fragile lives. *The New York Times*, 1, 28.

Benard, B. (1990). An overview of community-based prevention. In K. H. Key, C. L. Faegre, & P. Lowery (Eds.), *Prevention research findings: 1988* (pp. 126–147). OSAP Prevention Monograph. Rockville, MD: Office of Substance Abuse Prevention.

Benjamin, M. P. (1994). Research frontiers in building a culturally competent organization. *Focal Point, 8*, 17–18.

Benson, P. (1996). Random acts of asset building. *Wingspread Journal, 18*, 7–9.

Bernal, G., & Shapiro, E. (1996). Cuban families. In M. McGoldrick, J. Giordano, & J. K. Pearce (Eds.), *Ethnicity & family therapy* (pp. 141–154). New York: Guilford Press.

Billups, J. O. (1994). The social development model as an organizing framework for social work practice. In R. G. Meinert, J. T. Pardeck, & W. P. Sullivan (Eds.), *Issues in social work: A critical analysis* (pp. 21–37). Westport, CT: Auburn House.

Black, L. (1996). Families of African origins: An overview. In M. McGoldrick, J. Giordano, & J. K. Pearce (Eds.), *Ethnicity & family therapy* (pp. 57–65). New York: Guilford Press.

Black, R. B., & Walter, V. N. (1995). The practitioner-researcher team: A case example. In P. M. Hess, & E. J. Mullen (Eds.), *Practitioner-researcher partnerships: Building knowledge from, in, and for practice* (pp. 151–161). Washington, D.C.: National Association of Social Workers.

Blackwell, J. E. (1985). *The Black community*. New York: Harper & Row.

Bletzer, K. V. (1995). The use of ethnography in the evaluation and targeting of HIV/AIDS education among Latino farm workers. *AIDS Education and Prevention, 7*, 178–191.

Blum, A., Biegel, D. E., Tracy, E. M., & Cole, M. J. (1995). Agency-university collaboration: Partnerships for implementing and studying practice innovations. In P. M. Hess, & E. J. Mullen (Eds.), *Practitioner-researcher partnerships: Building knowledge from, in, and for practice* (pp. 162–188). Washington, D.C.: National Association of Social Workers.

Bond, L., Bowden-Proctor, J., Lauby, J., Walls, C., & Woll, M. (1997). Developing non-traditional print media for HIV prevention: Role model stories for young urban women. *American Journal of Public Health, 87*, 289–290.

Borrello, M. A., & Mathias, E. (1977). Botanicas: Puerto Rican folk pharmacies. *Natural History, 86*, 64–73.

Boston Foundation. (1994). *Guiding principles for a new social contract.* Boston: Author.

Boston Herald. (1997, April 9). Hub churches' crime fight goes national, 21.

Bouvier, L. F., & Grant, L. (1994). *How many Americans?: Population, immigration and the environment.* San Francisco: Sierra Club Books.

Boyce, J. N. (1990, July 26). More blacks embrace self-help programs to fight urban ills. *The Wall Street Journal*, 1.

Boyce, J. N. (1991, April 1). Struggle over hospital in Los Angeles pits minority vs. minority. *The Wall Street Journal*, 1.

Boyte, H. C., & Kari, N. N. (1996). *Building America: The democratic promise of public work.* Philadelphia: Temple University Press.

Bracho de Carpio, A., Carpio-Cedraro, F., & Anderson, L. (1990). Hispanic families learning and teaching about AIDS: A participatory approach at the community level. *Hispanic Journal of Behavioral Sciences, 12,* 165–176.

Brashears, F., & Roberts, M. (1996). The black church as a resource for change. In S. L. Logan (Ed.), *The black family: Strengths, self-help, and positive change* (pp. 181–192). Boulder, CO: Westview Press.

Brooks, R. B. (1994). Children at risk: Fostering resilience and hope. *American Journal of Orthopsychiatry, 64,* 545–553.

Brown, C., & Broderick, A. (1994). Asian and Pacific Island elders: Issues for social work practice and education. *Social Work, 39,* 252–259.

Brown, D. W. (1995). *When strangers cooperate: Using social conventions to govern ourselves.* New York: The Free Press.

Browne, C., & Broderick, A. (1996). Asian and Pacific Island elders: Issues for social work practice and education. In P. L. Ewalt, E. M. Freeman, S. A. Kirk, & D. L. Poole (Eds.), *Multicultural issues in social work* (pp. 322–335). Washington, D.C.: NASW Press.

Bruzy, S., & Segal, E. A. (1996). Community-based research strategies for social work education. *Journal of Community Practice, 3,* 59–69.

Bryant, J. (1994b, April 7). Walk organizer's aim for greater outreach. *Austin American-Statesman,* 2.

Buning, E., Brussel, G. V., & Santen, G. V. (1992). The impact of harm reduction drug policy on AIDS prevention in Amsterdam. In P. A. O'Hare, R. Newcombe, A. Matthews, & E. C. Buning (Eds.), *The reduction of drug-related harm* (pp. 30–38). London: Routledge.

Burawoy, M. (1991a). Reconstructing social theories. In M. Burawoy et al. (Eds.), *Ethnography unbound: Power and resistance in the modern metropolis* (pp. 8–27). Berkeley: University of California Press.

Burawoy, M. (1991b). The extended case method. In M. Burawoy et al. (Eds.), *Ethnography unbound: Power and resistance in the modern metropolis* (pp. 271–287). Berkeley: University of California Press.

Burawoy, M., Burton, A., Ferguson, A. A., Fox, K. J., Gamson, J., Gartrell, N., Hurst, L., Kurzman, C., Salzinger, L., Schiffman, J., & Ui, S. (1991). *Ethnography unbound: Power and resistance in the modern metropolis.* Berkeley: University of California Press.

Burleson, B. R., Albrecht, T. L., Goldsmith, D. J., & Sarason, I. G. (1994). Introduction: The communication of social support. In B. R. Burleson, T. L. Albrecht, & I. G. Sarason (Eds.), *Communication of social support: Messages, in-*

teractions, relationships, and community (pp. xi–xxx). Newbury Park, CA: Sage Publications.

Burros, M. (1990, July 18). Supermarkets reach out to Hispanic customers. *The New York Times*, C1, C6.

Burton, L. M., Dilworth-Anderson, P., & Bengtson, V. L. (1992). Creating culturally relevant ways of thinking about diversity and aging: Theoretical challenges for the twenty-first century. In E. P. Stanford, & F. M. Torres-Gil (Eds.), *Diversity: New approaches to ethnic minority aging* (pp. 129–140). Amityville, NY: Baywood Publishing Co.

Butterfield, F. (1992, July 19). Are American jails becoming shelters from the storm? *The New York Times*, 4E.

Campbell, R. (1996, December 26). Urban regains its good name: They're keen, not mean, streets these days. *The Boston Globe*, D1, D7.

Campinha-Bacote, J. (1991). *The process of cultural competence: A culturally competent model of care.* Wyoming, OH: Transcultural C.A.R.E. Associates.

Caraballo, J. M. (1992). *The role of the Pentecostal church as a service provider in the Puerto Rican community in Boston, Massachusetts: A case study.* Doctoral Dissertation, Brandeis University.

Carmody, D. (1972, May 2). Bodega owners gain strength in co-op here. *The New York Times*, 31.

Carr, E., & Perez, A. (1993, May 16). The rites of the ancient ones: Spiritualists are often regarded as charlatans, but to practitioners a visit to a curandero is as spiritual as a Sunday church service. *Los Angeles Times*, 16.

Castex, G. M. (1994). Providing services to Hispanic/Latino populations. *Social Work, 39*, 288–296.

Chachkes, E., & Jennings, R. (1994). Latino communities: Coping with death. In B. O. Dane, & C. Levine (Eds.), *AIDS and the new orphans* (pp. 77–120). Westport, CT: Auburn House.

Chacon, R. (1997, February 19). A bumpy road for small auto shops. *The Boston Globe*, B1, B8.

Chan, Y. (1992, September 16). "Safe-sex" fortune cookies. *New York Daily News*, 16.

Chapin, R. K. (1995). Social policy development: The strengths perspective. *Social Work, 40*, 506–514.

Chase, M. (1990, February 14). Volunteers' distress cripples huge effort to provide AIDS care. *The Wall Street Journal*, 1.

Chavis, D. M., & Wandersman, A. (1990). Sense of community in the urban environment: A catalyst for participation and community development. *American Journal of Community Psychology, 18*, 55–80.

Chavis, M. E. (1997). *Altars in the street: A neighborhood fights to survive.* New York: Bell Towers.

Chideya, F. (1995). *Don't believe the hype: Fighting cultural misinformation about African-Americans.* New York: Plume.

Cisneros, H. G. (1996). *Higher ground: Faith communities and community building.* Washington, D.C.: The Urban Institute.

City of Englewood, Department of Health. (1994). *Annual Report.* Englewood, NJ: Author.

Cohen, E., Mowbray, C. T., Gillette, V., & Thompson, E. (1992). Preventing homelessness: Religious organizations and housing development. In K. I. Pargament,

K. I. Maton, & R. E. Hess (Eds.), *Religion and prevention in mental health* (pp. 317–333). New York: Haworth Press.

Collins, A. H., & Pancoast, D. L. (1976). *Natural helping networks: A strategy for prevention.* Washington, D.C.: National Association of Social Workers.

Colon, H. M., Sahai, H., Robles, R. R., & Matos, T. D. (1995). Effects of a community outreach program in HIV risk behaviors among injection drug users in San Juan, Puerto Rico. *AIDS Education and Prevention, 7,* 195–209.

C.O.S.T. (1995). *Churches organized to stop tobacco (COST).* Boston: The Medical Foundation.

Cothran, G. (1996, July 3). Merchant of redemption during his first three decades on sixth street. *San Francisco Weekly,* 1–3.

Coulton, C. J. (1995a). Research for initiatives in low-income communities. In P. McCartt Hess, & E. J. Mullen (Eds.), *Practitioner-researcher partnerships: Building knowledge from, in, and for practice* (pp. 103–121). Washington, D.C.: NASW Press.

Coulton, C. J. (1995b). Riding the pendulum of the 1990s: Building a community context for social work research. *Social Work, 40,* 437–439.

Cowger, C. D. (1994). Assessing client strengths: Clinical assessment for client empowerment. *Social Work, 39,* 262–268.

Cox, H. (1995). *Fire from heaven: The rise of Pentecostal spirituality and the reshaping of religion in the twenty-first century.* New York: The Free Press.

Crocker, J. (1994). *Folk medicine and its influence on access and delivery of modern health services: A case study of the Latino population in Lawrence, MA.* Unpublished manuscript.

Cross, T. L. (1988). Services to minority populations: Cultural competence continuum. *Focal Point, 3,* 1–4.

Daley, J. M., & Wong, P. (1994). Community development with emerging ethnic communities. *Journal of Community Practice, 1,* 9–24.

Daly, A., Jennings, J., Beckett, J. O., & Leashore, B. R. (1995). Effective coping strategies of African-Americans. *Social Work, 40,* 240–248.

Deck, A. F., & Nunez, J. A. (1982, October 23). Religious enthusiasm and Hispanic youth. *America,* 232–234.

De Jong, P., & Miller, S. D. (1995). How to interview for client strengths. *Social Work, 40,* 729–736.

De La Cancela, V., & Zavalas, I. (1983). An analysis of culturalism in Latino mental health: Folk medicine as a case in point. *Hispanic Journal of Behavioral Sciences, 5,* 251–274.

De La Rosa, M. (1988). Natural support systems of Hispanic Americans: A Key dimension of their well-being. *Health and Social Work, 13,* 181–190.

Delgado, M. (1974). Social work and the Puerto Rican community. *Social Casework, 55,* 117–123.

Delgado, M. (1977). Puerto Rican spiritualism and the social work profession. *Social Casework, 58,* 451–458.

Delgado, M. (1979). Herbal medicine in the Puerto Rican community. *Health & Social Work, 4,* 24–40.

Delgado, M. (1979–80). Accepting folk healers: Problems and rewards. *Journal of Social Welfare, 6,* 5–16.

Delgado, M. (1982). Use of key informants in assessing Hispanic mental health needs. *Journal of Mental Health Administration, 9,* 2–4.

Delgado, M. (1989). Alcoholism among Hispanics. In T. D. Watts, & R. Wright, Jr. (Eds.), *Alcoholism in minority populations* (pp. 77–92). Springfield, IL: Charles C. Thomas.

Delgado, M. (1994). Hispanic natural support systems and the AODA field: A developmental framework for collaboration. *Journal of Multicultural Social Work, 3,* 11–37.

Delgado, M. (1995a). Hispanic natural support systems and alcohol and other drug services: Challenges and rewards for practice. *Alcoholism Treatment Services, 12,* 17–31.

Delgado, M. (1995b). Puerto Rican elders and natural support systems: Implications for human services. *Journal of Gerontological Social Work, 24,* 115–130.

Delgado, M. (1995c). Community asset assessment and substance abuse prevention: A case study involving the Puerto Rican community. *Journal of Child and Adolescent Substance Abuse, 4,* 57–77.

Delgado, M. (1995d). Natural support systems and AOD services to communities of color: A California case example. *Alcoholism Treatment Quarterly, 13,* 13–24.

Delgado, M. (1996a). Religion as a caregiving system for Puerto Rican elders with functional disabilities. *Journal of Gerontological Social Work, 26,* 129–144.

Delgado, M. (1996b). Puerto Rican food establishments as social service organizations. *Journal of Community Practice, 3,* 57–77.

Delgado, M. (1996c). Puerto Rican elders and botanical shops: A community resource or liability. *Social Work in Health Care, 23,* 67–83.

Delgado, M. (1996d). A guide for school-based personnel collaborating with Puerto Rican natural support systems. *New Schools, New Communities, 12,* 38–42.

Delgado, M. (1996e). Community asset assessments by Latino youths: Lessons from the field. *Social Work in Education, 18,* 169–178.

Delgado, M. (1996f). Implementing a natural support system AOD project: Administrative considerations and recommendations. *Alcoholism Treatment Quarterly, 14,* 1–14.

Delgado, M. (1997a). Interpretation of Puerto Rican elder research findings: A community forum of research respondents. *Journal of Applied Gerontology, 16,* 317–332.

Delgado, M. (1997b). The role of small businesses in Latino community revitalization: Beauty parlors as a case in point. *Social Work, 42,* 445–453.

Delgado, M. (1997c). Strength-based practice with early adolescent Puerto Ricans: Lessons from an ATOD prevention project. *Social Work in Education, 19,* 101–112.

Delgado, M. (Ed.). (in press a). *Alcohol use/abuse among Latinos: Issues and examples of culturally competent services.* New York: Haworth Press.

Delgado, M. (in press b). Cultural competence and the field of ATOD: Latinos as a case example. *Alcoholism Treatment Quarterly, 18.*

Delgado, M. (in press c). Alcoholism services and community settings: Latina beauty parlors as case examples. *Alcoholism Treatment Quarterly, 18.*

Delgado, M. (in press d). Puerto Rican elders and merchant establishments: Natural support systems or simply businesses? *Journal of Gerontological Social Work.*

Delgado, M. (in press e). *Strategies for researching and serving Puerto Ricans and other Latinos: Rewards and challenges.* New York: Haworth Press.

Delgado, M. (in press f). Latina-owned businesses: Community resources for the prevention field. *Journal of Primary Prevention, 18.*

Delgado, M., & Barton, K. (in press). Murals in Latino communities: Social indicators of community strengths. *Social Work*.

Delgado, M., & Humm-Delgado, D. (1980). Interagency collaboration to increase community resources in serving Hispanics. *Hispanic Journal of Behavioral Sciences, 2,* 269–285.

Delgado, M., & Humm-Delgado, D. (1982). Natural support systems: Source of strengths in Hispanic communities. *Social Work, 27,* 83–89.

Delgado, M., & Rosati, M. (in press). Religion, asset assessment and AOD: A case study of a Puerto Rican community in Massachusetts. *Journal of Health and Social Policy* (Special Issue).

Delgado, M., & Santiago, J. (in press a). HIV/AIDS in a Puerto Rican/Dominican community: A collaborative project with a botanical shop. *Social Work*.

Delgado, M., & Santiago, J. (in press b). Latino barbershops as indigenous resources for outreach to males. *Journal of Prevention Intervention in the Community,*

Delgado, M., & Santiago, J. (in press c). Botanical shops in a Puerto Rican/Dominican community in New England: Implications for health and human services. *Journal of Health and Social Policy.*

Denby, R. W. (1996). Resiliency and the African American family: A model for family preservation. In S. L. Logan (Ed.), *The black family: Strengths, self-help, and positive change* (pp. 144–163). Boulder, CO: Westview Press.

Devore, W., & Schlesinger, E. G. (1996). *Ethnic-sensitive social work practice.* Boston: Allyn & Bacon.

DiAna, D. (1995). *Curlers and condoms.* Unpublished manuscript

Diaz, T., Buehler, J., Castro, K. G., & Ward, T. W. (1993). AIDS trends among Hispanics in the United States. *American Journal of Public Health, 83,* 504–509.

Dorrington, C. (1995). Central American refugees in Los Angeles: Adjustment of children and families. In R. E. Zambrana (Ed.), *Understanding Latino families: Scholarship, policy, and practice* (pp. 107–153). Thousand Oaks, CA: Sage Publications.

Drachman, D. (1995). Immigration statuses and their influence on service provision, access, and use. *Social Work, 40,* 188–197.

Drucker, E. (1994). Epidemic in the war zone: AIDS and community survival in New York City. *Centro de Estudios Puertorriquenos, 6,* 94–107.

Dugger, C. W. (1996, March 10). Immigrant voters reshape politics. *The New York Times,* 1, 28.

Eckenrode, J. (Ed.). (1991). *The social context of coping.* New York: Plenum Press.

Editorial. (1994). Puerto Ricans and AIDS: It's time to act! *Centro de Estudios Puertorriquenos, 6,* 1–13.

Eng, E., & Hatch, J. W. (1992). Networking between agencies and black churches: The lay health advisor model. In K. Pargament, K. I. Maton, & R. E. Hess (Eds.), *Religion and prevention in mental health* (pp. 293–316). New York: Haworth Press.

Epstein, J. A., Dusenbury, L., Botvin, G. J., & Diaz, T. (1994). Acculturation, beliefs about AIDS, and AIDS education among New York City Hispanic parents. *Hispanic Journal of Behavioral Sciences, 16,* 342–354.

Evans, S. M., & Boyte, H. C. (1986). *Free spaces: The sources of change in America.* New York: Harper & Row.

Ewalt, P. A., Freeman, E. M., Kirk, S. A., & Poole, D. L. (Eds.). (1996). *Multicultural issues in social work.* Washington, D.C.: NASW Press.

Featherstone, D. (1992, August 17). Shop where business is a religion. *Newsday*, p. 32.

Feldman, E. J., & Suskind, A. (1995). Foreword. In P. M. Hess, & E. J. Mullen (Eds.), *Practitioner-researcher partnerships: Building knowledge from, in, and for practice* (pp. ix–xiii). Washington, D.C.: National Association of Social Workers.

Fellin, P. (1995). *The community and the social worker*. Itasca, IL: F.E. Peacock.

Fetterman, D., Kaftarian, S., & Wandersman, A. (1996). *Empowerment evaluation*. Thousand Oaks, CA: Sage Publications.

Fiffer, S., & Fiffer, S. S. (1994). *50 ways to help your community*. New York: Doubleday.

Firestone, D. (1995, March 29). Major ethnic changes under way. *The New York Times*, B1–B2.

Fisch, S. (1968). Botanicas and spiritism in a metropolis. *Milbank Memorial Fund*, 41, 377–388.

Fisher, I. (1997, February 8). Bartender, bartender, make them a match. *The New York Times*, 23, 27.

Fisher, R., & Kling, J. M. (1987). Leading people: Two approaches to the role of ideology in community organizing. *Radical America*, 21, 31–45.

Fitzpatrick, J. P. (1987). *Puerto Rican Americans: The meaning of migration to the mainland*. Englewood Cliffs, NJ: Prentice Hall.

Flanagan, W. G. (1993). *Contemporary urban sociology*. New York: Cambridge University Press.

Florin, P., & Wandersman, A. (1990). An introduction to citizen participation, voluntary organizations, and community development: Insights for empowerment through research. *American Journal of Community Psychology*, 18, 41–53.

Forester, J. (1989). *Planning in the face of power*. Berkeley: University of California Press.

Forte, J. A. (1997). Calling students to serve the homeless: A project to promote altruism and community service. *Journal of Social Work Education*, 33, 151–166.

Fox, K. J. (1991). The politics of prevention: Ethnographers combat AIDS among drug users. In M. Buraway (Ed.), *Ethnography unbound: Power and resistance in the modern metropolis* (pp. 227–249). Berkeley: University of California Press.

Freeman, E. M. (1997). Alternative stories and narratives for transforming schools, families, communities, and policymakers. *Social Work in Education*, 19, 67–71.

Freudenberg, N., Israel, B. A., & Germain, L. M. (1994). A case study of the Hartford Hispanic health council's comunidad y responsabilidad AIDS prevention project. *Centro de Estudios Puertorriquenos*, 6, 228–237.

Frisbie, W. P., & Bean, F. D. (1995). The Latino family in comparative perspective: Trends and current conditions. In C. K. Jacobson (Ed.), *American families: Issues in race and ethnicity* (pp. 29–71). New York: Garland Publishing.

Froland, C., Pancoast, D. L., Chapman, N. J., & Kimboko, P. (1981). *Helping networks and human services*. Beverly Hills, CA: Sage Publications.

Gaiter, D. J. (1980, December 24). At Christmas, Hispanic Pentecostal church puts stress on 'gifts' without price tags. *The New York Times*, B1, B4.

Galper, J. H. (1975). *The politics of social services*. Englewood Cliffs, NJ: Prentice Hall.

Gans, S., & Horton, G. T. (1975). *Integration of human services: The state and municipal levels*. New York: Praeger.

Garbarino, J. (1983). Social support networks: Rx for the helping professions. In

J. K. Whittaker, & J. Garbarino (Eds.), *Social support networks: Informal help-ing in the human services* (pp. 3–28). New York: Aldine.

Garbarino, J., Dubrow, N., Kostelny, K., & Pardo, C. (1992). *Children in danger: Coping with the consequences of community violence.* San Francisco: Jossey-Bass.

Gardner, J. W. (1994). Forward. In M. W. McLaughlin, M. A. Irby, & J. Langman (Eds.), *Urban sanctuaries: Neighborhood organizations in the lives and futures of inner-city youth* (pp. ix–xii). San Francisco: Jossey-Bass.

Garr, R. (1995). *Reinvesting in America.* Reading, MA: Addison-Wesley.

Gaston Institute. (1992a). *Latinos in Holyoke.* Boston: University Of Massachusetts.

Gaston Institute. (1992b). *Latinos in Lawrence.* Boston: University of Massachusetts.

Gaston Institute. (1994a). *Latinos in Holyoke: Poverty, income, education, employ-ment and housing.* Boston: University of Massachusetts.

Gaston Institute. (1994b). *Latinos in Lawrence: Poverty, income, education, employ-ment and housing.* Boston: University of Massachusetts.

George, L. (1992). *No crystal star: African-Americans in the city of angels.* New York: Doubleday.

Ghali, S. B. (1982). Understanding Puerto Rican traditions. *Social Work, 27,* 98–102.

Gidron, B., & Chesler, M. (1994). Universal and particular attributes of self-help: A framework for international and intranational analysis. In F. Lavoie, T. Borkman, & B. Gidron (Eds.), *Self-help and mutual aid groups: International and multicultural perspectives* (pp. 1–44). New York: Haworth Press.

Glugoski, G., Reisch, M., & Rivera, F. G. (1994). A wholistic ethno-cultural para-digm: A new model for community organization teaching and practice. *Journal of Community Practice, 1,* 81–98.

Goldberg, C. (1997, January 30). Hispanic households struggle as poorest of the poor in the U.S. *The New York Times,* A1, A16.

Gonzalezs, D. (1992, September 1) Dominican immigration alters Hispanic New York. *The New York Times,* A1.

Gonzalez, D. (1994, November 16). A mission to the South Bronx: Mormons live the Gospel and work for converts. *The New York Times,* B1.

Googins, B., Capoccia, V., & Kaufman, V. A. (1983). The interactional dimension of planning: A framework for practice. *Social Work, 28,* 273–277.

Gordon, K. A. (1996). Resilient Hispanic youths' self-concept and motivational pat-terns. *Hispanic Journal of Behavioral Sciences, 18,* 63–73.

Gorov, L. (1997, April 20). In LA, rebuilding has a price. *The Boston Globe,* A1, A26.

Gottlieb, B. H. (Ed.). (1981). *Social networks and social support.* Beverly Hills, CA: Sage Publications.

Gottlieb, B. H. (1983). *Social support strategies: Guidelines for mental health prac-tice.* Beverly Hills, CA: Sage Publications.

Gottlieb, B. H. (Ed.). (1988). *Marshaling social support: Formats, processes, and ef-fects.* Newbury Park, CA: Sage Publications.

Gould, K. H. (1995). The misconstruing of multiculturalism. The Stanford debate and social work. *Social Work, 40,* 198–205.

Graham, E., & Boyce, J. N. (1989, August 22). A South Bronx street rises through the toil of poor homesteaders. *The Wall Street Journal,* p. 1.

Grant, L. M. (1996). Are culturally sophisticated agencies better workplaces for so-cial work staff and administrators? *Social Work, 41,* 163–171.

Grant, L. M., & Gutierrez, L. M. (1996). Effects of culturally sophisticated agen-cies on Latino social workers. *Social Work, 41,* 624–631.

Gray, B. (1989). *Collaborating: Finding common ground for multiparty problems.* San Francisco: Jossey-Bass.

Green, J. (1996, September 15). Flirting with suicide. *The New York Times Magazine,* 38–45, 54–55, 84–85.

Green, J. W. (1995). *Cultural awareness in the human services: A multi-ethnic approach* (2nd ed.). Boston: Allyn & Bacon.

Greene, G. J., Jensen, C., & Jones, D. H. (1996). A constructivist perspective on clinical social work with ethnically diverse clients. *Social Work, 41,* 172–180.

Gutierrez, L. (1990). Working with women of color: An empowerment perspective. *Social Work, 35,* 149–154.

Gutierrez, L. (1992). Empowering ethnic minorities in the twenty-first century. In Y. Hasenfeld (Ed.), *Human services as complex organizations* (pp. 320-338). Newbury Park, CA: Sage Publications.

Gutierrez, L., Alvarez, A. R., Nemon, H., & Lewis, E. A. (1996). Multicultural community organizing: A strategy for change. *Social Work, 41,* 501–508.

Gutierrez, L. M., GlenMaye, L., & DeLois, K. (1995). The organizational context of empowerment practice: Implications for social work. *Social Work, 40,* 249–258.

Gutierrez, L. M., & Ortega, R. M. (1991). Developing methods to empower Latinos: The importance of groups. *Social Work with Groups, 14,* 23–43.

Gutierrez, L., Ortega, R. M., & Suarez, Z. (1990). Self-help and the Latino community: In T. J. Powell (Ed.), *Working with self-help* (pp. 218–236). Silver Springs, MD: National Association of Social Workers.

Hacker, G. A., Collins, R., & Jacobson, M. (1987). *Marketing booze to blacks.* Washington, D.C.: Center for Science in the Public Interest.

Halpern, R. (1995). *Rebuilding the inner city: A history of neighborhood initiatives to address poverty in the United States.* New York: Columbia University Press.

Halter, M. (Ed.). (1995a). *New migrants in the marketplace.* Boston: University of Massachusetts Press.

Halter, M. (1995b). Introduction—Boston's immigrants revisited: The economic culture of ethnic enterprise. In M. Halter (Ed.), *New migrants in the marketplace* (pp. 1–22). Boston: University of Massachusetts Press.

Hardcastle, D. A., Wenocur, S., & Powers, P. R. (1997). *Community practice: Theories and skills for social workers.* New York: Oxford University Press.

Harper, B. C. O. (1990). Blacks and the health care delivery system: Challenges and prospects. In M. L. Logan, E. M. Freeman, & R. G. McRoy (Eds.), *Social work practice with black families* (pp. 239–256). White Plains, NY: Longman.

Harrington, M. (1994). The community research initiative (CRI) of New York: Clinical research and prevention treatments. In J. P. Van Vugt (Ed.), *AIDS prevention and services: Community based research* (pp. 153–178). Westport, CT: Bergin & Garvey.

Hathaway, W. L., & Pargament, K. I. (1992). The religious dimensions of coping: Implications for prevention and promotion. In K. I. Pargament, K. I. Maton, & R. E. Hess (Eds.), *Religion and prevention in mental health* (pp. 129–154). New York: Haworth Press.

Harwood, A. (1977). *Rx: Spiritist as needed: A study of a Puerto Rican community mental health resource.* New York: John Wiley & Sons.

Hawkins, J. D., & Fraser, M. W. (1981). Social support networks in treating drug abuse. In J. K. Whittaker, & J. Garbarino (Eds.), *Social support networks: Informal helping in the human services* (pp. 357–380). New York: Aldine.

Hayes-Bautista, D. E., Schink, W. O., & Chapa, J. (1988). *The burden of support: Young Latinos in an aging society.* Stanford: Stanford University Press.

Haymes, S. N. (1995). *Race, culture, and the city.* Albany: State University of New York Press.

Henderson, J. N. (1994). Ethnic and racial issues. In J. F. Gubrium, & A. Sankar (Eds.), *Qualitative methods in aging research* (pp. 33–50). Thousand Oaks, CA: Sage Publications.

Hernandez, M., & Isaacs-Shockley, M. (1997). *Promoting cultural competence in systems of care.* Baltimore, MD: Paul H. Brooks.

Hernandez, R. (1994, July 12). Where Hispanic merchants thrive: In Westchester, growth of businesses bolsters economy. *The New York Times,* 1.

Herszenhorn, D. M., & Hirsh, S. (1996, December 8). Healing neighborhoods with comprehensive community building. *The New York Times,* 61.

Hess, P. M. (1995). Reflecting in and on practice: A role for the practitioner in knowlege building. In P. M. Hess & E. J. Mullen (Eds.), *Practitioner-researcher partnerships: Building knowledge from, in, and for practice* (pp. 56–82). Washington, D.C.: NASW Press.

Hill, R. (1972). *Strengths of the black family.* New York: Hall Publishers.

Hoffman, A. V. (1994). *Local attachments: The making of an American urban neighborhood.* Baltimore: Johns Hopkins University Press.

Holmes, G. E. (1992). Social work research and the empowerment paradigm. In D. S. Saleebey (Ed.), *The strengths perspective in social work practice* (pp. 158–168). New York: Longman.

Holmstrom, D. (1996a). Asset-building: A Minnesota city mobilizes around kids. *The Christian Science Monitor Series Reprint,* 6, 7, 8.

Holmstrom, D. (1996b). Black churches put 'spirit' into children's afternoons. *The Christian Science Monitor Series Reprint,* 6–7.

Howe, M. (1986, November 19). Bodegas find prosperity amid change. *The New York Times,* 8.

Hudson, M. (Ed.). (1996). *Merchants of misery: How corporate America profits from poverty.* Monroe: Common Courage Press.

Hurtado, A. (1995). Variations, combinations, and evolutions: Latino families in the United States. In R. E. Zambrana (Ed.), *Understanding Latino families: Scholarship, policy, and practice* (pp. 40–61). Thousand Oaks, CA: Sage Publications.

Hutzler, C. (1991, October 31). Haircut, shave, and AIDS info in New Jersey. *United Press International–Thursday BC Cycle,* 2.

Hynes, H. P. (1996). *A path of Eden: America's inner-city gardeners.* White River Junction, VT: Chelsea Green.

Iglehart, A. P., & Becerra, R. M. (1995). *Social services and the ethnic community.* Boston: Allyn & Bacon.

Indian Health Service. (1993). *Trends in indian health.* Rockville, MD: U.S. Department of Health and Human Services.

IPR Datanote. (1995). Puerto Ricans and other Latinos in the United States: March 1994. *Institute for Puerto Rican Policy,* 17, 1–2.

Israel, B. A. (1985). Social network and social support: Implications for natural healer and community leader interventions. *Health Education Quarterly,* 12, 65–80.

Jackson, A. A. (1992, December 15). AIDS effort targets minorities: 2 agencies join in 8-week drive to inform, counsel blacks and Hispanics. *The Dallas Morning News,* 1V.

Jackson, D. Z. (1989, June 18). Why blacks, Latin-Americans are at a higher risk for AIDS. *The Boston Globe,* 86.

Jarman-Rohde, L., McFall, J., Kolar, P., & Strom, G. (1997). The changing context of social work practice: Implications and recommendations for social work educators. *Journal of Social Work education, 33,* 29–46.

Jenkins, S. (1981). *The ethnic dilemma in social services.* New York: The Free Press.

Jones, L., Newman, L., & Isay, D. (1997). *Our America: Life and death on the south side of Chicago.* New York: Scribner.

Kaplan, C. P., Turner, S., Norman, E., & Stillson, K. (1996). Promoting resilience strategies: A modified consultation model. *Social Work in Education, 18,* 158–168.

Kaplan, F. (1997, April 12). In NYC, Dominicans feeling political clout. *The Boston Globe,* A1, A8.

Keating, W. D. (1996). Introduction: Neighborhoods in urban America. In W. D. Keating, N. Krumholz, & P. Star (Eds.), *Revitalizing urban neighborhoods* (pp. 1–6). Lawrence: University of Kansas Press.

Keating, W. D., Krumholz, N., & Star, P. (Eds.). (1996). *Revitalizing urban neighborhoods.* Lawrence: University of Kansas Press.

Kelly, J. A., St. Lawrence, J. S., Stevenson, L. Y., Hauth, A. C., Kalichman, S. C., Diaz, Y. E., Brasfield, T. L., Koob, J. J., & Morgan, M. G. (1992). Community AIDS/HIV risk reduction: The effects of endorsements by popular people in three cities. *American Journal of Public Health, 82,* 1483–1489.

Keys, P. R. (1994). *School social workers in the multicultural environment: New roles, responsibilities, and educational enrichment.* New York: Haworth Press.

Kilbourne, B. W., Gwinn, M., Castro, K. G., & Oxtoby, M. J. (1994). HIV infection and AIDS among women: Impact on Hispanic women and children residing in the United States. In G. Lamberty, & C. Garcia Coll (Eds.), *Puerto Rican women and children: Issues in health, growth, and development* (pp. 103–117). New York: Plenum Press.

Killilea, M. (1976). Mutual help organizations: Interpretations in the literature. In G. Caplan, & M. Killilea (Eds.), *Support systems and mutual aid: Multidisciplinary explorations* (pp. 37–93). New York: Grune & Stratton.

Kim, I. (1987). The Koreans: Small business in an urban frontier. In N. Foner (Ed.), *New immigrants in New York* (pp. 219–242). New York: Columbia University Press.

Koester, S. (1994). Applying ethnography to AIDS prevention among IV drug users and social policy implications. In J. P. Van Vugt (Ed.), *AIDS prevention and services: Community based research* (pp. 35–57). Westport: Bergin & Garvey.

Korrol, V. E. S. (1983). *From colonia to community: The history of Puerto Ricans in New York City, 1917–1948.* Westport, CT: Greenwood Press.

Kostarelos, F. (1995). *Feeling the spirit: Faith and hope in an evangelical Black store-front church.* Columbia: University of South Carolina.

Kozol, J. (1995). *Amazing grace: The lives of children and the conscience of a nation.* New York: Crown Publishing, Inc.

Kraus, W. A. (1984). *Collaboration in organizations: Alternatives to hierarchy.* New York: Human Sciences Press.

Kretzmann, J. P., & McKnight, J. L. (1993). *Building communities from the inside out: A path toward finding and mobilizing a community's assets.* Evanston, IL: Center for Urban Affairs and Policy Research, Northwestern University.

Kreuger, L. W. (1997). The end of social work. *Journal of Social Work Education, 33,* 19–27.

Lavoie, F., Farquharson, A., & Kennedy, M. (1994). Workshop on "good practice" in the collaboration between professionals and mutual aid groups. In F. Lavoie, T. Borkman, & B. Gidron (Eds.), *Self-help and mutual aid groups: International and multicultural perspectives* (pp. 303–313). New York: Haworth Press.

Lazarus, R. S., & Folkman, S. (1991). The concept of coping. In A. Monat & R. S. Lazarus (Eds.), *Stress and coping: An anthology* (pp. 189–207). New York: Columbia University Press.

Lazzari, M. M., Ford, H. R., & Haughey, K. J. (1996). Making a difference: Women of action in the community. *Social Work, 41,* 197–205.

Lee, E. (1996). Asian American families: An overview. In M. McGoldrick, J. Giordano, & J. K. Pearce (Eds.), *Ethnicity & family therapy* (pp. 227–248). New York: Guilford Press.

Lee, F. R. (1994a, September 8). On a Harlem block, hope is swallowed by decay. *The New York Times,* A1, B8.

Lee, F. R. (1994b, September 9). Harlem family battles weight of the past. *The New York Times,* A1, B4.

Lee, F. R. (1994c, September 10). A drug dealer's rapid rise and ugly fall. *The New York Times,* 1, 22.

Lee, J. (1995, July 25). Coffeehouse for gay youth: Alcohol-free Farmingdale site seeks to boost self-esteem. *Newsday* (Nassau and Suffolk Edition), A18.

Lee, J. A. B. (1994d). *The empowerment approach to social work practice.* New York: Columbia University Press.

Lenrow, P. B., & Burch, R. W. (1981). Mutual aid and professional services: Opposing or complementary? In B. H. Gottlieb (Ed.), *Social networks and social support* (pp. 233–257). Beverly Hills, CA: Sage Publications.

Levett, P. (1995). A todos les llamo primo (I call everyone cousin): The social basis for Latino small businesses. In M. Halter (Ed.), *New migrants in the market-place* (pp. 120–140). Boston: University of Massachusetts Press.

Levy, S. J., & Rutter, E. (1992). *Children of drug abusers.* New York: Lexington Books.

Life Force. (1994). *Life force: History of the organization, area and population served.* New York: Author, Agency Document, 1–4.

Logan, S. L. (Ed.). (1996a). *The black family: Strengths, self-help, and positive change.* Boulder, CO: Westview Press.

Logan, S. L. (1996b). A strengths perspective on black families: Then and now. In S. L. Logan (Ed.), *The black family: Strengths, self-help, and positive change* (pp. 8–38). Boulder, CO: Westview Press.

Logan, S. L. (1996c). Strengthening family ties: Working with Black female single-parent families. In S. L. Logan (Ed.), *The black family: Strengths, self-help, and positive change* (pp. 164–180). Boulder, CO: Westview Press.

Longres, J. F. (1988). *Human behavior in the social environment.* Itasca, IL: F.E. Peacock.

Longres, J. F., & Seltzer, G. B. (1994). Racism: Its implications for the education of minority social work students. In P. R. Key (Ed.), *School social workers in the multicultural environment: New roles, responsibilities, and educational enrich-ment* (pp. 59–75). New York: Haworth Press.

Lum, D. (1996). *Social work practice & people of color.* Monterey, CA: Brooks/Cole.

Luther, S. S., & Ziegler, E. (1991). Vulnerability and competence: A review of research on resilience in childhood. *American Journal of Orthopsychiatry, 57,* 317–331.

Lyon, L. (1989). *The community in urban society.* Lexington: Lexington Books.

Maguire, L. (1991). *Social support systems in practice.* Washington, D.C.: NASW Press.

Malony, H. N. (1992). Congregational consultation. In K. Pargament, K. I. Maton, & R. E. Hess (Eds.), *Religion and prevention in mental health* (pp. 277–292). New York: Haworth Press.

Maluccio, A. N. (1981). *Promoting competencies in clients.* New York: The Free Press.

Mangaliman, J. (1994, August 22). Nailing AIDS: Disease battlefront enters multicultural beauty world. *Newsday,* A12.

Manoleas, P. (1994). An outcome approach to assessing the cultural competence of MSW students. In P. R. Keys (Ed.), *School social workers in the multicultural environment: New roles, responsibilities, and educational enrichment* (pp. 43–57). New York: Haworth Press.

Margolin, L. (1997). *Under the cover of kindness: The invention of social work.* Charlottesville: University Press of Virginia.

Marin, B. V. (1996). Cultural issues in HIV prevention for Latinos: Should we try to change gender roles? In S. Oskamp & S. C. Thompson (Eds.), *Understanding and preventing HIV risk behavior: Safer sex and drug use* (pp. 157–176). Thousand Oaks, CA: Sage Publications.

Marshack, E. F., Ortiz-Hendricks, C., & Gladstein, M. (1994). The commonality of difference: Teaching about diversity in field instruction. In P. R. Keys (Ed.), *School social workers in the multicultural environment: New roles, responsibilities, and educational enrichment* (pp. 77–89). New York: Haworth Press.

Martin, E. P., & Martin, J. M. (1995). *Social work and the black experience.* Washington, D.C.: National Association of Social Workers.

Martin, J. M., & Martin, E. P. (1985). *The helping tradition in the black family and community.* Washington, D.C.: National Association of Social Workers.

Martinez-Brawley, E. E. (1990). *Perspectives on the small community: Humanistic views for the practitioner.* Washington, D.C.: NASW Press.

Mason, J. L. (1994). Developing culturally competent organizations. *Focal Point, 8,* 1–8.

Mathias, R. (1996). Protective factors can buffer high-risk youths from drug abuse. *NIDA Notes,* May/June, 7–8.

Maton, K. I., & Pargament, K. I. (1992). Religion as a resource for preventive action: An introduction. In K. I. Pargament, K. I. Maton, & R. E. Hess (Eds.), *Religion and prevention in mental health* (pp. 1–15). New York: Haworth Press.

Maxwell, B., & Jacobson, M. (1989). *Marketing disease to Hispanics: The selling of alcohol, tobacco, and junk foods.* Washington, D.C.: Center for Science in the Public Interest.

McKnight, J. (1995). *The careless society: Community and its counterfeits.* New York: Basic Books.

McKnight, J. L., & Kretzmann, J. (1990). *Mapping community capacity.* Evanston, IL: Center for Urban Affairs and Policy Research, Northwestern University.

McLane, D. (1991, December 11). Along 90 blocks of New Jersey, a new world of Latin tastes. *The New York Times,* C1, C6.

McLaughlin, M. W. (1993). Embedded identities: Enabling balance in urban contexts. In S. B. Health & M. W. McLaughlin (Eds.), *Identity & inner-city youth: Beyond ethnicity and gender* (pp. 36–68). New York: Teachers College Press.

McLaughlin, M. W., Irby, M. A., & Langman, J. (1994). *Urban sanctuaries: Neighborhood organizations in the lives and futures of inner-city youth.* San Francisco: Jossey-Bass.

Mecca, A. M., Smelser, N. J., & Vasconcellos, J. (Eds.). (1989). *The social importance of self-esteem.* Berkeley: University of California Press.

Meinert, R. G. (1994). Introduction: Scanning for critical issues in social work. In R. G. Meinert, J. T. Pardeck, & W. P. Sullivan (Eds.), *Issues in social work: A critical analysis* (pp. 1–19). Westport, CT: Auburn House.

Mendoza, L. (1980). Los servidores: Caretakers among the Hispanic elderly. *Generations, 5,* 24–25.

Menedez, B., Blum, S., Singh, T. P., & Drucker, E. (1994). Trends in AIDS mortality rates among residents of Puerto Rico and among Puerto Rican immigrants and other Hispanic residents of New York City, 1981–1989. *Centro de Estudios Puertorriquenos, 6,* 14–21.

Monat, A., & Lazarus, R. S. (Eds.). (1991). *Stress and coping: An anthology.* New York: Columbia University Press.

Moore, T. (1992). The African-American church: A source of empowerment, mutual help, and social change. In K. I. Pargament, K. I. Maton, & R. E. Hess (Eds.), *Religion and prevention in mental health* (pp. 237–257). New York: Haworth Press.

Morales, J. (1992). Community social work in Puerto Rican communities in the United States: One organizer's perspective. In F. Rivera & J. Ehrlich (Eds.), *Community organization in a diverse society* (pp. 110–118). Boston: Allyn & Bacon.

Mulroy, E. A., & Shay, S. (1997). Nonprofit organizations and innovation: A model of neighborhood-based collaboration to prevent child maltreatment. *Social Work, 42,* 515–524.

Navarro, M. (1989, December 29). In Hispanic community, many ignore AIDS. *The New York Times,* A1, B4.

Neighbors, H. W., Elliot, K. A., & Grant, L. M. (1990). Self-help and black Americans: A strategy for empowerment. In T. J. Powell (Ed.), *Working with self help* (pp. 189–217). Silver Spring, MD: NASW Press.

Nelkin, D. (1987). AIDS and the social sciences: Review of useful knowledge and research needs. *Reviews of Infectious Diseases, 9,* 980–986.

New York Times. (1994, April 22). Americans in 2020: Less white, more southern, p. 34.

Newcomb, M. D. (1992). Understanding the multi-dimensional nature of drug use and abuse: The role of consumption, risk factors, and protective factors. In M. Glantz, & R. Pickens (Eds.), *Vulnerability to drug abuse* (pp. 255–298). Washington, D.C.: American Psychological Association.

Niebuhr, G. (1994, December 11). A ceremony in Mexico City shows growth in Mormonism. *The New York Times,* 36.

Novas, H. (1994). *Everything you need to know about Latino history.* New York: Plume/Penguin Books.

Oboler, S. (1995). *Ethnic labels, Latino lives: Identity and the politics of (re)presentation in the United States.* Minneapolis: University of Minnesota Press.

O'Hare, W. P., & Felt, J. C. (1991). Asian Americans: America's fastest growing minority group. *Population Reference Bureau, 19,* 1–16.

Ojito, M. (1997, January 29). More Spanish accents, but fewer are Cuban. *The New York Times,* B1, B4.

Oldenburg, R. (1991). *The great good place.* New York: Paragon House.

Olsen, M. R. (1983). Forward: Social support networks from a British perspective. In J. K. Whittaker, & J. Garbarino (Eds.), *Social support networks: Informal helping in the human services* (pp. xi–xx). New York: Aldine.

Onishi, N. (1996, May 20). New sense of race arises among Asian-Americans. *The New York Times,* 1, B6.

Ortiz, V. (1995). The study of Latino families: A point of departure. In R. E. Zambrana (Ed.), *Understanding Latino families: Scholarship, policy, and practice* (pp. 18–39). Thousand Oaks, CA: Sage Publications.

Ortiz-Torres, B. (1994). The politics of AIDS research and policies and the Latino community. *Centro de Estudios Puertorrequenos, 6,* 108–114.

Owen, J. M. (1993). *Program evaluation: Forms and approaches.* St. Leonards, Australia: Allen & Unwin.

Padilla, F. M. (1993). *The gang as an American enterprise.* New Brunswick, NJ: Rutgers University Press.

Paulino, A. (1994). Dominicans in the United States: Implications for practice and policies in the human services. *Journal of Multicultural Social Work, 3,* 53–65.

Pearlman, R., & Gurin, A. (1972). *Community organizing and social planning.* New York: Council on Social Work Education.

Pears, R. (1992, December 4). New look at the U.S. in 2050: Bigger, older and less white. *The New York Times,* A1, D18.

Pearson, R. E. (1990). *Counseling and social support: Perspectives and practice.* Newbury Park, CA: Sage Publications.

Perez-Stable, M., & Uriate, M. (1997). Cubans and the changing economy of Miami. In D. Y. Hamamoto, & R. D. Torres (Eds.), *New American destinies: A reader in contemporary Asian and Latino immigration* (pp. 141–162). New York: Routledge.

Pfeffer, M. J. (1994). Low-wage employment and ghetto poverty: A comparison of African-American and Cambodian day-haul farm workers in Philadelphia. *Social Problems, 41,* 9–29.

Pina, T. (1995, June 21). Spreading the word about AIDS: Dedicated women go into the Hispanic community to warn about the fatal disease. *Providence Journal-Bulletin,* 1C.

Pollio, D. E. M., McDonald, S. M., & North, C. S. (1996). Combining a strengths-based approach and feminist theory in group work with persons "on the streets." *Social Work With Groups, 19,* 5–20.

Popple, K. (1996). Community work: British models. *Journal of Community Practice, 3,* 147–180.

Portes, A., & Rumbaut, R. G. (1996). *Immigrant America: A portrait.* Berkeley: University of California Press.

Portes, A., & Sensenbrenner, J. (1993). Embeddedness and immigration: Notes on the social determinants of economic action. *American Journal of Sociology, 98,* 1320–1350.

Powell, T. J. (1987). *Self-help organizations and professional practice.* Silver Spring, MD: National Association of Social Workers.

Powell, T. J. (1990). Professional help and informal help: Competing or complimentary systems. In T. J. Powell (Ed.), *Working with self-help* (pp. 31–49). Silver Spring, MD: National Association of Social Workers.

Rapp, C. A. (1992). The strengths perspective of case management with persons suffering from severe mental illness. In D. C. Saleebey (Ed.), *The strength perspective in social work practice* (pp. 45–58). New York: Longman.

Raynor, V. (1991, July 7). Charting the migration of Puerto Ricans, and their resilience. *The New York Times*, 14.

Razin, E., & Langlois, A. (1996). Metropolitan characteristics and entrepreneurship among immigrants and ethnic groups in Canada. *International Migration Review, 30*, 703–727.

Reed, S. (1994, March 13). San Francisco bath house opens with nineties message. *CNN News Network Program*.

Reed-Victor, E., & Stronge, J. (1997). Building resiliency: Constructive directions for homeless education. *Journal of Children and Poverty, 3*, 67–91.

Ribadeneira, D. (1997, February 24). Hands together against AIDS: Black clergy unite in service of healing. *The Boston Globe*, B1, B7.

Rierden, A. (1992, February 16). Problems temper Puerto Ricans' success. *The New York Times*, section 12 CN, 1.

Rivera, E. (1994). The compadres project: Puerto Rican children orphaned by AIDS. *Centro de Estudios Puertorrequenos, 6*, 216–227.

Rivera, F. G., & Erlich, J. L. (Eds.). (1992). *Community organizing in a diverse society*. Boston: Allyn & Bacon.

Rivera, Jr., G. (1990). AIDS and Mexican folk medicine. *Social Science Research, 75*, 3–7.

Rivera, R. (1992). Latinos in Massachusetts: Growth and geographical distribution. *New England Journal of Public Policy, 8*, 51–65.

Roberts, B., & Thorsheim, H. (1992). Reciprocal ministry: A transforming vision of help and leadership. In K. Pargament, K. I. Maton, & R. E. Hess (Eds.), *Religion and prevention in mental health* (pp. 259–275). New York: Haworth Press.

Roberts, S. (1994, October 16). Hispanic population outnumbers blacks in four cities as nation's demographics shift. *The New York Times*, 39.

Rogler, L. H., & Hollingshead, A. B. (1961). The Puerto Rican spiritualist as a psychiatrist. *American Journal of Sociology, 67*, 17–21.

Rohter, L. (1985a, January 12). Protestantism gaining influence in Hispanic community. *The New York Times*, 23, 26.

Rohter, L. (1985b, August 11). New York's thriving Hispanic banks. *The New York Times*, 4.

Rohter, L. (1985c, October 10). El Barrio residents worry and wait. *The New York Times*, B16.

Ronnau, J. P. (1994). Teaching cultural competence: Practical ideas for social work educators. In P. R. Keys (Ed.), *School social workers in the multicultural environment: New roles, responsibilities, and educational enrichment* (pp. 29–42). New York: Haworth Press.

Rooney, R. H. (1988). Socialization strategies for involuntary clients. *Social Casework: The Journal of Contemporary Social Work, 69*, 131–140.

Rooney, R. H. (1992). *Strategies for work with involuntary clients*. New York: Columbia University Press.

Rothman, J. (1994). *Practice with highly vulnerable clients: Case management and community-based service.* Englewood Cliffs, NJ: Prentice Hall.

Rusk, D. (1995). *Cities without suburbs.* Baltimore: Woodrow Wilson Press.

Rutter, M. (1987). Psychosocial resilience and protective mechanisms. *American Journal of Orthopsychiatry, 57,* 317–331.

Ryan, A. S. (Ed.). (1997). *Social work with immigrants and refugees.* New York: Haworth Press.

Saleebey, D. S. (Ed.). (1992). *The strengths perspective in social work practice.* New York: Longman.

Saleebey, D. S. (1996). The strengths perspective in social work practice: Extensions and cautions. *Social Work, 41,* 296–305.

Sanchez, C. (1987). Self-help: Model for strengthening the informal support system of the Hispanic elderly. *Journal of Gerontological Social Work, 9,* 117–130.

Sanchez-Ayendez, M. (1988). Puerto Rican elderly women: The cultural dimension of social support network. *Women & Health, 14,* 239–252.

Sandler, I. N., Miller, P., Short, J., & Wolchik, S. A. (1989). Social support as a protective factor for children in stress. In D. Belle (Ed.), *Children's social networks and social support* (pp. 277–307). New York: John Wiley & Sons.

Santiago, J. (1995). *"Botanicas" (herbalists): Helping the Latino community cope with AIDS.* Unpublished Manuscript.

Sarri, R. C., & Sarri, C. M. (1992). Organizational and community change through participatory action research. *Administration in Social Work, 16,* 99–110.

Saulnier, C. F. (1994). Twelve step programs for everyone? Lesbians in Al-Anon. In T. J. Powell (Ed.), *Understanding the self-help organization: Frameworks and findings* (pp. 247–271). Thousand Oaks, CA: Sage Publications.

Schon, D. A. (1983). *The reflective practitioner: How professionals think in action.* New York: Basic Books.

Schwartz, D. B. (1997). *Who cares?: Rediscovering community.* Boulder, CO: Westview Press.

Seelye, K. Q. (1997, March 27). The new U.S.: Grayer and more Hispanic. *The New York Times,* A32.

Segal, E. J. (1994). Forward. In S. Fiffer, & S. S. Fiffer (Eds.), *50 ways to help your community* (pp. ix–x). New York: Doubleday.

Seigel, J. (1994, April 10). San Francisco debates reopening gay baths. *Chicago Tribune,* 22.

Sells, S. P., Smith, T. E., & Newfield, N. (1997). Teaching ethnographic research methods in social work: A model course. *Journal of Social Work Education, 33,* 167–184.

Sengupta, S. (1996, January 7). Asians are not immune. *The New York Times,* 37.

Sexton, J. (1995, September 17). A church's daily rite of sadness: Strangers build bonds in familiarity of death. *The New York Times,* 43, 49.

Shapiro, J. P., & Wright, A. R. (1996, September 9). The faith factor: Can churches cure America's social ills? *U.S. News & World Report,* 46–53.

Shepard, P. (1997, April 9). Black pastors plan program to curb crime. *The Boston Globe,* A6.

Simon, B. L. (1994). Are theories for practice necessary? Yes! *Journal of Social Work Education, 30,* 144–147.

Simoni, J. M., & Perez, L. (1995). Latinos and mutual support groups: A case for considering culture. *American Journal of Orthopsychiatry, 65,* 440–445.

Sims, C. (1992, November 29). Under siege: Liquor's inner-city pipeline. *The New York Times*, section 3, 1, 6.

Singer, M. (1984). Spiritual healing and family therapy: Common approaches to the treatment of alcoholism. *Family Therapy, 11,* 155–162.

Singer, M. (1991). Confronting the AIDS epidemic among IV drug users: Does ethnic culture matter? *AIDS Education and Prevention, 3,* 258–283.

Singer, M., Castillo, Z., Davison, L., & Flores, C. (1990). Owning AIDS: Latino organiations and the AIDS epidemic. *Hispanic Journal of Behavioral Sciences, 12,* 196–211.

Singer, M., Flores, C., Davison, L., Burke, G., & Castillo, Z. (1991). Puerto Rican community mobilizing in response to the AIDS crisis. *Human Organization, 50,* 73–81.

Singer, M., Gonzalez, W., Vega, E., Centeno, I., & Davison, L. (1994). Implementing a community based AIDS prevention program for ethnic minorities: The communidad y responsibilidad. In J. P. Van Vught (Ed.), *AIDS prevention and services: Community based research* (pp. 59–92). Westport, CT: Bergin & Garvey.

Singleton, S. M. (1994). Faculty personal comfort and the teaching of content on racial oppression. In P. R. Key (Ed.), *School social workers in the multicultural environment: New roles, responsibilities, and educational enrichment* (pp. 5–16). New York: Haworth Press.

Smelser, N. J. (1989). Self-esteem and social problems: An introduction. In A. M. Mecca, N. J. Smelser, & J. Vasconcellos (Eds.), *The social importance of self-esteem* (pp. 1–23). Berkeley: University of California Press.

Smith, H. Y. (1996). Building on the strengths of black families: Self-help and empowerment. In S. L. Logan (Ed.), *The black family: Strengths, self-help, and positive change* (pp. 21–38). Boulder, CO: Westview Press.

Snowden, L. R., & Lieberman, M. A. (1994). African-American participation in self-help groups. In T. J. Powell (Ed.), *Understanding the self-help organization: Frameworks and findings* (pp. 50–61). Thousand Oaks, CA: Sage Publications.

Solomon, B. B. (1976). *Black empowerment: Social work in oppressed communities.* New York: Columbia University Press.

Solomon, B. B. (1985). Community social work practice in oppressed minority communities. In S. H. Taylor, & R. W. Roberts (Eds.), *Theory and practice of community social work* (pp. 217–257). New York: Columbia University Press.

South Carlina AIDS Education Network. (1995). *A history and overview of programs.* Columbia: Author.

Specht, H., & Courtney, M. E. (1994). *Unfaithful angels: How social work has abandoned its mission.* New York: The Free Press.

Spencer, G. (1986). *Projections of the Hispanic population: 1983–2080.* Current Population Reports, Series P-25, No. 995. Washington, D.C.: U.S. Department of Commerce, Bureau of the Census.

Spencer, S. (1995, May 20). Glorious garden rises in midst of urban decay. *The Record* (Strockton, CA), D6.

Spencer-Molloy, F. (1994, March 2). Doctor negotiates path between folk and traditional medicines. *The Hartford Courant*, D9.

Spradley, J. P. (1979). *The ethnographic interview.* New York: Holt, Rinehart and Winston.

Stake, R. E. (1995). *The art of case study research.* Thousand Oaks, CA: Sage Publications.

Staples, L. (Ed.). (1984). *Roots to power: A manual for grassroots organizing.* New York: Praeger.

Staples, R. (1995). Socio-cultural factors in black family transformation: Toward a redefinition of family functions. In C. K. Jacobson (Ed.), *American families: Issues in race and ethnicity* (pp. 19–27). New York: Garland Publishing.

Stewart, M., Banks, S., Crossman, D., & Poel, D. (1994). Partnerships between health professionals and self-help groups: Meanings and mechanisms. In F. Lavoie, T. Borkman, & B. Girdon (Eds.), *Self-help and mutual aid groups: International and multicultural perspectives* (pp. 199–240). New York: Haworth Press.

Stimson, G. V. (1992). Public health and health behavior in the prevention of HIV infection. In P. A. O'Hare, R. Newcombe, A. Matthews, & E. C. Buning (Eds.), *The reduction of drug-related harm* (pp. 39–48). London: Routledge.

Stout, H. (1988, June 26). What's new in Hispanic business: Out of the Barrio and into the mainstream. *The New York Times,* 13.

Stover, H., & Schuller, K. (1992). AIDS prevention with injecting drug users in the former West Germany: A user-friendly approach on a municipal level. In P. A. O'Hare, R. Newcombe, A. Matthews, & E. C. Buning (Eds.), *The reduction of drug-related harm* (pp. 186–194). London: Routledge.

Su Salud. (1996). *The largest all volunteer health education fair in the U.S.A.* Stockton, CA: Author.

Sufian, M., Friedman, S., Neaigus, A., Stepherson, B., Rivera-Beckman, J., & Des Jarlais, D. (1990). Impact of AIDS on Puerto Rican intravenous drug users. *Hispanic Journal of Behavioral Sciences, 12,* 122–134.

Sullivan, W. P. (1992). Reconsidering the environment as a helping resource. In D. S. Saleebey (Ed.), *The strengths perspective in social work practice* (pp. 148–157). New York: Longman.

Sullivan, W. P., & Rapp, C. A. (1996). Breaking away: The potential and promise of a strengths-based approach to social work practice. In R. G. Meinert, J. T. Pardeck, & W. P. Sullivan (Eds.), *Issues in social work: A critical perspective* (pp. 83–104). Westport, CT: Auburn House.

Sutton, C. T., & Broken Nose, M. A. (1996). American Indian families: An overview. In M. McGoldrick, J. Giordano, & J. K. Pearce (Eds.), *Ethnicity & family therapy* (pp. 31–44). New York: Guilford Press.

Terry, D. (1992a, September 13). More familiar, life in a cell seems less terrible. *The New York Times,* 1, 40.

Terry, S. (1992, August 22). A wave of immigration is fast changing Boston. *The New York Times,* 5.

The Medical Foundation. (1995). *Creating a community of prevention.* Boston: Author.

The Compact Edition of the Oxford English Dictionary (1971). New York: Oxford University Press.

Thompson, M. S., & Peebles-Wilkins, W. (1992) The impact of formal, informal, and societal support networks on the psychological well- being of Black adolescent mothers. *Social Work, 37,* 322–328.

Thyer, B. A. (1994). Are theories for practice necessary? No! *Journal of Social Work Education, 30,* 148–151.

Triandis, H. C. (1995). *Individualism & collectivism*. Boulder, CO: Westview Press.

Trolander, J. A. (1987). *Professionalism and social change: From the settlement house movement to neighborhood centers 1886 to the present*. New York: Columbia University Press.

Trolander, J. A. (1988). *Professionalism and social change: From the settlement house movement to neighborhood centers*. New York: Columbia University Press.

Tuller, D. (1994, March 5). Gay bathhouse planned for San Francisco. *The San Francisco Chronicle*, 17.

Tye, L. (1996a, November 13). Faith, hope and multitudes: Across nations, races, Pentecostal gains 50,000 members per day. *The Boston Globe*, 1, 28, 29.

Tye, L. (1996b, November 14). Pentecostal world reach: Faith finds millions underground in China. *The Boston Globe*, 1, 7, 8.

Tye, L. (1996c, November 15). Brazil's poor hear Pentecostalism's call. *The Boston Globe*, 1, 16, 17.

Tye, L. (1996d, November 16). Pentecostalism's U.S. crossroads. *The Boston Globe*, 1, 20, 21.

Unger, D. G., & Wandersman, A. (1985). The importance of neighbors: The social, cognitive, and affective components of neighboring. *American Journal of Community Psychology, 13*, 139–169.

U.S. Bureau of Census. (1983). *Projections of the Hispanic population: 1983–2080*. Current Population Reports, Series P- 25, No. 995. Washington, D.C.: U.S. Government Printing Office.

U.S. Bureau of Census. (1986). *Projections of the Hispanic population: 1983–2028*. Current Population Reports, Series P- 20, No. 449. Washington, D.C.: U.S. Government Printing Office.

U.S. Bureau of Census. (1991). *American Indian and Alaska Native Areas: 1990*. Washington, D.C.: U.S. Government Printing Office.

U.S. Bureau of Census. (1992). *Persons of Hispanic origin in the United States: 1990*. Washington, D.C.: U.S. Government Printing Office.

Valdes, A. (1994, December 15). A faith emerges from the shadows. *The Boston Globe*, pp. 74, 78.

Valdes, A. (1994, January 25). Sales down, but loyalty remains. *The Boston Globe*, B1, B4.

Valdiserri, R. O., Aultman, T. V., & Curran, J. W. (1995). Community planning: A national strategy to improve HIV prevention programs. *Journal of Community Health, 20*, 87–100.

Valdivieso, R., & Davis, C. (1988). U.S. Hispanics: Challenging issues for the 1990s. *Population Reference Bureau, 17*, 1–16.

Van Soest, D., & Byrant, S. (1995). Violence reconceptualized for social work: The urban dilemma. *Social Work, 40*, 549–557.

Van Vught, J. P. (Ed.). (1994). *AIDS prevention and services: Community based research* (pp. 35–57). Westport, CT: Bergin & Garvey.

Vazquez, B. (1994). St. Ann's corner of harm reduction. *Centro de Estudios Puertorriquenos, 6*, 193–204.

Vazquez, J. D. (1974). La Bodega—A social institution. In *The Puerto Rican curriculum development workshop: A report* (pp. 31–36). New York: Council on Social Work Education.

Vergara, C. J. (1995). *The new American ghetto*. New Brunswick, NJ: Rutgers University Press.

Verhovek, S. H. (1996, February 13). With detentions up, border is still porous: Halted on Rio Grande, Vowing to Return. *The New York Times*, A12.

Vulliamy, E. (1994, May 21). Steamy battle in the city of AIDS. *The Observer*, 24.

Wagner, C. (1985). San Diego's "hotel alert." *Aging, 351*, 7–11.

Watts, T. D., & Wright, Jr., R. (Eds.). (1989). *Alcoholism in minority populations.* Springfield, IL: Charles C. Thomas.

Weber, G. H. (1982). Self-help and beliefs. In G. H. Weber, & L. M. Cohen (Eds.), *Beliefs and self-help: Cross-cultural perspectives and approaches* (pp. 13–30). New York: Human Sciences Press.

Weeks, M. R., Schensul, J. J., Williams, S. S., Singer, M., & Grier, M. (1995). AIDS prevention for African-American and Latino women: Building culturally and gender-appropriate interventions. *AIDS Education and Prevention, 7*, 258–283.

Weick, A., Rapp, C., Sullivan, W. P., & Kisthardt, W. (1989). A strengths perspective for social work practice. *Social Work, 34*, 350–354.

Weil, M. O. (1996). Community building: Building community practice. *Social Work, 41*, 481–499.

Werner, E. M. (1991). *Against the odds.* Ithaca, NY: Cornell University Press.

Werner, E. E., & Smith, R. S. (1992). *Overcoming the odds: High risk children from birth to adulthood.* Ithaca, NY: Cornell University Press.

Whitcher, P. M., Gallagher, A. C., & Perz, M. C. (1997). *Final report of the Southeastern Michigan chapter and national headquarters HIV/AIDS evaluation study: Project Headsup.* Washington, D.C.: American National Red Cross.

Whittaker, J. K. (1983). Mutual helping in human service practice. In J. K. Whittaker, & J. Garbarino (Eds.), *Social support networks: Informal helping in the helping profession* (pp. 29–67). New York: Aldine.

Whittaker, J. K., & Garbarino, J. (Eds.), (1983). *Social support networks: Informal helping in the human services.* New York: Aldine.

Williams, S. E., & Wright, D. F. (1992). Empowerment: The strengths of black families revisited. *Journal of Multicultural Social Work, 2*, 23–36.

Williamson, M. (1997). *The healing of America.* New York: Simon & Schuster.

With, T. M. (1996, April 14). From Mexico to Massachusetts: Northeast migration linked to jobs, Prop. 187, and family. *The Boston Globe*, 1,8,9.

Wlazelek, A. (1995, May 24). The AIDS fight: Grant to fund AIDS outreach efforts. *The Morning Call (Allentown)*, B1.

Wolchik, S. A., Beals, J., & Sandler, I. N. (1989). Mapping children's support networks: Conceptual and methodological issues. In D. Belle (Ed.), *Children's social networks and social support* (pp. 191–220). New York: John Wiley & Sons.

Woodard, C. (1993, April 26). AIDS awareness: Passion patrol, safe-sex monitor helps club patrons on the up-and-up. *Newsday*, 15.

Wuthnow, R. (1991). *Acts of compassion: Caring for others and helping ourselves.* Princeton, NJ: Princeton University Press.

Wuthnow, R. (1996). *Learning to care: Elementary kindness in an age of indifference.* New York: Oxford University Press.

Wysocki, B. (1991, January 15). Influx of Asians brings prosperity to Flushing, a place for newcomers. *The Wall Street Journal*, 1.

Yamashiro, G., & Matsuoka, J. K. (1997). Help-seeking among Asian and Pacific Americans: A multiperspective analysis. *Social Work, 42*, 176–186.

Yee, B. W. K., & Weaver, G. D. (1994). Ethnic minorities and health promotion: Developing a 'culturally competent' agenda. *Generations, 18*, 39–44.

Yin, R. K. (1994). *Case study research: Design and methods.* Thousand Oaks, CA: Sage Publications.

Zorrilla, C., Diaz, C., Romaguera, J., & Martin, M. (1994). Acquired immune deficiency syndrome (AIDS) in women and children in Puerto Rico. In G. Lamberty, & C. Garcia Coll (Eds.), *Puerto Rican women and children: Issues in health, growth, and development* (pp. 55–70). New York: Plenum Press.

Zukin, S. (Ed.). (1995). *The cultures of cities.* Cambridge, UK: Blackwell.

Zunz, S. J., Turner, S., & Norman, E. (1993). Accentuating the positive: Stressing resilience in school-based substance abuse prevention programs. *Social Work in Education, 15,* 169–176.

Author Index

Subject Index

Printed in the United States
135378LV00002B/163/P